DON PACIFI

DON PACIFICO

The Acceptable Face of Gunboat Diplomacy

DEREK TAYLOR

VALLENTINE MITCHELL
LONDON • PORTLAND, OR

First published in 2008 by Vallentine Mitchell

Suite 314, Premier House,
112–114 Station Road,
Edgware, Middlesex HA8 7BJ

920 NE 58th Avenue, Suite 300,
Portland, OR
97213-3786

www.vmbooks.com

British Library Cataloguing in Publication Data:
A catalogue record has been applied for

ISBN 978 0 85303 762 0 (cloth)
ISBN 978 0 85303 763 7 (paper)

Library of Congress Cataloging-in-Publication Data
A catalogue record has been applied for

Typeset by FiSH Books, Enfield, Middx
Printed by Biddles Ltd, King's Lynn, Norfolk

Contents

List of Plates

DON DAVID PACIFICO'S FAMILY TREE

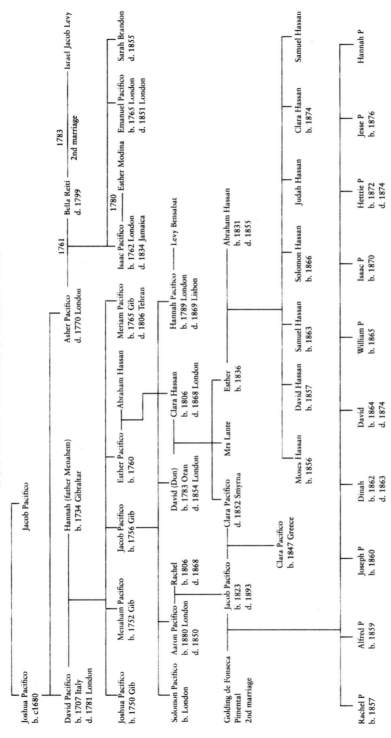

NOTES

1. All dates of birth and death supplied where known.

2. There is no evidence that Moses Hassan (b. 1856) ever lived. Except that otherwise David Hassan (b. 1857) should have been called Moses after his paternal grandfather.

3. Whoever Jacob Pacifico (b. 1756) married, her father was called Solomon. Aaron must have been named after his mother's senior uncle.

4. Esther Pacifico (b. 1836) would have been named after Esther Pacifico (b/ 1760).

1 Prologue

The mob started to gather that Easter Sunday in 1847 as soon as the church services ended at noon. It wasn't long before the crowd numbered several hundred, filling the square at the front of the palace. The old Jew watched them with growing anxiety from the rear of the first-floor balcony of his big house opposite the palace and its grounds. He knew that the Easter celebrations had gone on all night and if this was a drunken mob, then they were the worst.

All his life he had seen mobs and they were invariably very bad news. He had watched them at work in war and peace. Would he ever forget what they had done to General Jordao when they finally caught up with him in Faro? Or the results of Archbishop Gregorios going to Constantinople? He had seen them at their worst in town and country, out for revenge and out for plunder. Sometimes they had good cause, but they had in common that they didn't wait for justice to take a measured course.

He had thought that in this year, at least, the anniversary of the resurrection might go off quietly. In Athens on Easter Sunday the inspiration for a demonstration had for years been anti-Semitism. The people gathered to burn an effigy of Judas Iscariot. They would try to recreate on it the face of a prominent Greek Jew. The same thing happened in the old man's home town of Gibraltar, except that the dummy was just depicted as Jewish and the garrison would make sure the mob didn't get out of hand. This, had he known it, would go on until 1917. He had been in England on 5 November when he was young, and seen the bonfires burned to commemorate the failure of Guy Fawkes' efforts to blow up Parliament – but the villains in England were supposed to be the Catholics. Here it was the Jews who were in the dock for betraying Jesus, and the Greek Catholics had shown their hatred of them many times in the past.

He'd had his breakfast: matzo, of course, for this was the fourth day of Passover, the ancient celebration of the deliverance of the children of Israel from Egypt. The two Seder night services on Wednesday and Thursday had told the story yet again of those momentous days, thousands of years before. Passover and Easter usually coincided because the Last Supper that Jesus attended was the Seder night meal. It was one of the old man's favourite family celebrations and the table had looked beautiful when Clara had finished laying it. Everybody had been there, except his oldest girl and he didn't want to think about her.

The offence which the effigy-burning in Athens gave to the Jewish community at Easter was of no importance to anyone except themselves. In this year, however, the government had banned it. The reason was not a sudden outbreak of brotherly love. It was because the state was in terrible financial trouble again and a Rothschild banker was visiting the city 'to discuss the repayment of the loan to the Greek government'.[1] As it was well known that the Greeks hadn't paid even the interest on the loan ever since they'd received it more than fifteen years before, the feeling was that, at this delicate time, it would be somewhat inappropriate to mount an anti-Semitic demonstration as part of their core welcome to their distinguished visitor. It was considered a small sacrifice to deprive the mob of its traditional entertainment. The government knew that Britain, France and Russia, the co-guarantors of Greek independence, were substantial creditors of the state, and the progress of the talks with the bankers was being watched with great interest. As the British Minister reported to London: 'It has been the custom in Athens for some years to burn an effigy of Judas on Easter Day, but this year the government, in consequence of the Baron C. M. de Rothschild being here, took measure to prevent it taking place.'

The traditional setting for the burning happened to be nearly outside the old Jew's house and he knew a rumour had been spread that the cancellation of the bonfire had been at his request, as president of the local Jewish community. It was an important city landmark, like the Plaza Mayor in Madrid, where they had burned the actual bodies of heretics at autos-da-fé for centuries.

The mob swelled by the minute and in the front of the crowd were two easily recognized figures: the adolescent sons of Lieutenant General Kitsos Tzavellas, one of the less attractive bandit chiefs in the Greek government, who held the portfolio of Minister of War. It was about as wise to tangle with Tzavellas in Athens as with Genghis Khan a few hundred years before in Asia. For any complainant to be successful was out of the question, and to remain, physically, in one piece at the end of any argument, was an unlikely outcome.

In the strict Greek Orthodox communities, the Jews were not popular for all the usual reasons; they were perceived as not having seen the light as far as the arrival of Jesus was concerned, and they were believed to have been responsible for the crucifixion. The rumour would be useful. The government didn't want to acknowledge the power of the Rothschilds, because that would result in their losing face. Better to see the blame shifted onto the local Jews.

As the mob grew more menacing, the old man probably thought that at least his house would be quite safe. After all, it was one of the best in the city. Indeed, it had been good enough to have been the home of the first regent in modern Greece, the Bavarian Count Joseph von Armansperg.

The drawing room occupied half of the first level, with the outside wall being made up of French doors leading onto a terrace and providing an admirable view of the royal gardens. The library formed an anteroom to the office and gave him an area of complete quiet from the the activities of the rest of the household. Kitchen and storerooms filled the rest of the first floor, and were well stocked. The second-floor bedrooms were furnished with those handsome, richly carved pieces he had brought with him from Portugal: mahogany bedsteads, chests and looking glasses; music boxes and brass-bound Morocco trunks; sheets of embroidered cambric fringed with lace and damask coverlets; armchairs, footstools and scented Brazil-wood chests. Overall, it was a handsome two-storied building and its double doors were protected by a massive ironwork gate.

It might just as well have been a scout tent. The riot was well planned. The mob were already armed with large pieces of stone, which were unlikely to have been taken by them to their church services. As the old Jew wrote later:

> threatening groups of people from whom you can hear threats of 'Death to the Jews' had assembled in front of the church next to the house...Then the mob increased and was moving to the front of the house...The violence had doubled in force, stones flew everywhere, doors were forced, furniture was broken. They have been thrown out on the street; furniture, linen, papers, house effects etc. These things had been left on the pavement, on crossings and in the street, where the fanatics, under the very eyes of the police agents had divided the loot; the police agents, who instead of opposing those thefts, were saying to the thieves 'Be quick! Before the chiefs arrive'.

The old Jew had sent for the police immediately and appealed for help to the nearby gendarmerie post. There were guards at the palace opposite but as the afternoon dragged on, the authorities, who were in charge of public security, heard no riot, saw no riot, and many would later not speak of what they knew about the riot. It was only when there was nothing left to break or steal that armed police finally appeared. The Greek Foreign Minister later denied that there had been any delay. He said that as soon as the old Jew had asked for police help, they hurried to the scene of the crime: that the mob had 'formed in the blink of an eye but the rioters were dispersed with great speed'.[2] They still had ample time to steal everything movable and if the king had looked out of his window, he could have seen it happening.

The old Jew preferred to be known, and signed his name, as The Chevalier, D. Pacifico. He has come down in history by another of his titles, Don Pacifico, which will help us to distinguish him from his grandfather. His given name was David Pacifico and in his time he had been the Portuguese consul-general in Athens. He was, consequently, well known in diplomatic and court circles, but none of this helped him that Sunday:

> How can the authorities justify letting three hours pass before bringing help to evil that had been declared with such publicity? The Gendarmerie, the guards, the police offices were too near the scene of the crime not to be able to organize help in five or ten minutes. Had they been more prompt and ran to the clamour of the populace and to the cry of distress of the victims, or to say more correctly had they been more willing, these bad acts would have been much less, but they wanted to let loose the rage of the rioters, they wanted the attackers to be enriched by the goods of an honest man, they wanted to arrest only the poor who were unfortunate and whose guilt cannot be proven. They did not want to involve the real guilty party. Had they been quicker, there would have been more arrests, more proofs against the guilty and severe punishment would have ensued.

While all this was true, one highly significant fact was never commented upon; if the mob was sufficiently inflamed to cry out 'Death to the Jews' then Pacifico had obvious top billing for the role of the victim. Yet nobody touched Pacifico himself. He was over 60 years old, so he was an easy target, but in spite of the bloodthirsty shouts, the mob left him strictly alone. As an anti-Semitic riot it made no sense. Usually in such circumstances, the Jews were lucky to escape with their lives, especially if the mob had three hours to do its worst.

When Pacifico saw the attack was imminent, he sent staff to appeal to the British minister for help. The message reached the ambassador, Sir Edmund Lyons, who was in church. Lyons, a former naval captain, acted immediately, sending Philip Griffiths, the secretary of the legation, post-haste to Ionnis Kolettis, who doubled up his job as Prime Minister with the responsibilities of Minister of the Interior. It was an official complaint by the ambassador of one of the major powers guaranteeing Greek independence, but nothing happened for those three long hours on that Easter Sunday, 4 April 1847. Griffiths had reached Kolettis, but the minister had done nothing. Lyons, who was a prickly individual at the best of time, would have fumed. You simply didn't ignore the British minister and, over the years, he had built up an amply sufficient reputation to ensure that everyone knew he was ignored at their peril. Unless, of course, it was even more important to avoid the disruption of some well-laid plan. Pacifico wrote 'prayers and entreaties, we begged them to do so', but these had no effect either. The old Jew and his family had to watch helplessly as their house was looted:

> These brigands, in number about 300 or 400, entered my house, and swearing dreadfully, began beating my wife, my innocent children, and my son-in-law. After having broken the windows, doors, tables, chairs, and every other article of furniture, they robbed me of my jewels, forcing open the closets in which were vases, candlesticks, gold and silver ornaments, diamonds, and lastly a box containing money to the amount of 9,800 drachmas [£20,000 in today's money], of which 2,300 [£5,000 in today's money] were my own private property, and 7,500 which had been deposited with me by the Jewish Community of Italy for the projected erection of a temple [synagogue], and for the poor of this kingdom.

It was a terrifying experience for the whole family as they watched their keepsakes and mementoes, family heirlooms and religious vestments carried off or smashed. For the old man, however, the worst moment came when the mob found his papers. A lot of these were written in languages the mob couldn't even understand, but they must have thought they would realise some money if a friend could be found to translate them. The papers had official-looking seals and headings and, if they were worthless, they could always be thrown away. To Pacifico's intense chagrin, they were carted away like all the rest of his belongings. For years he had pored over those papers. The injustice they spoke of, in great detail, produced feelings of bitter betrayal in the old man. How could he have been discarded by those he had worked with so closely? 'These barbarians did not even leave me the Consular Portuguese Archives which were torn by them to pieces. These papers being my security from that nation for the sum of £21,295 sterling...'.

In today's money that £21,000 is about £1.35 million. Now that's a great deal just for lost papers, if you're not talking about bank drafts, currency or share certificates – which Pacifico wasn't. The biggest items in the Portuguese claim dated back to the War of the Two Brothers in Portugal almost fifteen years before. What had the old Jew been doing in the middle of a war?

At the end of the day, Pacifico and his family ran for refuge to the embassy. 'I asked the Greek justice who went on the scene and I helped all I could, but was told it was not enough! I was forced to hide, pursued by a frantic mob, in the British Ministry.' Again, 'a frantic mob' which never caught him. It was reminiscent of a stage fight. If they'd wanted to catch him – several hundred men against one old Jew – nothing could have stopped them. Unless it wasn't planned that way.

Pacifico had lost all his money and anything on which he could raise money. Clara, his wife, was badly shaken up by the experience and Jacob, his son-in-law, had plenty of bruises. So had Clara, his daughter, who was terrified by the events. Even worse, who could tell what the memories of that dreadful day might do to his 11-year-old daughter, Esther? They had suffered only comparatively minor physical injuries, however, where entire Jewish Greek communities had been massacred throughout the country only thirty years before in the War of Independence against the Turks.

When the Athens dust died down, the question was, what could be done about it? The complexion of the current Greek government had been severely criticised by the British foreign secretary, Viscount Palmerston. On many occasions he had said that the Greek King Otho was 'supporting a system of corruption and tyranny' and that Kolettis governed Greece 'corruptly, illegally, prodigally, unconstitutionally and tyrannically'. Furthermore, the prime minister had created The System: 'by means of patronage and corruption, and by constant interference with the processes of law, he managed to get under control the nomarchs, eparchs...etc.'. Everybody was corrupted – the gendarmerie and the tax and law officers as well. To make matters worse: 'In keeping his grip upon the provinces, he had recourse to brigands who continued to play an important part in Greek political life.' Many Athens politicians doubled up as gang leaders outside Parliament.

From the outset, Lyons, who had served in Greece for nearly twenty years and knew the territory, had little doubt that the riot was not simply motivated by anti-Semitism:

> The brigands who infest the capital took advantage of the occasion [the burning of the effigy] to spread a report that M. Pacifico, who is a Jew, was the cause of the discontinuance of this annual custom, and to excite the people against him in order that they might plunder his house. [The mob was] aided, instead of being repressed, by soldiers and gendarmes, and who were accompanied and encouraged, if not headed, by persons whose presence naturally induced a belief amongst the soldiers and the mob that the outrages they were committing would be indulgently treated by the Government. I have not failed to represent to M. Coletti [Ionnis Kolettis], that there is a great distinction between a common burglary and a protracted attack upon a large and conspicuous house in the middle of the day by several hundred persons who were aided, instead of being repressed by soldiers and gendarmes.

It had been designed to look like anti-Semitism, and it would enter the historical records of the time as just another anti-Semitic outrage, but Lyons could recognize a hidden agenda when he saw one. Pacifico would have been in no doubt either. Tzavellos and Kolettis were types he knew well. Their methods were no tougher than the Portuguese, Saldanha, Terceira or Sá de Bandeira even if they weren't as smooth as that poisonous Loulé. After the likes of Pedro and Miguel, he wasn't about to trust those who held the throne either.

So the King was crooked, the government was crooked and the courts were crooked. The government had felt itself quite safe in ignoring the British advice that a riot was taking place. The Jews were a tiny minority in Athens and thoroughly unpopular at the best of times. Pacifico was now broke, out of business, and in a foreign country. Obviously, the chances of his getting any compensation were practically non-existent and lesser men would have retired beaten from the battlefield and disappeared from sight for ever. The Greeks certainly expected him to do just that, after the usual token British protests. The government would, of course, see that the courts went through the motions in a properly judicial manner, but it would be easy to find a pliable judge who would hand down the decision they gave him in advance of the evidence.

There was only one thing the perpetrators of the riot had overlooked; they weren't, in fact, dealing with a decrepit old Jewish businessman. As far as fighting anti-Semitism, brigands, tyrannical

kings and political corruption – even full-scale wars – was
concerned, Pacifico had been there and done that. He was very well
trained indeed in how, if necessary, to take on the entire Greek
establishment. He had been taught how to go about it from his
earliest youth in Gibraltar and he didn't lack friends.

The Greeks might not realise it that Easter day, but they had
picked on the wrong man and they were now going to have a major
fight on their hands.

For Don David Pacifico, there had been a battle to be won for
most of his life. To understand his story you have to go back to its
beginning in Gibraltar and follow the tumultuous road which finally
led to his house in Athens on that fateful April day.

NOTE

1   Don Pacifico's account of the riot was sent to the British
    minister within a few days. The correspondence between the
    Greek authorities and the British embassy is all to be found in
    Foreign Office File 881 443. The quotations are from these
    sources.

2 Between a Rock and a hard place

When David Pacifico applied for a passport in 1833 – the aristocratic 'Don' was in all likelihood a Portuguese title he had earned on merit – he told the lieutenant governor of Gibraltar that he had been born in Oran in Morocco and that he was 43 years old. That would make the year of his birth 1789, but his death certificate pinpoints 1783 or 1784. The year 1789 is likely to have been untrue because his sister, Hannah, was born in that year. He also stated publicly in 1850 that he was born in Gibraltar. Whatever the truth – and, when his back was to the wall, Pacifico ducked and dived – he was definitely a British citizen because his parents were born in Gibraltar.

The Pacificos were Sephardi Jews and the Sephardic communities were particularly strong in the Mediterranean countries. Those Jews who lived in eastern Europe were mostly Ashkenazim. There isn't a great deal of difference between the two Orthodox religious communities except that they sing different melodies, which makes it difficult to join in their respective services, if you're a member of the other side. We can trace the Pacifico family to Venice in Italy at the end of the seventeenth century. There were two Pacificos we know about, Joshua and Jacob. They were cousins and their descendants can be traced initially because of an almost inviolable habit of the Sephardi Jews at the time.

They almost always named the family's first son after his paternal grandfather. The second was named after the maternal grandfather and the third after the senior paternal uncle. Everything springs from that. Joshua had a son, David. David married Jacob's niece, Hannah. David and Hannah had their first son in 1750 and he was named Joshua after his grandfather The second son (born 1752) was named after the maternal grandfather, Menahem. The third son was, of course, called Jacob (born 1756) and he was Don David Pacifico's father. As David Pacifico was named after his paternal grandfather, he must have been the first son of that generation.

David Pacifico, the Elder, is listed in the 1776 Gibraltar census and is also in a massive five-volume record of the genealogies of all Gibraltar Jewish families.[1] You can see the family tree on page vii.

A minor problem for the Jews in Gibraltar was that they weren't allowed to live there. There was a settlement between Spain and Britain in 1713, the Treaty of Utrecht, which clearly set down this restriction. Gibraltar had officially become British only as a result of the treaty, but then adding the Rock to the British Empire was, initially, very much an accident, which successive Spanish governments have tried unsuccessfully to reverse for the last 300 years.

The process had started when Charles II, king of Spain, died without leaving any children to succeed him in 1699. As a consequence, he decided to bequeath the Spanish throne to the Duke of Anjou, the grandson of Louis XIV of France. Combining France and Spain as a European superpower would have removed the safety net in that delicate seventeenth-century political high wire act we call the Balance of Power. As could have been expected, England, Austria, Holland, Portugal, and Savoy in Italy did not like the idea of a nearby superpower one little bit. So they all decided to go to war with France and Spain in what history has called the War of the Spanish Succession.

One result of this was that an Anglo–Dutch fleet sailed into the Mediterranean in 1704. Always keen to find something to conquer, they overcame the Spanish governor's small force defending Gibraltar and took possession of the territory in the name of their candidate for the vacant Spanish throne, who was known as King Charles III. It took only a four-day siege in the end but the allies lost sixty dead and over 200 wounded. Four thousand of the Spanish inhabitants of Gibraltar departed in high dudgeon and only seventy stayed behind. So, as nobody else seemed to want to take a permanent interest in a very large, but 80 per cent empty Rock, albeit with an excellent harbour and 1,200 houses, the island was occupied.

The original main objective of the fleet had been to start a revolt in southern Spain and crown Charles in Seville. Unfortunately, Charles' father died before this could take place, and so the Pretender had to go home to rewrite the script, at which point the allies abandoned the plan.

This left the British with a practically uninhabited Gibraltar. It could be supplied from Europe. It was always more sensible, however, to get what was needed in a hurry from Morocco on the other side of the Strait. Tetuan was its main trading centre, but the native Moroccans, divorced from cosmopolitan Europe, could hardly be described as international traders. So they left the vast majority of their imports and exports to be handled by the Sephardic Jewish communities in their midst, who knew all about such things.

Indeed, the Sephardim were world experts in this area. They had centuries of experience; European Sephardic merchants were trading with China in the eleventh century. In addition, they had the invaluable advantage of being able to trust completely the majority of their contacts in other countries, because these fellow traders were also Jews. The ancient Talmud laid down the rules which were to govern trade between Jews, and these were strictly adhered to, which facilitated the payment of bills as nothing else could. In addition, as the Christians stopped the Jews from joining guilds and becoming manufacturers, or becoming farmers by owning land, the international trade option was one of the few occupations left open to them, and many became specialists.

The sultan in Morocco was perfectly happy to leave his foreign commerce in the hands of the Sephardim, but most sultans tended to be uncomfortably unpredictable; not for nothing was the incumbent at the time, the Emperor Mulay (which means Lord) Ismael, nicknamed The Bloodthirsty. You never knew when a trusted Jewish merchant was suddenly going to cease being flavour of the month and suddenly be proclaimed an enemy of the state, which could have very unpleasant consequences indeed. To make matters worse, although they could trust their contacts overseas, unscrupulous local Jewish competitors were, on occasion, not averse to spreading rumours which could lead to their rivals' imprisonment and execution; the sultan suspected there were traitors under every bed and, as a top trader could easily amass a vast fortune, there was a great deal of jealousy.

As a result, many Sephardic merchants in Tetuan decided that Gibraltar, under the British, would be a far safer harbour, and so they emigrated to the Rock. They were joined by other Sephardim who were agents of the London and Leghorn trading houses; the Mediterranean had always been a very busy commercial area.[2]

The British were happy to see the Jews come to Gibraltar. They gave the new naval base an economic foundation and they could handle the booty that the navy seized from ships they captured – the ships as well if they were worth salvaging. As naval pay was poor and often irregular, prize money was the reason why almost everybody was in the service. The problem, however, was that the authorities back in London were often intent on keeping the prize money for themselves under various pretexts. What was worse, if a captain went to court to oppose the robbers at the Admiralty, the place men could ruin their naval careers even if they won. And if they did win they could be told that the court costs outweighed the value of the prize money and they were now deeply in debt. It was a moot point whether the enemy or the Admiralty were the more difficult opponents.

Another reason for the governor of Gibraltar to welcome Jews was that they could be made to pay twice the licence fees charged to anybody else for permission to trade: two *moeda* gold coins a month, compared to the normal one. Nevertheless, within a few years of the 1704 occupation, there were 300 Jews in Gibraltar.

The double fee charged to the Jews was a typical example of the international discrimination from which they suffered, although conditions were far worse throughout the Continent than they were in Gibraltar. The autocratic ruler could always fleece the Jews who had no popular support among the Christian majority of the populations. The Jews could never oppose discrimination with military might and they were hopelessly outnumbered. It was always possible to whip up public opinion to expel or massacre them, particularly if the state found itself in debt to their Jewish merchant bankers – or moneylenders, as they were called at the time.

In the face of this totally inexcusable oppression by the all-powerful monarchs, the Jewish merchants were expected to accept their fate with stoicism and behave at all times with total commercial integrity. The allegations against Don Pacifico in the future would constantly home in on the suggestion that he had not reached this lofty peak, irrespective of how he was, himself, treated. Any deviation from such standards would be roundly condemned by those who committed infinitely worse offences against Jews in the name of their nation or religion. Not surprisingly, the Jews were not always prepared to play ball. To survive in a hostile world they needed to develop as many alternative strategies as they could.

Consequently, they perfected a great ability to do favours for those who discriminated against them. They helped out many rulers financially and they used charm in abundance – and bribery if it came to the crunch. If they were going to survive at all, it might be necessary, on occasion, to bend the rules.

The reality of the situation was succinctly summarised by a Christian MP, the great historian, Thomas Macaulay. When William Cobbett, the nineteenth-century journalistic champion of rural England, attacked the Jews in Parliament in the 1830s, he said: 'usury is the only pursuit for which they are fit'. Macaulay got up and buried him: 'Such, sir, has been in every age the reasoning of bigots. They never fail to plead in justification of persecution the vices which persecution has engendered.'

Major Bucknall, the governor in Gibraltar, twisted the anti-Semitic taxation screw a little tighter. Besides the double monthly payment, he threatened to expel the Jews unless they each gave him a one-off payment of two or three *moeda*. Even so, the good news for the Jews was that they were safe, because the colony was under secure military discipline. Moreover, in fairness, extortion was commonplace in any empire; everybody knew that.

So, after the Treaty of Utrecht, the British were committed to expelling the Jews. The Spanish had a virulent hatred of the Sephardim, which was reciprocated in full measure. When the Spanish expelled the Jews from Spain in 1492, they created an implacable multitude of determined enemies for centuries: victims who were devoted to doing anything possible to undermine those who had treated them so cruelly, by burning their relatives at the stake or sending them to the galleys. In 1717 the Bishop of Cadiz found 300 Jews living in Gibraltar and he immediately complained to the Spanish ambassador in London, who asked for an explanation. The British could come up with no valid excuses, and slowly and reluctantly they started to throw the Gibraltarian Jews out of the colony.

At this point, however, the Sultan of Morocco, a somewhat unexpected white knight, rode to the rescue and announced that he was banning all trade between his country and both England and Gibraltar. The sultan might well have reasoned that the expulsion of the Jews was unfair and must be opposed. He might have been replete with humanitarian principles. He would certainly have resented that section of the treaty which also insisted on the Moors themselves being expelled. The Spanish and the Moors had struggled for control of the peninsula for centuries and, after many hundreds of years, the Catholics had won, but the enmity still continued. The sultan would also have recognized the benefits to Morocco already accruing from the Jewish contribution to the Gibraltar trade. It brought him much-needed foreign currency.

There was one final, pressing consideration for the potentate; if push came to shove, the Jews could always walk out on him in a body – and then who was going to handle the Moroccan exports and imports? That would have been bad news for his country: 'Jews were often the only traders, moneylenders or metalsmiths available. The withdrawal of services would have complicated and perhaps even significantly disrupted local economic life.'[3] For the British as well, a Moroccan embargo was unthinkable. To start with, building materials for the colony's expansion had to come from across the Strait, not to mention water for the passing British naval squadrons. As the Jews now recognized, Morocco could be a very useful ally and bolt-hole in troubled times. The Pacifico family would take due note.

A compromise didn't take long to reach. In 1721, the British and the Moroccans signed the pragmatic Treaty of Fes which acknowledged that all the Jews and Moors in Gibraltar would have the same rights as British citizens. Furthermore, if only Jews were involved in a dispute, the case could be resolved in their own court, the Beth Din. By this decision, the British effectively abrogated the anti-Semitic clauses in the Treaty of Utrecht. In 1727, Captain Stewart even went on a recruiting drive to Tetuan, on behalf of the governor of Gibraltar, to get the remaining Jews, of those who had been expelled, to come back.

The Spanish had been furious from the beginning at losing part of the Iberian Peninsula to the British. They started to refuse to supply the colony, even though it's only a ten-minute walk into Spain from the centre of the town. The 1721 Anglo–Moroccan agreement upset them even more. In about 1725 they closed the border and it stayed closed for forty years. This made absolutely certain that the Jews were fixtures in Gibraltar by the time normal relations were temporarily restored.

Not that the Jews were strangers to the Rock. With the aid of smugglers, a number had escaped to Gibraltar after the 1492 expulsion from Spain and 'for a time there was a plan to turn Gibraltar over to Spanish and Portuguese refugees'.[4]

By 1753 a third of the population of Gibraltar was Jewish. Over the years the community became unique in one particular way. The British naval and military forces came and went. The Spanish and Moors stayed a while and moved on, but the Jews had found a refuge where they were unmolested and well treated. The worst evidence of public anti-Semitism was parading the effigy of the Jew at Easter in the poorer part of the town.

As a consequence, the Jews became the only permanent fixture in the population. In 1796 the lieutenant governor, Major General Thomas Trigge, summed up their position: 'The Jews having been long established here and having no other country, are more interested in our keeping possession of this place, and have more to fear from our losing it, than any other person.'

The Sephardim in Gibraltar never deviated from their origins. They were powerfully led by chief rabbis who were all traditionally trained in the ancient community in Morocco. The Sephardim soon 'formed the quiet nucleus of the most industrious and able citizens on Gibraltar'.[5]

Into this haven came the Pacificos. David Pacifico, the Elder, Joshua's son, was born in 1707 in Italy and arrived in Gibraltar in 1726, at the age of 19. The family settled down and a legal document from 1759 has survived, bearing three signatures. One is that of a British officer called Mackenzie. The second is that of Isaac Lara, who would be the father-in-law of Aaron Cardozo, a name to be conjured with during the Napoleonic Wars. The third is David Pacifico, the Elder, the grandfather of Don David Pacifico. If the Pacifico family were already on such good terms with the Laras and the Cardozos, they were members of the Jewish Establishment.

David Pacifico and his wife, Hannah, had five children; Joshua was born in 1750, Menahem in 1752, Jacob in 1756, Esther in 1760 and Meriam in 1765. Hannah herself had been born in Gibraltar in 1734, so she had given birth to Joshua when she was only 16. There were twenty-seven years between husband and wife. Even so, with life expectancy so much lower than it is today, there was nothing exceptional about the bride being so young. 'Men tended to marry at an advanced age when they could afford their own houses'.[6]

In 1779 the Spanish decided to make another attempt to capture the colony. They besieged it for the next three-and-a-half years. For good measure, during the course of the siege, they fired 250,000 cannonballs at the town, so that most of the buildings were in ruins by the end of it.

The British had no intention of surrendering. A fleet was sent to bring supplies to the beleaguered garrison in the autumn of 1779, under Admiral Rodney. Its plans were betrayed and the French set out to destroy it with a massive, combined Franco–Spanish fleet of sixty-six men-of-war. The British admiral, Rodney, caught the Spanish fleet before it had time to join up with the French. The result, in foul weather and total darkness, was the destruction of half the Spanish flotilla. Rodney sailed on into Gibraltar pretty well unscathed. It was this sort of action which gave the Pacificos and the Gibraltarians confidence in the effectiveness of the British navy.

Relief convoys managed to sail into harbour in 1781, 1782 and 1783. During the siege, however, the British wanted to concentrate on defending the town, rather than bothering about the problems of the civilians. It was, therefore, decreed that any family without food supplies for three months would have to leave the Rock.

In 1777 the Jews had owned 25 per cent of the houses in the colony. As they weren't officially allowed to own houses, they lent the money to buy them to Christian friends and then took mortgages from them. Staying during the blitz, however, was hardly attractive and many Jews did decide to be evacuated. This was primarily after April 1782, when the French and Spaniards started the serious bombardment. A considerable number of Jews went to England as early as 1781 when the fleet returned to its home port, and they joined the Sephardic community in London's Bevis Marks Synagogue.

Others went across the Strait to Oran, and a number of the Pacificos were probably among them. Several Pacificos were to have Moroccan connections in the future. Joshua Pacifico, the eldest grandson, became the secretary to Rabbi Mordekhay De la Mar in Mazagon in southern Morocco. Jacob, Don Pacifico's father, served as British consul in Rabat, the capital of Morocco, towards the end of the eighteenth century.[7] This was an important diplomatic post. Pacifico followed in the footsteps of Mark Milbanke, who was a naval captain. Milbanke had been described by the sultan as a man of 'great sense, very proper, agreeable and courteous'. Whoever took over from him had to be able to live up to the standard he had set and it was considered that Jacob Pacifico could do that.

Jews were recruited as consuls by the rulers in North Africa and in a number of the European countries. Samuel Palache was the first Moroccan envoy to Holland, and General Cornwallis sent Jacob Benider to serve as envoy in Morocco in 1772.[8] The advantage of using Jews was that they could speak foreign languages and understood both the Arab and Christian cultures.

It is, therefore, quite likely that the Pacifico family departed for Morocco during the siege, and while some stayed, others moved on. There is no record of a Pacifico in the Gibraltar 1791 census. David Pacifico, the Elder, took ship for Britain during the siege but he was well over 70 and it was an arduous journey. He died in London in 1781.[9]

The conflict ended in February 1783 but the town of Gibraltar was so badly damaged that the original population drifted back only very slowly. There were just 3,300 living there in 1787, but life eventually got back to normal and ten years later numbers had risen to 8,000. Even so, by 1791 the Jewish percentage of the population was down to a fifth from a third and most of the houses were still in ruins. So whether Don Pacifico was born in 1783, 1784 or 1789, it is still most likely that the birth took place in Oran or Rabat. As his parents were Gibraltarian, it didn't affect his British nationality anyway.

The loss of the American colonies proved a boon to Gibraltar as the British turned, perforce, to expanding their trade with India and the Far East: 'The shortest and most economic route to India was not round the Cape of Good Hope but through the Mediterranean to Egypt, then by caravan across the isthmus of Suez to the Red Sea, and finally by ship again to India. Gibraltar was the first port of call on this trade route.'[10]

After his stint as consul in Rabat, Jacob Pacifico went to London, where his son, Aaron, was born in 1800. Another son, Solomon, was born there somewhat earlier, although he is a more shadowy figure.[11] There is no information about how Don Pacifico was educated, except for the implications of the position he attained later in life as president of the Athens Jewish community. This office would always be held by someone who was well versed in Talmudic studies. Indeed, the Gibraltarians who went to London soon gained the reputation of being among the most religious members of the Sephardic community. Don Pacifico definitely excelled in foreign languages. By the time he died he spoke fluent English, Portuguese, Greek, Ladino and Hebrew, and could speak and write beautiful French. He would be referred to in the British Parliament as an educated man.

It was probably a few years after Aaron's birth that the family returned to Gibraltar. Economic conditions in London were very difficult because of the earlier war with France. There was, of course, a lull in the fighting after the Treaty of Amiens in 1802, but this broke down in 1803. The Gibraltarian economy had already been boosted in the first conflict and now hostilities had restarted, its economic position improved even more:

> Between 1793 and 1801, British exports and imports rose by 30 per cent and Gibraltar – as the port in Europe where fewer questions were asked than anywhere else about the provenances and destinations of goods landed there by Merchantmen and Privateers, and as the most suitable place to which naval vessels could take their prizes captured in the Mediterranean or the Atlantic – benefited more than proportionately.[12]

The governor in those days was 'The Old Cock of the North', Major General Charles O'Hara, who took over the command at the end of 1795. O'Hara had expensive tastes, including two mistresses, and he governed strictly in his own interests. If, however, he didn't benefit financially by breaking the law, O'Hara stuck to it. He had a cosy arrangement with the Spanish General Castanos to stop tobacco smuggling by allowing Spanish gunboats from Algeciras and Ceuta to fire on British merchant shipping without retaliation. The deal was that if the Spanish didn't fire on the fortress, then Gibraltar's guns would remain silent in return. Admiral Jervis, Nelson's boss, who had the job of protecting British shipping, was furious when he arrived on the station and found he had to defend them without the help of the shore batteries.

In 1798 the Spanish were emboldened by The Old Cock of the North's relaxed attitude to think that Gibraltar might be taken from within. Spanish civilians on the Rock tried to raise a revolt, but the plot was discovered as a result of too much gossiping in the taverns, and O'Hara expelled over 1,000 Spanish citizens as a result. The Jews had no intention of becoming involved in anything illegal unless the governor had already permitted it. They carried on with their businesses.

When the Peace of Amiens broke down in 1803, Napoleon controlled Europe from the English Channel to the south of Spain and Italy, and east to Austria. Only the British and the Portuguese were outside his empire. Napoleon had a two-track strategy; he was going to invade England and, until he was ready for that, he was going to starve her out.

The plans for the invasion of England were ruined when Nelson beat the daylights out of the French and Spanish fleets at the Battle of Trafalgar off the Portuguese coast. The victory is, of course, famous, but the massive storm immediately afterwards is less so. A lot more damaged ships went down as a result and the Spanish navy never recovered. Admiral Collingwood estimated, with considerable regret, that an additional £4 million of prize money from the French and Spanish surrenders had disappeared beneath the waves. The captured ships that survived were taken to Gibraltar, where they and their contents were sold off. The agents were men like Aaron Cardozo, whose father-in-law, Isaac Lara, was mentioned earlier as a friend of David Pacifico, the Elder.

There was a great deal of extra money to be made now as an agent for the ships of the British navy. In 1807 alone 320 prizes were handled. Everything that could be moved was sold. As it was the booty rather than the pay that attracted men to the service, they welcomed professional help in dealing with the proceeds of their battles. In addition, of course, they were happy for any assistance in fighting the French, and this came from Gibraltarian privateers. In 1804 these small, fast, armed ships were given permission by the lieutenant governor, General Henry Fox, to attack the ships of the French and their allies.

Any blockade-running neutral ships trying to beat the British traps were also considered fair game. The privateers went to work with a will. Many merchants, including Jews, simply became official pirates, as they had in previous sieges as well. On one occasion a Jewish privateer had captured a Dutch cargo ship and alleviated the famine which threatened Gibraltar at the time. There is a record of a privateer called *Pacifico*[13] and that must have belonged to the family.

Where did the money come from to buy a small warship? Possibly from Aaron Cardozo or from Judah Benoliel, the 'King of Gibraltar' who took pleasure in having himself weighed in gold, like the Aga Khan. Benoliel was also the Gibraltar end of the flow of money from London to pay Wellington's troops in Spain and Portugal.

Cardozo did not own any privateers. He preferred to be well in with the navy and handle their prizes. He was also a good friend of Nelson, who often dined with him when he was in town. When Cardozo acted as an intermediary between the British and the Sultan of Morocco, Mawley Sulayman, on a question of supplies, Nelson lent him a ship to take him over the Straits. Cardozo managed to get permission for Nelson to water the fleet in Morocco's Mazri Bay, and he did deals for cattle and corn to feed the colony.

The whole of Gibraltar's commerce, however, was totally undermined in the spring of 1804 by an outbreak of yellow fever. Only cold weather could destroy the mosquitoes and when the worst was over, in January 1805, no less than 40 per cent of the population of Gibraltar was dead: 6,000 out of a total of 15,000 – 1,082 military fatalities and 4,864 civilian.

Apart from that dreadful interlude, the war continued to create boom times for Gibraltar. The colony was repopulated far faster than had been the case after the Great Siege. By 1808 it was back to 7,500 civilians. It was the Gibraltar merchants, shipping agents and bankers who profited most. A lot of the food Britain needed came from America. Gibraltar and the ports in southern Portugal were vital staging posts. After 1809, when the war was going badly for France, the French besieged Cadiz in Spain. At this point, to the considerable benefit of the colony, the South American merchants handling the export trade on the European side moved to Gibraltar.

There had been Jewish merchants in South America for at least 200 years, so the lines of communication were easily readjusted. Only during the height of the epidemic did Cardozo temporarily shift his headquarters to Morocco.

David Pacifico's own financial position was also improved by that same yellow fever epidemic which had killed so many in Gibraltar in 1804. Meriam, Don Pacifico's aunt, had married Moses Bensabat and gone to live in Tetuan. When the disease hit Morocco, they died in 1806 and as they had no children, they left their estate to their nephews, Don David, Solomon and Aaron.

The money supply didn't come only from piracy. The cost of running any war is likely to be very large and the Napoleonic Wars went on for the best part of twenty years. The British national debt increased by some £200 million. Part of that money was needed to pay the troops. There was always a warship in Gibraltar harbour taking on money to send to the army in Portugal. They shipped between £100,000 to £200,000 a month in that way. Money was also available to anybody who had something to sell which would facilitate the winning of the war.

The opportunities for graft were considerable. Cardozo, of course, was heading up an organisation rather than acting on his own. Jews owned most of the supply boats. They brought food to the Rock from Portugal, and food and water from Morocco.

The French plan to starve England was to be achieved by what became known as the Continental Blockade. Napoleon decreed that nobody in Europe was to trade with Britain or her colonies. All the continental ports were closed to British shipping. All British ships in those ports were to be seized. In retaliation, Britain declared that it would blockade French-occupied Europe. These grandiose declarations were easier to publicise than to achieve, but Gibraltar had a new role as one of the few allied entry ports to Europe, and Lisbon was another. One inevitable result of the blockade was, of course, a massive increase in smuggling. Many of those involved profited greatly and the officials on both sides were often not averse to accepting bribes, to allow the contraband to continue on its journey without undue interference. Another effect of the smuggling, of course, was to send the prices of the goods in demand through the roof.

The French forces didn't stand idly by while the British set out to beat the blockade. Their Spanish allies still had armed customs boats to intercept tobacco smugglers and they could attack Gibraltarian shipping on its way to Portugal. From the other side, Aaron Cardozo provided fast boats to carry messages for the British navy commanders. When looking for support in later years, he pointed to the secret missions he had personally carried out, without reward, which could have involved him in considerable danger. His old friends in the military were happy to confirm his accounts.

One of the main challenges in running a resistance movement in wartime, often behind enemy lines, is to avoid being betrayed. Who is on your side and who is an enemy plant? This was, of course, long before sophisticated electrical equipment, encoding machines and computers. For their own security system the British relied partly on freemasonry.

The advantages of freemasonry as a way of cementing good race relations and promoting better citizenship had led to the foundation of the first lodge in Gibraltar as early as 1727 – the St John of Jerusalem Lodge. Sometimes the lodges were restricted; the Friendship Lodge accepted no Jews. The Hiram Lodge, on the other hand, was for Jews. Members of the different lodges were, however, invited to each other's meetings and they all accepted the same rules of conduct.

The British realised that lodges had another advantage. You could scrutinise applications to make sure that the potential freemason was on your side. Then, when he had been initiated into the Craft, he could be given the secret passwords and handshake. In a foreign country, even in the dark, he could then identify friend from foe. How, though, could you avoid accepting Catholics, whose beliefs might be compatible with the masonic principles, but who might equally still be loyal citizens of their own countries?

The Catholics solved that problem for the British by forbidding their co-religionists to become masons. As a secret society, freemasonry was frowned upon. As a society whose members swore an oath not to divulge their secrets to anybody who was not a mason – which would include a Catholic's confessor – membership of it was out of the question.

It was the perfect solution for the British. The method of creating a new lodge is for an existing one to sponsor the newcomer, and the resulting bodies are called daughter lodges. The Gibraltar lodges could do that anywhere they liked, and they did.

For the Jews, freemasonry was enormously attractive. As freemasons were all equal, anyone could become more senior in freemasonry than military officers, vicars or knights of the realm. There was certainly nothing to stop Don Pacifico becoming a member after he turned 21 in 1805.

As far as most of the British were concerned, they were in the Gibraltar area to fight the enemy; they didn't pretend to know the lie of the land as well as the locals and they weren't businessmen. So the Jews provided an immensely useful backup, as they had so often in the past. In the War of the Spanish Succession, the Duke of Marlborough, the British general, had relied on Sir Solomon de Medina to arrange a lot of the food supplies for the troops on the Continent. Marlborough was also accused of taking a £6,000-a-year bribe for handing Medina the contract – which, in today's money, is about £450,000!

The number of soldiers eventually gathered in Gibraltar was substantial. In 1808 Sir John Moore arrived on the Rock with 10,000 men drawn from Sicily. At the same time another 5,000 men were brought in from England under General Spencer. 'Jewish merchants from Gibraltar were required to negotiate the purchase of supplies, particularly fresh food'.[14]

Jewish merchants were also needed in Portugal where there was a much larger infrastructure for handling goods. Ports in the south, like Lagos, had safe harbouring for hundreds of ships and were easy to reach from the Rock. So Jewish merchants started to set up operations at both ends of the line. Among them was David Pacifico, now in his middle 20s, and with an office in Lagos in 1812. He also opened a warehouse in Mertola, about fifty miles inland, in the rich farming country of the Alentejo. Officially he described himself as a corn merchant and there was plenty of money to be made in wartime if you had access to large stocks of corn. Although he had now, effectively, emigrated to Portugal, Pacifico would have had no difficulty in returning to Gibraltar to see the family; indeed, he was there in August 1811 and again in March 1812.

How do we know? When a boy is born in a Jewish family, the child is circumcised when it is eight days old. It is a religious service as well as an operation, and it is a great honour to be asked to be the *sandek*, the one who holds the child securely while the *mohel* (the surgeon) is removing the foreskin. That honour was given to David Pacifico in 1811 at the *briss* (circumcision) of Jacob Wanano. In 1812 he was there again for Judah Pariente.[15]

By 1812 the war was continuing to take its toll. Gibraltar was overcrowded, dirty and indifferently managed. The civil population had to be left to fend for itself, but by now David Pacifico was settled in Portugal and it is in Portugal, that we can pick up the story again.

NOTES

1 José Maria Abecasis, *Genealogia Hebraica, Portugal e Gibraltar* (Lisbon, 1991).

2 Tito Benady, 'The Jewish Community of Gibraltar', in Richard Barnett and Walter Schwab (eds), *The Western Sephardim* (Gibraltar Books, 1989).

3 Allan R. Meyers, *Jews among Muslims* (New York: New York University Press, 1996).

4 Bernard Postal and Samuel Abramson, *The Travellers Guide to Jewish Landmarks of Europe* (Fleet Press, 1971).

5 Ernle Bradford, *Gibraltar* (Rupert Hart Davis, 1971).

6 Benady, 'The Jewish Community of Gibraltar'.

7 Abecasis, *Genealogia Hebraica, Portugal e Gibraltar*.

8 Cecil Roth, *Miscellanies*, vol. 2 (Jewish Historical Society of England, 1935).

9 Bevis Marks records.

10 Sir William G. F. Jackson, *The Rock of the Gibraltarians* (Gibraltar Books, 1987).

11 Don Pacifico's daughter, Esther, named her third son, Solomon. By Sephardi custom, that would have been the name of the boy's senior maternal uncle – which would have been Solomon, Don Pacifico's brother who, therefore, must have been older than Aaron. None of the children of Esther and her husband, David Hassan, was named Aaron.

12 George Hills, *Rock of Contention* (Robert Hale, 1974).

13 Gibraltar records.

14 Benady, 'The Jewish Community of Gibraltar'.

15 Abecasis, *Genealogia Hebraica, Portugal e Gibraltar*.

3   The Portuguese connection

When Don Pacifico was born, the Jews weren't officially allowed to live in Portugal, just as they weren't allowed to live in Gibraltar. This was in spite of the fact that they had originally settled in Portugal more than 1,000 years before. On the Largo de Carmo, on top of the Santa Justa Hill in Lisbon, is the ruin of the Church of the Carmo. In the grounds is a tombstone inscribed in Hebrew and it dates from the sixth century.

Nearly a millenium later in 1497, King Manuel the Fortunate was determined to deal, once and for all, with the stubborn congregations of Jews who rejected his faith. So he had all the Portuguese Jewish children aged between 4 and 14 arrested and forcibly converted to Christianity. If their parents wanted them back, they had to convert to Catholicism as well. The Jewish families agonised over their terrible dilemma but a large number, very naturally, couldn't resist the infernal pressure and agreed to apostatise. As a result of their conversion it was then possible to consider the *marranos*, as the apostates were called (it means pigs), as heretics if they tried to practice their old religion. That brought them within the aegis of those the Inquisition could punish for backsliding heresies. Over the next couple of hundred years about 1,500 Portuguese *marranos* were burnt at the stake by the Inquisition for just that.

Pacifico would have known of the barbarities of the Inquisition. When he was attending Bevis Marks in London as a youngster, he would have found, on Yom Kippur, the Day of Atonement, that prayers were said for 'our brethren who are imprisoned in the dungeons of the Inquisition'.[1] By 1800 the vast majority of Portuguese *marranos* had been absorbed into the main body of the population, although with typical Jewish pertinacity, these new Christians still dominated that part of Portuguese trade which wasn't in the hands of foreigners. There was little competition because the Portuguese nobility were forbidden to become merchants. As a consequence, the Portuguese nobility had to make do with working for the crown, entering the church or serving in the armed forces. It was a strange anomaly, that a great trading nation had nothing much in the way of a merchant class, except for unwilling converts to the official religion.

Portugal is split almost into two by the river Tagus. To the north is the mountainous area with unnavigable rivers, deep gorges and heavy rainfall, making communications very difficult. In the mountains you can get 100 inches of rain (2.75 metres) a year. If northern Portugal was invaded, the conditions would favour the defenders.

In the south, below the Tagus, the country is flat, with a pleasant climate and little in the way of natural obstacles. The Algarve today has room for plenty of golf courses. Lisbon, the capital, is a port on the Tagus, and in the eighteenth century the heaviest concentration of the Portuguese population was in the Lisbon area. Conquer Lisbon and Porto to the north, and you had the headquarters of the country.

Within Portugal the economy had been substantially reliant for hundreds of years on the income from the colonies. Most of the Crown's revenue came from overseas, notably from Brazil. The Portuguese had been among the earliest of the European empire builders. Three-quarters of Portugal's trade with other countries originated in her colonies and became re-exports. Three-quarters of her imports came from Brazil, India and Africa. At home, the country was mostly agricultural, with olive oil and wine being useful exports. Seventy per cent of the population worked on the land.

As Britain proved an excellent export market for port wine, and as the Methuen Treaty in 1703 encouraged trading between the two countries, the links between Portugal and Britain had become very close. The British dominated many of the largest commercial operations and were prepared to help maintain Portuguese independence, by force if necessary.

The movement to modernise Portugal in the mid-eighteenth century came, primarily, from the Marquês de Pombal, Prime Minister under King Joseph Emanuel, who reigned from 1750 to 1777. He attacked the power of the church and the nobility and expelled the Jesuits. That made the country more tolerant, and Jews from Gibraltar, whose nationality protected them from the Inquisition, started to establish a community in Lisbon. More Jews but less British was Pombal's objective. He felt that London had far too large a say in Portugal's economy and he 'more than halved the numbers of British merchants and factors as well as the value of their trades'.[2] So the expats were not sorry when Pombal was dismissed by Queen Maria I when she succeeded her father in 1777.

Maria was not a strong queen. She was very much dominated by her mother and went on to suffer from melancholia after her husband and eldest son died. She virtually stopped reigning in 1792 before going mad in 1798. As a consequence the effective ruler of the country was her only surviving son, John, who became the regent. John was known to be 'irresolute, wanting in willpower and insight'.[3] It has to be said in his favour, however, that if he had these shortcomings, he still managed to survive in at least nominal power for over a quarter of a century during extremely difficult times for his country.

The church and the nobility recovered their positions under John but, when he took over, he recognized that one of the the ingredients he lacked in order to achieve his economic objectives was a substantial group of Jewish businessmen. As a consequence, he invited them to live in Portugal again – but keeping their religion to themselves. John's initial idea was that they should pretend to be Christians, but the first two Jewish merchants he approached, Moses Levy and Isaac Aboab, refused to pass themselves off as any such thing. Either they got safe conduct from John or they weren't coming.

The Inquisition was not pleased, but it was only a shadow of its former self. It had burnt its last heretic in 1761 and in any case it had never had a remit to deal with Jews. If they converted – forcibly or otherwise – the Inquisition could insist they didn't practice Judaism. If they remained Jews, the Inquisition could only try to get them expelled. John gave Levy and Aboab what they wanted, and the first Jewish grave in Portugal for hundreds of years is dated 1800.

More Jews arrived from Britain, Morocco and Tangier because, with the French controlling so much of Europe during the Napoleonic Wars, Portugal was bound to become an even more important staging post for British trade. Where trade flourished, the Jews were keenly interested in participating and would travel. By 1820 there was also a resuscitated congregation in Faro, about thirty-five miles up the road from Lagos and convenient for Gibraltar.

It was during John's time that 'a new upper middle class of wealth and potential influence was beginning to emerge. It was made up of elements of the commercial bourgeoisie in the coastal towns, an elite of educated bureaucrats and officeholders, and some of the non-aristocratic and petty noble landholders in central and south-central Portugal.'[4] It was, however, a slow process.

When the wars against the French started after the 1789 Revolution, Portugal signed treaties of mutual assistance with Spain and Britain in 1793. Unfortunately the Spanish made peace with

France without telling their allies. As a consequence France and Spain were able to threaten Portugal with invasion if it didn't enter the war on the French side. The French then tried to get the Portuguese to agree to close their ports to British shipping, but this would have been a total economic disaster for the Portuguese, who prevaricated. When the British, in their turn, announced that they were blockading France in 1804, the Portuguese, with all the firmness they could muster, proclaimed that they were neutral.

Lisbon grew slowly in population from 180,000 in 1800 to 200,000 in 1820. It had been the largest Iberian city in 1620 but had long been surpassed by Madrid. Porto, the second city, went from 40,000 to 50,000 but the south generally declined over the period. Lisbon became a British naval base in 1797 with a squadron anchored in the mouth of the river Tagus outside the capital. Ostensibly there only to protect British interests, Portugal may have remained an independent country, but if you wanted to conquer the Portuguese, you'd have to beat the British navy first – and later the British army as well.

The importance of Portugal in the Napoleonic Wars rested on a number of factors. It was the easiest place for the Americans to land sorely needed food for the British Isles. From Portugal the merchantmen's grain could be shipped by the navy to British ports, mainly from Lagos. The same applied to Portuguese wheat. There were a number of excellent harbours along the south coast of the peninsula, including Faro, but the advantage of Lagos was its location on the bay of Segras, which covered a very large area. Over 400 warships had once anchored there many years before. Loading and unloading was sometimes difficult on the Tagus, which had many storms; the weather was normally calmer in the south.

It was in the peninsula that Arthur Wellesley, later Duke of Wellington, became really famous. His campaigns weren't fought in the south of the country, however, and, as Lisbon was the main enemy objective, the battles were mostly in the area between the capital and Porto to the north. For the French to attack the south would mean either dangerously extending their lines of communication and supply, or tackling the British navy based on Gibraltar. Neither option was attractive.

In 1807 French pressure did eventually lead to a Portuguese declaration of war against Britain, but Napoleon's patience had run out by that time and he sent Marshal Jean Andoch 'The Tempest' Junot to invade Portugal. Napoleon told Junot to take the shortest route to Lisbon, but the terrain was dreadful and the weather worse:

'The army suffered incessantly from the bad weather. In Portugal the autumnal rains are a positive deluge...twenty times a day the columns of infantry were broken in fording the...swollen rivers.'[5] As Junot's target was twenty miles a day, he lost a lot of troops, and this was to be typical of France's efforts to subdue Portugal. The physical conditions were as damaging as the cost of battle. There was little resistance from the Portuguese army, however, and the French finally reached Lisbon on 30 November. In the meantime, there had been a stampede to get as many as possible of the Portuguese VIPs, and much of the valuables, out of the country and over to Brazil. On 29 November, just one day before the French entered the city: 'The Tagus being filled with the sails of a large convoy of shipping heading for the open sea. Going with them were the Portuguese Royal Family, the Portuguese navy, the contents of the treasury, and thousands of the country's leading citizens. Napoleon, in short, had been foiled.'[6]

Nothing was left to chance. Eight men-of-war, four frigates and twenty-four merchantmen sailed out of the Tagus and were met by the British naval squadron which was now blockading the mouth of the river. Loaded with half the coinage in Portugal and the majority of the British expat merchants and their stock, the fleet made landfall safely some weeks later on the other side of the Atlantic.

There was a price, however, for all this British support; the Portuguese economy back home suffered a terrible blow when in 1808 John had to agree to the British proposal that the Brazilian ports be opened to the shipping of all nations. When other countries' merchant shipping could carry goods to anywhere in Europe, without going via Portuguese ports first, the Portuguese balance of payments took a pounding. In 1810 the British then forced a new commercial treaty on their allies, which undermined more of the foundations of the Portuguese economy, by giving foreign countries much freer access to all the Portuguese colonial markets. Exports to Portugal went down by two thirds by 1813.

In any case, Napoleon didn't plan for Portugal to exist for much longer. Junot's victory came quickly and most of the large towns found themselves with French garrisons. The Portuguese nobility and the army were quiescent but the peasantry was decidedly not. Financed by subsidies in gold from John in Brazil, it fought back.

The French occupation was deeply resented in the countryside because the peasants' economic activity was severely reduced. It was also the case that a lot of the nobility fled abroad, which meant that a lot of servants lost their livelihoods. As a result there was a major outbreak of guerilla warfare and this led to some horrific French retaliation. The French, however, found that, while they could hold the towns, the countryside was out of their control. To make Junot's life more difficult, the British eventually decided to send troops to help the Portuguese, and Sir Hew Dalrymple from Gibraltar was appointed interim commander. Under him was Wellington.

In 1808 the French had an ample force of 26,000 troops in Portugal, but from now on they would encounter serious resistance. They were well beaten at the Battle of Vimeiro, suffering 2,000 casualties to Wellington's 720. Wellington was still dissatisfied because he could easily have mopped up the rest of Junot's forces if he'd been allowed to do so. Dalrymple, however, made peace with the French marshall at the Convention of Cintra, allowing the French army to be taken home in British ships. Not for nothing was he known to his troops as Dowager Dalrymple. There was a piece of doggerel which went the rounds in London at the time:

> This is John Bull, in great dismay / at the sight of the ships which carried away / the gold and silver and all the spoil / the French had plundered with so much toil / after the Convention which nobody owns / which saved old Junot's Baggage and Bones / altho' Sir Arthur (whose Valour and Skill / began so well but ended so ill) / had beaten the French, who took the Gold / that lay in the city of Lisbon.[7]

In 1809 Napoleon tried again. The Peace of Vienna in that year ended war in the north of Europe. Napoleon had won by a landslide and had neutralised the armed forces of the whole of the Continent except Britain, Spain and Portugal. He knew he couldn't invade England, but he was now able to turn all his attention to the last continental outposts of resistance in the Iberian Peninsula.

For the new campaign he sent 60,000 troops, divided into three divisions, to Portugal under Marshall Massena. The first two corps occupied the land between the Douro and the Tagus. Wellington had 30,000 British troops and another 30,000 poorly-trained Portuguese with which to oppose them. The Portuguese Regency Council could weigh in with another 15,000 and was also able to order the whole population into arms through the *levée en masse*. Should the people became sufficiently annoyed with the French, the whole population could rise in arms – if there were enough weapons to go round. Britain provided most of what was available of any quality and paid for it as well. The French weren't too concerned; they didn't rate the Portuguese fighting man highly after their previous experiences.

Things had changed though. The job of training the Portuguese
army was now under Charles Beresford. Wellington admired his
administrative capabilities, so he gave him the job with the
Portuguese army a few weeks after the Battle of Corunna in
February 1809, and he was elevated to the rank of marshal. Of
course, in wartime Portugal, if you controlled the army in the
absence of the king, you were a major player.

Beresford was helped by a large number of British army officers
and sergeants who were placed alongside their Portuguese
counterparts, on the basis of three per battalion. They provided a
reliable corps of good trainers, they were Beresford's eyes and ears
throughout the army and their higher professional standards made
them good role models for the local soldiery. Beresford improved the
effectiveness of the Portuguese until they were a match for the
French.

One of Beresford's most serious problems in making the
Portuguese army a good fighting unit was getting the feeding and the
pay of the troops right, which was the task of his commissariat.
There was neither sufficient money nor effective organisation:
'Lacking funds, the army had to muddle through on the basis of
wagons, pack mules and draught animals hired on a short-term basis
from the local populace. As for its debts it had to rely on bills of
credit presented to the central Junta ... and generally only settled
months in arrears.'[8] If the Portuguese army was to be a meaningful
force in any future war, those problems would need to be remembered and addressed by subsequent commanders.

Portuguese patriotism, fuelled by a desire for vengeance for past
atrocities, also went some way to make up for the lack of hardware.
The Portuguese knew they were fighting one of the finest armies
Europe had produced up to that time. The French were well trained,
experienced in battle and well commanded. The main strength of the
Portuguese was that they knew they were fighting for their national
independence. On their home patch they did the French a lot of
damage, but away from the countryside they knew so well, they
were useless. It was in their own gorges and mountains that they
were almost impossible to dislodge because they knew every nook
and cranny from which to hit and run.

Wellington ignored the French taunts and challenges to battle and
stayed in the hills. He realised that if he ventured into the plains for
a set piece battle, his forces would be destroyed by the great French
cavalry and that would have been particularly awkward as he had
the only major British standing army.

The French invaded in August, and Marshall Massena soon thought he had spotted that the British had left open the route to the city of Coimbra. In the fighting that followed, the British and Portuguese held the high ground and, despite the French army's admirable discipline and courage in attack, their troops were easily picked off as they advanced. The French lost 1,800 killed and 3,000 wounded while the allies had only 1,235 casualties. It was the first of many similar conflicts.

Massena then tried a flanking movement and got into Coimbra as the allied forces retreated to avoid being surrounded. The French scented victory and were sure they could push Wellington into the sea. It was a rude shock for them when they encountered those tremendous defences Wellington had constructed on the chain of mountains which stretch from Alhandra to Torres Vedras. Passes, geographically impenetrable, had been augmented with strong fortifications and bristled with the best artillery British workshops could manufacture. The troops could also be supplied from the British ships in the Tagus and, all round, the defensive position was impregnable.

Wellington still refused to give battle and left the French to die of hunger and disease, harried by the guerilla warfare of the local population. The local people agreed to leave the area altogether, burning the crops and taking all their animals and food stocks with them. As a French officer reported: 'I found only deserted towns and villages, mills made useless, wine flowing in the streets, corn burned to ashes and even furniture broken to pieces. They saw neither horse, mule, ass, cow nor goat.'⁹ Wellington had, in fact, got the people to undertake a scorched earth policy. Everything of use to the enemy was destroyed and the French army was reduced to spending much of its time trying to find something to eat. The French commissary system which had that responsibility – the quartermasters and pay corps – simply couldn't cope.

The war had raged from the border across to Lisbon and the north, but the south was 100 miles away and the internal communications were very poor. Portugal had the most antiquated road system in Europe and it got more pockmarked as the war stamped across it.

The Alentejo area in the south was normally a fertile agricultural region and the landowners continued to gather in a good harvest in most years. Foreigners were accepted because of the commercial contribution they could make. This was certainly beneficial, but they couldn't affect the weather, and in 1811 the crop failed, which led to substantially higher prices. Overall, there was also an inevitably deep economic crisis between 1808 and 1813 as the war disrupted business. The trade gap increased by 800 per cent between 1810 and 1811 and 15 per cent of the grain the country needed had to be imported.[10] The government's income, which went into the king's coffers, halved, and not until 1842 was the level of revenues achieved in 1805 recorded again. There was obviously still money to be made in the cereal market, though, as the price per bushel had more than doubled since 1789.

This was, presumably, the attraction which brought David Pacifico to Mertola in 1812 to set up as a corn merchant. There were plenty of large magnates in the area and 'all these landowners had direct contact with the big dealers in the nearest town, to whom they sold their wheat'.[11] Any newcomer with solid contacts in Gibraltar would be an ideal go-between. Pacifico had set up well away from the battle zone but, in the years to come, there would be plenty of people to recount their first-hand stories of the terrible times they had survived in the north. It would take a lot to have any sensible man raise his head over the parapet in some future conflict. Anybody who thought war was glamorous should have read George Simmons' recollections:

> Our present quarters are truly miserable; on all sides stupendous mountains, the people wretched in the extreme, clothes hardly sufficient to cover themselves, and positively not a degree above savages... Of a morning they will turn out of their wretched cabins and are to be seen in rows upon the ground... picking lice off themselves and out of each other's heads.[12]

When Wellington forced the French out of Portugal and moved on with his army to fight in Spain, he left the control in Lisbon to Viscount Beresford, who became the effective ruler of the country as head of the transitional government.

The question which could be considered, when there was some spare time, was what would happen after the war was over. The intelligentsia, as a whole, didn't fancy a further dose of absolutist rule. In present conditions the fiat of the central government was only as strong as the military forces it could bring to bear on a region. These were usually very small and so most of the interior of the country was effectively run by local juntas, with each isolated by the lack of good roads. This situation would continue for a number of years. At the same time, the French might be unpopular for their invasions, but their ideas had taken root. As democracy and communism fought each other on many fronts in the twentieth century, so liberalism and absolutism were the main protagonists in the nineteenth.

For the Portuguese there was a power vacuum during the early years of the century, with the king in Brazil and the country struggling with an ineffectual Regency Council. The leader of the new liberal movement was General Gomes Freire Andrade. It is at this point that the normally unexceptional influence of freemasonry also becomes important in Portugal.

When freemasonry in Britain was transformed into a patriotic national organisation after the defeat of the Old Pretender in 1715, membership was soon much prized and in Portugal the British merchants founded the Lodge of the Heretical Merchants as early as 1727 – so they were practically in at the start. In 1738, however, Pope Clement XII banned freemasonry for all Catholics on the threat of excommunication, so freemasonry had to become an anti-Catholic organisation to survive. The oath to keep the secrets of freemasonry and the demands of the confessional produced contradictory obligations impossible to bridge.

Periods of persecution and toleration followed throughout the latter part of the century in Portugal. One enthusiastic police chief, Pina Manique, hunted down clandestine freemasons for more than twenty-five years. Pombal tolerated freemasonry but Queen Maria didn't. Over the years lodges were formed and disbanded, recruiting members publicly and then secretly.

The British, for their part, had helped the infant Liberal Party, partly by creating masonic lodges in Portugal. These were linked to British ships and army corps. This development started when the British expeditionary force was sent to the Tagus in 1797. The British recognized the benefits of forming lodges; it cemented friendships with important local notables, and it continued to sort out friends from enemies.

The process had begun that year on board the frigate *Fenix*, anchored near Lisbon, when a lodge was formed for Portuguese and British masons. There were French masons too.[13] At the same time three army lodges were created, linked to British regiments, and a fourth for Portuguese and British officials. In 1801, 200 masons decided to form the Grand Lodge of Portugal. The government knew of this but now, in wartime, the British allies were deeply involved and, at their request, the Portuguese government agreed not to persecute the masonic brethren. The Grand Lodge was established in

May 1802; Portuguese lodges became an independent district of the Grand Lodge of England, and a focus for liberal ideas and future revolutionary uprisings. With senior British officers involved, aristocrats flocked to join the now fashionable movement.

General Andrade had decided to support the British cause in 1801 and it was in Andrade's palace that a masonic constitution was drawn up in 1806. This would be the model for the way the whole government of the country was run in later years and a prototype for the formulation of the 1826 and 1838 constitutions. The division of church and state was particularly emphasised. A legislative system of two chambers was agreed: a Chamber of Worshipful Masters and a Chamber of Representatives. The Representatives were responsible for the executive and the judiciary, and this bicameral system roughly translates into a House of Lords and a House of Commons.

When Junot had invaded Portugal in 1807, he was received respectfully by the masons in Lisbon. Napoleon had decided that he would legalise freemasonry, as it would placate a lot of potential opponents and be an opposing force to the powerful French church. Junot was also a mason but he overplayed his hand. He wanted a bust of Napoleon to be displayed at all masonic meetings, instead of that of the prince regent in Brazil, and he wanted to be Grand Master himself. Both demands upset the Portuguese, and the British special relationship was reinforced. Rebuffed, Junot went back to persecuting the masons during his time and getting the lodges dissolved.

Andrade found the French liberal ideas so attractive that he switched to Napoleon's side in 1808. He thereby became an opponent of Beresford and his autocratic system of government. During the latter parts of the war, Andrade went so far as to serve with the French on the Russian front. A lot of the Portuguese nobles and intellectuals had been exiled in France during the war and they returned dedicated to the French form of freemasonry, which was known as the Grand Orient. Those exiles who had reached Britain often came home to Portugal brimming with enthusiasm for constitutional monarchy. They found, however, that while the British would defend the system to the death in the United Kingdom, they were more inclined to absolutism on the ground in Portugal. The feeling grew increasingly in the Portuguese salons that this might be excusable in emergency wartime, but it wouldn't do when the war was over.

Freemasonry was still looked upon with suspicion within the Portuguese Regency Council. In 1810, thirty masons were arrested and sent to the Azores, condemned as French supporters. Nevertheless freemasonry developed as a very upper-crust organisation and, by 1812, the thirteen lodges in Portugal had a membership which included a considerable proportion of the most senior officials and dignitaries in the country. Andrade became the Portuguese Grand Master in 1815, establishing a precedent that the head of the Liberal Party would also be the head of the masons.

By 1817 Andrade was working hard for the country to have a new constitution, but his officially subversive activities were betrayed by three fellow masons to the Regency Council. He was arrested by Beresford, together with eleven other conspirators, and charged with trying to overthrow the government. When the court found the defendants guilty, Beresford hanged them all, but the harshness of the sentences made him very unpopular indeed. Beresford was, however, a soldier through and through, and mutineers were not tolerated in his world. He also recognized the fragile nature of his control of the nation; there were plenty of bandits in the countryside, and the state of law and order was similar to that of the American frontier later in the century. As far as Beresford was concerned, the lawless elements had to be taught that the administration he headed could be very tough on rebels if it needed to be.

In 1816 Queen Maria had died after eighteen years of insanity, and John had become John VI of Portugal, even though he was still living in Brazil. After the executions he forbade membership of all secret societies on pain of imprisonment and death, and so the lodges became totally clandestine. In Porto a group of masons formed a society called the *Sinedrio* (Greek for assembly) to fight for their liberal beliefs, which certainly didn't include an absolute monarchy. Porto was always to be the centre of liberal unrest in the future. The liberals wanted popular suffrage and freedom of the press, religion and speech. They also wanted far less bureaucracy in trade and industry. Something drastic certainly had to be done to help the economy; the interest rate at the end of the Napoleonic Wars had risen to 16 per cent and the national debt was £18 million.

The carnage of war finally ended with the Battle of Waterloo in 1815. The death toll in Portugal had been 250,000 – four times the entire population of Porto, the second largest city in the country. The Portuguese had fought hard on the victorious allied side, but their representatives at the peace negotiations were simply ignored. Little was demanded on Portugal's behalf by way of reparations from the French for all the damage they had done to the country's infrastructure in three major invasions. The economy had been left in a hopeless mess.

In 1815 Brazil was raised to the nominal status of a kingdom and John decided to stay in South America rather than help tackle the problems of his Portuguese inheritance on the spot. He had become an indecisive man, unable to decide which was the right way forward, and falling back on hoping that something would turn up. He had little willpower and he was no political economist. He watched, helpless, as the economically crucial Brazilian trade became more and more controlled by the British, depriving Portugal of much-needed foreign currency and markets.

After the war David Pacifico stayed on as a merchant in Lagos and was joined by his two brothers, Solomon and Aaron. They still kept in touch with their family and friends in Gibraltar. Solomon was *sandek* at two *brissim* in the colony in 1818 and 1823. The latter circumcision was for another Bensabat baby, Jacob Bensabat.

David Pacifico lived partly in Portugal and partly in Gibraltar.[14] He owned property in the colony and Solomon was one of the merchants who gave generously to build the fine Exchange Building in Gibraltar's town centre, which stands to this day. His name is among those of the good and the great on the memorial plaque in the building, so he must have been in a substantial way of business. Gibraltar, however, was having to adjust to the new conditions of peacetime. When the war ended in 1815, the Rock lost its key position as one of the few allied bases in western Europe. The colony's privateers could no longer attack French and Spanish shipping with legal impunity, and the smuggling opportunities were reduced as trade flowed freely. There was, therefore, little incentive for David Pacifico to abandon his business in Portugal, but Gibraltar remained the base camp.

There were still commercial problems in Portugal. One of the great advantages for Pacifico was that, as a British subject, he felt he could rely on British support in times of trouble. The interests of their merchant expats were important to Britain. For the Portuguese, the price of getting rid of the French remained a high degree of British tutelage. From a merchant's point of view, however, the Continent was now able to trade with Britain again and the wheat business wasn't all it had been. So the Pacificos spread their wings and diversified: 'He was able to offer many foreign productions at one half the cost in this capital', said *The Times*' correspondent in Lisbon thirty years later.[15] The Pacificos became general traders. If you wanted it, Pacifico could probably get it for you.

There was certainly money to be made in Portugal but it was a fairly primitive location, even by the standards of the day. Lisbon was a dilapidated village by comparison with the great capitals of Europe.

It might be the capital but it was a good city to avoid. One old soldier remembered it as 'the most filthy town I had ever seen'.[16] Another said that 'on setting your foot on land, you are almost overcome with the stench'.[17] Thirty years later there would be only 135 miles of macadamised road in the whole country. There were bandits in the countryside, very little manufacturing and masses of poverty. Nevertheless, in a primitive society, a sophisticated merchant finds far less competition than in more highly developed surroundings.

In 1817 Pacifico had a very nasty hiccough in the improvement of his fortunes. The cause of the problem was a ship called the *Berwick Packet* which was sold in Villa Nova, a port about 150 miles south of Lisbon. One of the part-owners didn't like the idea of the proceeds being carried hundreds of miles back to London in wads of currency, and preferred the greater safety of a bill of exchange, for which he paid 2,000 Spanish dollars. In today's money that would be £24,000. He bought the bill from Solomon Pacifico.

David was acting as a ship's agent for a ship called the *Swallow*: 'being the only person there who spoke the English language'.[18] The *Swallow* was owned by the same man as the *Berwick Packet*, which would account for Pacifico being entrusted with the financial arrangements. When, however, the son of the owner of the *Swallow* tried to present Pacifico's bill for payment in London, he was told it was forged and he was arrested for trying to cash it. He explained to the judge what had happened and was released. The court held, however, that it couldn't help him recover his money, because the negotiations had been concluded in Portugal, and so the case came up in Lisbon some months later.

As British subjects, the Pacificos were able to take advantage of the special arrangements for British merchants which had been in force for well over a hundred years in Portugal. When the two countries first started to discuss reciprocal trading in earnest, back in the seventeenth century, the British merchants were concerned about being subject to the Portuguese courts. These were held to be corrupt, slow and Catholic – which last criticism meant that if a judge didn't like your Protestant witness, he could always rule the evidence out of court on no better grounds than that the witness was a heretic. It was consequently agreed that, in non-criminal cases, the British merchants could have their own system.

This consisted of a conservator – a minor judge – being agreed, who would settle disputes between Portuguese and British traders. From this came the British Court of Conservancy in Pacifico's time, but he needed – like all the other British merchants – to get permission to be covered by its rules. This involved getting the privilege granted by Don John, and in 1822 Pacifico made a statement in court during the dispute over the *Berwick Packet* payment, that he was 'privileged in this kingdom by the British Court of Conservancy, under a patent from his Majesty, Don John VI'.

The case was settled by Pacifico repaying the owner his money in hard cash, and the court was satisfied with that. It might be suggested in future that Aaron had paid the captain over the odds to hush the whole thing up, but in fact he offered no more than the original figure involved. Solomon said that he bought the bill in good faith in Lisbon and had himself been cheated.

The affair does not seem to have been of any great importance, except that 20,000 Spanish dollars was a very large sum to lose. Pacifico continued to be a respected merchant in Portugal; he was accepted in the ranks of the liberals, and the proceedings in court would not be held against him by the Portuguese government in the future. Nevertheless, the *Berwick Packet* case would return to haunt Pacifico in the years to come.

When it was all over Pacifico stayed in the south. He wanted to belong to the new upper class, but the problem was that they were not of one political opinion. In particular, there was unrest among those Portuguese expats who remained in Britain but who felt that they had lost control of their own country. A Brazilian wrote to *The Times* in April 1820 to reassure the readers that the best jobs in Portugal didn't all go to foreigners and that there were plenty of senior Portuguese officers in the army: also that there were only a small number of British officers, and jobs in the civil service were restricted to Portuguese citizens. In truth, Beresford was still running the country. In 1819 Pacifico was 35 and, in trading terms, a seasoned professional. It was still possible to make a good living if you knew what you were about. There was a major problem, however; the rumble of a political volcano was beginning to be heard. Liberal influence was growing within the army, and the military was the strongest body in the country. In 1820 the rumble would turn into an eruption.

NOTES

1   Cecil Roth, *Essays and Portraits in Anglo-Jewish History* (Jewish Publication Society of America, 1962).

2   L. M. E. Shaw, *The Anglo-Portuguese Alliance and the English Merchants in Portugal 1654–1818* (Ashgate, 1998).

3 Stanley G. Payne, *A History of Spain and Portugal*, vol. 2 (The Library of Iberian Resources online).
4 Ibid.
5 M. Foy, *History of the War in the Peninsula under Napoleon* (London: 1827).
6 Charles Esdaile, *The Peninsular War* (Penguin Books, 2002).
7 David Birmingham, *Concise History of Portugal* (Cambridge University Press, 1993).
8 Esdaile, *The Peninsular War*.
9 Rocca's *War in Spain*, ch. 9.
10 A. H. de Oliveira Marques, *History of Portugal* (Columbia University Press, 1972).
11 H. V. Livermore, *Portugal* (Edinburgh University Press, 1973).
12 W. Verner (ed.), *A British Rifleman: Journals and Correspondence of George Simmons during the Peninsular War and the Campaign of Waterloo* (London: 1899).
13 Pelo Irmao A.M. Gonçalves, *A Shortened History of Freemasonry in Portugal*.
14 *The Times*, 19 March 1850.
15 Ibid.
16 G. Bell, *Rough Notes of an Old Soldier*, ed. B. Stuart (London: 1956).
17 *Peninsula Portrait: The Letters of Captain William Bragge* (London: 1963).
18 *The Times*, 12 December 1817.

4   Portugal: Peace of a sort

The Pacifico brothers were living in Lagos and obviously doing well. David was the senior and had made a good living from the corn business for some years. He had inherited money from the Bensabats and could afford to buy two houses back in Gibraltar. He had also diversified into being a ships agent and was a well-known importer of luxury merchandise. The time had now come when he could afford to get married, and his bride was his first cousin, Clara Hassan, the daughter of Esther Pacifico, his father's sister. Clara was born in 1806 and would have been in her teens when the marriage took place. The prospect of leaving Gibraltar and living in Portugal must have been a challenge, but Clara was going to stick by her new husband through thick and thin for well over thirty years. Aaron married around the same time and his new wife, Rachel, was the same age as Clara.

Both wives soon gave birth. Aaron and Rachel had a boy in 1823. They called him Jacob. David and Clara had a daughter who would have been named after her grandfather Jacob's wife. Both brothers may well have got married in Faro, not far from Lagos, where there was a structured Jewish community, for there is no record of their marriages in the Gibraltar archives. There seems nowhere else in Portugal where the marriages could have been solemnized by a rabbi who could provide them with a *ketubah* (an official marriage certificate). Without this it was more difficult to prove the Jewish legitimacy of any children they produced. They certainly went back and forth to the colony.

There was always likely to be a power vacuum in Portugal after the war was over, unless Britain stepped in. In 1815 the French were gone, the king was overseas, the country's economy was rudderless and there was no effective national government. To make matters worse for Britain, it had very substantial assets at risk in the country. For example, two of its most senior military commanders, Wellington and Beresford, had large estates in Portugal, thanks to the generosity of those they had liberated. Something would have to be done to give the country some momentum and to create stability. The Anglo–Irish Beresford had became the governor of Portugal, but he was there primarily to protect British interests. Backing up Beresford was the British ambassador, Sir Charles Stuart, and a British naval squadron in the Tagus, with a careful watching brief. If the Portuguese ruling classes weren't happy, they knew at least that the British had no aggressive intentions. Temporarily, the Portuguese were prepared to put up with the situation as they bided their time.

The British were certainly instrumental in saving Portugal from being conquered by the French but, with that threat removed, they managed to outstay their welcome within a few years. Napoleon might be imprisoned on St Helena, but the liberal ideas of the French Revolution were still very much at liberty in many parts of the peninsula. Portuguese refugees had started several magazines and newsletters abroad which found their way clandestinely back to the homeland. The information in them kept their readers abreast of the progress of revolutionary movements in Europe and helped to encourage sedition. As the tide of unrest grew, Beresford soon had to deal with political chaos and military insurrections; the absence of the king in Brazil became more and more of an embarrassment. Beresford realised that the monarch was the unifying factor the country needed and so, in 1820, he set sail for South America to try to get John to come back.

By now an additional problem was that Portugal's balance of payments had worsened and the country was in economic turmoil. The loss of the Brazilian revenues was a catastrophe and for the first time in 400 years the country had to try to make do with an economy based on home production. The balance of payments deficit in 1820 was 21 million *cruzados* and it was difficult to borrow money in the international markets at anything like a reasonable rate of interest. Portugal's fiscal debts were, in fact, minute compared to the British national debt. This had ballooned from £240 million in 1793 to £900 million in 1815, after paying for the war. In today's money that's another £25 billion. It was expected, however, that Britain could service her debts, but there was no similar confidence about the Portuguese. There was a growing feeling that change was desperately needed, and the two options available were either to continue with absolutist government or to turn to a constitutional form of ruler.

The battle between the liberal constitutionalists and the absolutists throughout Europe was heavily weighted on the side of the absolutists. They once again controlled the governments and military forces of every country except Britain. They also had the valuable support of the Catholic Church, whose senior members in Portugal were often recruited from the ranks of the ruling classes. The Portuguese peasants were also onside, as they had been brainwashed from birth to believe that the superiority of the absolutists was the natural status quo and, for the most part, they acquiesced in its continuance.

On the liberal side in Portugal, there was little actual power, although it had a large following among the intelligentsia. In many countries the liberals also attracted the new middle classes who wanted their place in the sun. The newcomers resented the fact that what they had achieved by hard work did not bring the reward of power in the government of the country. This was still enjoyed by the aristocracy who had inherited their position from birth and were not to be found in downmarket 'trade'. In Britain, by contrast, it was no disgrace for aristocrats to be merchants, and many successful entrepreneurs were given knighthoods or elevated to the peerage.

Napoleon had shown that the absolutist regimes could be overthrown. Moreover, Britain and the United States were examples of constitutional government. A successful liberal uprising in Spain in 1820 had been encouraging for their Portuguese neighbours. With sufficient courage and forbearance, victory was a possibility.

Beresford might have been a representative of constitutional Britain – albeit never written down at home – but abroad it was a different matter. In Portugal he wanted to continue to run the country without bothering to consult any voters for a mandate. He was particularly concerned that Ferdinand VII had agreed to a constitution for Spain and Beresford did not want John to have to deal with a similar movement from thousands of miles away. Instead, on 19 July 1820, John, who had become awkward, nervous and uncertain in exile, decided to give Beresford total control of the Portuguese armed forces as marshall general, and created him Duke of Portugal and the Algarve. The king then sent him back to Lisbon with one-and-a-half million Brazilian *cruzados* for the troops' back pay and told him he had his complete confidence. At the age of 53, John was beginning to prefer the sidelines.

The Portuguese liberal view was very different from that of Beresford. They believed that the true interests of the country were being subjugated to the benefit of Britain, particularly in terms of trade. So on 23 August a military and civilian rebellion broke out in Porto, five weeks after Beresford's elevation on the other side of the Atlantic. It gained power and the revolt spread to Lisbon in

September and proved equally successful. It was resolved to try to get rid of the British, restore the king and recover the Brazilian trade. A provisional junta was formed to govern the whole country until the ancient Portuguese parliament, the Cortes, could be summoned and a constitution written.

When Beresford came back from Rio, he arrived in the Tagus on the seventy-four-gun HMS *Vengeur* on 20 October. The Portuguese junta took its courage in both hands and refused to allow him to land, seventy-four-guns or not. The junta was worried that if Beresford landed, it would create the risk of a counter-revolution, but that couldn't be said openly. The excuse given to Beresford was that the junta was concerned he might be insulted, and that this could lead to a misunderstanding with England. It developed into a verbal chess match. Beresford said that he wanted to land because his health wasn't good: that he wasn't worried about being insulted and that he'd take full responsibility for ensuring there was no misunderstanding with England. Everybody was utterly charming but the junta still wouldn't let him land. It knew the power the king had given him. The Duke of Portugal left the country for England in very high dudgeon indeed and accompanied by a considerable number of British army officers, currently serving in the Portuguese army. Many, however, decided to remain.

The British influence on the Portuguese armed forces had been partly official and partly unofficial. Officially, the British continued to maintain a naval presence on the Tagus in order to safeguard British interests in an emergency. Unofficially, a considerable number of British army officers still held senior positions in the Portuguese army. This had suited everybody: the British military, because there was a lot of unemployed army talent after the end of the Napoleonic Wars; the Portuguese, because the British officers had saved them from the French and established their professional credentials on many Portuguese battlefields. The British were normally welcome in those roles and if, on occasion, they didn't get paid for months on end, they had a sufficiently comfortable lifestyle in kind to agree to wait for the money until better times came round. Most of them had no problem in leaving the Portuguese officers to decide which side they ought to back in a revolution. In the worst scenario, if mercenaries don't like the look of the probable outcome, they can always go home when the opportunity arises.

High society and the church kept the absolutists together but they had lost power. The liberals needed their own social framework to cement their relationships. Part of this still came from freemasonry.

Its own creed was strictly constitutional and democratic. It could attract royalty, like Pedro, John's eldest son, who was the Grand Master of the Brazilian Grand Lodge. The Craft could also attract senior politicians around the world with liberal leanings, like the Secretary at War in Britain, Viscount Palmerston, whose attitude towards Portuguese politics would be such a crucial factor in the future of the country.

There is no official record in the Grand Lodge of England archives that Palmerston was a freemason. What we do have is a letter to the editor of the *Freemasons Magazine and Masonic Mirror* at the time of Palmerston's death, which read: 'I am requested by the brethren present at a meeting of the New Concord Lodge of Instruction ... to express their united regret and deep sympathy at the death of our much-beloved Brother Henry John Temple, Viscount Palmerston ... his noble and distinguished character have endeared him to every class of society, and more especially to the Craft.'[1]

The Jews in Portugal remained attracted to freemasonry. If it was officially illegal, a lot of Jews would overlook this. They had many old scores to settle with the Portuguese absolutists. Their ancestors had been burnt at the stake, tortured and persecuted by them. Anything they could do to overthrow the Portuguese system of government and to destroy the influence of the Catholic Church would be some revenge for the treatment they had received at their hands.

There was also the same social advantage to masonry which had been found in the lodges in Gibraltar. By membership and by visiting other lodges, any brother could network with the good and the great of the country. If he worked hard enough, he could even become a member of the Grand Lodge. It was the perfect opening to high society. Whilst no evidence has survived that David Pacifico was a Portuguese freemason, it would certainly have been one of the only logical routes by which a Jewish corn merchant in a small provincial town could become known to, and friendly with, so many senior members of the liberal movement.

From whatever introduction, Pacifico became a loyal and enthusiastic member of the Liberal Party. He served it faithfully through all its trials and tribulations and, by the end of the 1820s, he had become highly regarded in its councils. The Jews fought for the countries in which they were citizens in the Napoleonic Wars. They were loyal to Britain and Russia, Austria and France. When the wars were over, however, it was the liberal movements which attracted them far more than the old absolutist philosophies.

The Cortes met in 1821 after the deputies had been elected by a three-tier system of semi-democratic suffrage, popularised by the Spanish. It meant that if you were a simple tax payer, you could vote in a man from a panel of candidates. Those standing who were successful then became voters in an election to choose deputies. It was a democratic election, once removed.

The result was the first representative body to meet in Portugal since 1689. When the polls closed, 60 per cent of the successful candidates came from the ranks of magistrates, teachers and the professions. The rest were made up of clergy, military officers and a few landowners and merchants. The handful of elected cardinals and patriarchs of the church refused to take the oath when the Cortes met, but they were in a tiny minority. Most of the deputies came from the families of the rural and land-holding upper middle class, and sat in the interests of those segments of the population.

When the news reached Brazil of the expulsion of Beresford and the establishment of the Cortes, John VI was in a dilemma. Did he stay in Brazil and let the Cortes get on with it, or did he return to Portugal and rule from there? The king dithered, but he wasn't popular in Brazil and in the spring he decided to leave, and make his son, Pedro, the regent. He knew that he would have to approve what the Cortes had done if he went home, but once in power, there was always the chance of changing things back to his liking.

The junta and the Cortes had always justified their actions by saying that they remained totally loyal to John. They said they wanted him back and when he decided to sail in June 1821, they proclaimed themselves delighted. There was, of course, the problem of paying for the upkeep of the royal family, and an appeal was made for donations from the public to make this possible, 'the public treasury being hardly able to meet the current expenses'.

The royal party arrived in Lisbon from London on 5 July and the king came straight to the Cortes, happily recognizing that 'on arrival, at a quarter before one, he was received with thousands of acclamations to the Constitutional King, by the countless multitude which covered the Terreiro de Paco, under a burning sun'.[2] He swore allegiance to the new constitution and it was completed in 1822. As a formula for a more just and democratic society, it was admirable. For those who lost power or income as a result of its implementation, it was a disaster.

To begin with, there was only one Chamber, and members had to be elected to it. There was no second House in which the nobility and the clergy could take their seats just because of their rank. Those

who supported the 1822 constitution were more radical than the
moderate wing, which developed in later years, although both sides
belonged to the Liberal Party. Naturally, the unicameral system was
supported by the radicals, democrats and republicans, while the
bicameral option had the support of the monarchists, conservatives
and the strict Catholics. The single House was elected for two years
by direct, universal male suffrage.

The intellectual majority of the deputies knew exactly what they
wanted to do and they set about the task of modernising the
country's laws with gusto. One of the first actions they took was to
abolish the Inquisition. It had been past its sell-by-date for years but
it was still a major symbolic institution. The next target was all the
feudal dues which had to be paid by the peasantry to church
landlords, and the tithes the church received as part of its ancient
privileges. All these were abolished as well, together with the
separate legal system for seigniorial and church domains, many
duties and a lot of internal tolls. In fact, every effort was made to cut
out the hindrances to free commerce.

The Cortes also abolished the ecclesiastical courts. Where
payments had to be made to landowners, the blow was softened on
occasion by allowing the rights to die with their owner. Some
merchants had bought estates which contained those rights – and
that number included David Pacifico. The profits from the corn
business had obviously been very good and his import business must
have flourished as well. In 1821 the customs duties on imported corn
were raised, favouring Pacifico's local customers. This would have
helped to counterbalance the effects of deflation as wartime prices
for scarce commodities subsided.

The practical effect of the 1822 constitution was that the monarch
would reign but not rule. He couldn't dissolve the Chamber and he
had no official representatives in it. He could delay legislation but he
couldn't stop it. The religious and economic interests of the Church
were maintained – there was no confiscation – and landowners were
left with no new social or economic reforms with which to contend.
Absolutist Europe was appalled but Britain was quite sanguine
about the changes.

For Pacifico, the Portuguese Liberal Party stood for everything he
believed in: the abolition of the Inquisition, a major reduction in the
power of the church, voting rights, equality before the law and
religious toleration. Run those principles up any flagpole and the
Jews would always salute. Furthermore, the Jews in Portugal had
reason to be grateful to John, who had invited them back to the

country more than twenty years before. They would not resent or fear his return from Brazil. Only a year before, 'in return for the assistance rendered by the Jews during the scarcity in Portugal, John VI... granted them the right to settle in Lisbon'. They could now have a synagogue in the capital and own property. It was a considerable extension to the level of toleration granted in 1800. In 1826 a decree would be made authorising religious toleration.

All the signs, however, were that constitutional government in Portugal would become the final form only as a result of civil war. The entrenched Establishment would fight to keep its privileges. Aaron Pacifico could see which way the wind was blowing. He decided that a good time had been had by all, but nothing goes on for ever. The corn business was no longer a licence to print money, he had a new wife and the unpleasant court case would take some living down. Perhaps he also disliked the prospect of always being junior partner to his older brother. For whatever combination of reasons, Aaron and David decided to dissolve their partnership and did so in 1822. Aaron and Rachel probably went home to Gibraltar, although only after Jacob was born in 1823. They were certainly living in the colony in 1833 because Aaron is listed in the census of that year as having a house in Irish Town.

Gibraltar had gone quiet since the end of the Napoleonic Wars. Everything had been geared up to winning the war, and other aspects of normal life were inevitably neglected. The Jews may have worked hard in the allied cause but officially they owned only thirty-nine houses. Instructions had been given in London in 1749 to restrict Catholic and Jewish house ownership. In 1818, however, under Lieutenant Governor Sir George Don, religious discrimination in holding property was finally abolished. The Pacificos would take advantage of this.

David, by contrast to Aaron, had found a cause. The conditions in post-war Europe were believed by many to herald the dawn of a new and fairer world, and Pacifico wanted to be instrumental in bringing it about. Far from leaving the scene, he decided to become a naturalized Portuguese. He was 38 now and a committed liberal. There would be those in the future who would support other versions of the constitution, but Pacifico had been in at the beginning and would always support the 1822 model.

Portugal still had appalling economic difficulties and looked to Britain for help, as its most important trading partner. The Rothschilds duly borrowed three million silver dollars from the Bank of England and lent half of it to the king.

The opposition to the constitution needed leadership, and this was provided by John's second son, Don Miguel, and, in the background, John's wife, Queen Colota Joaquina, the sister of King Ferdinand of Spain's. Colota was ambitious, ultra-conservative, authoritarian and promiscuous. For his part, Miguel was ambitious, clerical, equally authoritarian and fond of violent physical exercise. He had lived a military style of life in the country and, for Miguel, life was always cheap – as long as it was other people's lives.

Mother and son set out to put the clock back with a little help from their friends. The first attempt to overthrow the constitution came as early as February 1823 when the Count of Amarante led an insurrection in the Trás-os-Montes region north of Porto, although this was soon put down. At the end of April, Miguel besieged the king in his palace, on the grounds that there was a plot by the freemasons to assassinate him, and Miguel was there to protect his royal father. A few days later an infantry regiment revolted at Vila Franca de Xira, a few miles north of Lisbon. This uprising was called the *Vilafrancada*.

The mutiny was led by a young brigadier who would become one of the great survivors in nineteenth-century Portuguese history. His name was João Carlos Saldanha and, as Pombal's grandson, he was born to the purple. He would remain in power or in the senior ranks of the opposition for the next fifty years. Saldanha was born in 1790 and had fought against the British in the Napoleonic Wars. He was captured in 1810 and, on his release, went to Brazil, so he understood the policies on that side of the ocean. By 1823 he had risen through the ranks to become a general and, above all, he wanted to avoid what seemed to him an inevitable civil war, by reaching a compromise between the liberals and the absolutists.

Those who had managed to introduce a constitution to nearby Spain were suddenly faced by an invasion of the French in 1823, whose objective was to end that form of government. This the French achieved, restoring Ferdinand VII to the Spanish throne. Saldanha feared that Portugal might be the next on the French list and so he decided to pre-empt matters by getting rid of the constitutional Parliament himself. If there was no Parliament, there was no reason for the French to become involved. His army, therefore, arrived in Lisbon with the stated objective of driving out what he called the constitutional extremists.

What he hadn't bargained for was the other side of the coin; the absolutist extremists. So what Saldanha facilitated, a long way from the middle of the road, was the objectives of the absolutist Don

Miguel, working hard to try to take over the reins of power from his father as a result of the mutiny. Miguel immediately issued a statement to the Portuguese people which, like so many political appeals before and since, was long on rhetoric and short on facts:

> It is time in the name of the best of Kings, to break the iron yoke beneath which we live with such ignominy. We have long endured an intolerable despotism. It is not without extreme pain that I have withdrawn obedience from my august father; but I should blush if the evils which weigh down the generous nation to which I belong, could permit my resolution to be shaken... All classes of the nation are overturned by infernal wiles, and we shall be despised by Europe and the whole world, if we are so cowardly as longer to suffer such abasement.

The spin doctors working on the Miguelite proclamation went on in the same vein for a long time.

John did make the unrest and the successful mutiny an excuse to initiate some important changes in areas of the constitution he particularly disliked. He restored the monasteries which had been suppressed in 1822. On 20 June he condemned freemasonry again. The penalty for practising the Craft was set at five years' exile in Portuguese Africa and a fine of 100,000 *reis*. The freemasons started to flee to Britain, France and Gibraltar, and the lodges were told to disband by the Grand Master. They met only far away on the Portuguese island of Terceira.

John finally dissolved the Cortes on the all-embracing grounds of its alleged incompetence, disloyalty to the Crown and for being unrepresentative and inefficient. The Cortes was unpopular anyway because it was in its time that Brazil had finally declared independence of the homeland earlier in the year, by the treaty of Rio de Janeiro. A strong movement for separation from Portugal had grown up in the South American state. Brazil already had its own national government and Pedro was proclaimed emperor in 1822: 'Dom Pedro was a romantic and rather idealistic prince who was also unstable and afflicted with epilepsy. He was capable of outbursts of energy, but his behaviour was marked by sharp personal contradictions and occasional acts of highhandedness.'[3]

The Portuguese navy tried to prevent the separation, but Pedro declared war and, with the help of the British forces in the area, the Portuguese navy was defeated. This was the period when all the South American countries gained their independence from Spain or Portugal and one result of this was that the normal trading links between the Continent and the peninsula were severed. As a result, both Britain and Spain took to using Gibraltar as a neutral distribution centre.

There was a great deal of hype about the *Vilafrancada* insurrection, which was said by Miguel to be for the protection of the king's sovereignty. For the most part, Miguel and his mother encouraged the regressive changes made by John and then kept the king securely at the palace while they acted in his name. A climate of terror and persecution soon emerged and within a short time the army regretted that the constitution had been overthrown, as the country started to descend into chaos. In October 1823 *The Times* reported: 'The King, the Queen, Prince Michael [Miguel], each separate minister, the Superintendent of the Police, the Magistrates of the Barrios or wards of Lisbon, all independently of each other, issue orders to arrest, banish, confiscate property, and condemn to secret imprisonment.'[4]

At this point the diplomatic corps decided enough was enough and insisted on an audience with the king. In their supportive presence John felt strong enough to give Miguel a terrific dressing-down, as a result of which the prince literally grovelled on the ground in submission. John was triumphantly back in power and Saldanha was finally satisfied with the way things had worked out. Like anyone seeking the middle ground, however, he was attacked from both sides: as an enemy who had overthrown the Cortes by the constitutionalists and as a dangerous subversive freemason by the absolutists. Canning, the British Foreign Secretary, strengthened the Tagus flotilla in order to help John stop Miguel and his mother from trying again, and the warships were also there to dissuade any other European power from interfering. Even then John had to be smuggled onto a British ship to get him completely out of the hands of the queen and the prince.

Miguel learned little from this experience because, due to the initial duress, John had appointed him commander-in-chief of the army. This appointment wasn't retracted and John also permitted Amarante to recover his confiscated lands. Treason went unpunished; John continued to be very indecisive. He also had a bad habit of adopting the policy of the last person he spoke to and he was getting old and past it.

Miguel was nothing if not persistent. There were a dozen minor insurrections in 1823 and 1824. In April 1824 he led another uprising, called the *Abrilada*, and arrested the prime minister, the Marquês of Palmela, but this was altogether too much for everybody to stomach. The revolt soon failed but, for most of the effective rulers of the countryside, it was court intrigue rather than absolutism which was unacceptable.

The British did their best to back up the king. They gave John the Order of the Garter to provide him with added prestige. Beresford, whom the king had always liked, came back to provide advice. The pendulum swung the absolutist way again and, in May 1824, the king outlawed freemasonry once more and imprisoned hundreds of brethren. In June he unconditionally abolished what he called the 'monstrous' 1822 constitution, but promised to come up with another. He didn't try to go the whole hog and revert to European-style absolutism, but Beresford played his cards badly again. He entered into a conspiracy with the queen, that she would become regent and Beresford would become prime minister – if the king could be got out of the way. When John refused to abdicate to facilitate this cosy arrangement, the new scheme also collapsed.

The penalties for failure were still not onerous, though, encouraging the rebels to consider making another effort in the future. Beresford was allowed to go home to England again and the queen was told to choose between Rome and a nunnery for the rest of her life. Colota, however, feigned illness, got several doctor's notes and retired to her castle near Lisbon, where John weakly allowed her to continue to live unmolested. He treated Miguel as an indulgent father would, but at least he was firm enough to exile him to France.

As far as David Pacifico was concerned, the epicentre for all the political upheaval was going to be either Lisbon or Porto. With his set-up in Mertola and Lagos, he was a long way from both. He had been accustomed to changes of ruler in Gibraltar, and the Jews were very experienced in adjusting to new regimes. He remained, however, a keen believer in the importance of democratic institutions and, if he were asked to do so, was prepared to work for these to become a permanent part of Portuguese life.

When Miguel moved on to Vienna in disgrace, John profited by the opportunity to take more power for himself. A lot of the liberals, fearing the worst, fled the country, and many of them finished up in Gibraltar. An article in a Lisbon paper about Aaron Cardozo, commented: 'In this hospitality [to Liberal refugees] he received the efficient co-operation of the so honest and philanthropic inhabitants of Gibraltar.' John, however, confounded his liberal critics by ruling for the next two years as only a moderate absolutist.

In 1825 John named Maria Gloria, his granddaughter, as his successor, because of the behaviour of Miguel, whose claims he ignored. Pedro, the elder son, had not been born in Portugal which was technically a serious obstacle to his succession. Pedro was also Emperor of Brazil, whose independence John also acknowledged in that year. A notable appointment at the time was Saldanha as Minister of War – still operating his power base in Porto. The king eventually died in 1826, and now Beresford urged the Cortes to declare Pedro king, even though he was unpopular in the country for leading Brazil to independence. Neither the Portuguese nor the Brazilians wanted a unified monarchy; the Brazilians feared for their independence and the Portuguese wanted Brazil to be no more than a colony.

Pedro was allowed to succeed his father in return for an agreement to reintroduce a constitution, and sent his version of this long distance from Brazil in an urgent effort to 'dash off his Charter'.[5] The absolutists were still not satisfied and Saldanha had to force the Regency Council to issue the document: this was in spite of the fact that the 1826 charter did offer absolutists a number of concessions.

For example, there would now be two Houses of Parliament. One would be for 111 deputies, elected by indirect suffrage for four-year terms. The other would consist of peers chosen by the crown: one duke, twenty-four marquises, forty-one counts, three viscounts, four archbishops and eleven prelates. The judicial power would remain in the hands of the courts but there would be an executive consisting of ministers chosen by the king, who would be able in future to exercise an absolute veto on legislation he disliked. The civil rights of the people were considerably reduced below those granted to them in 1822 and, as the senior judges were chosen by the government, there was always a danger that they would be political rather than independent appointments. The new constitution denied the clergy any representation in the Chamber of Deputies. Such was the charter, whose supporters would be known as chartists, as against the constitutionalists who supported the 1822 document.

Pedro decided to go back to Brazil and, as his father had wanted, provisionally abdicated the Portuguese throne in favour of his daughter, Maria da Glória, who was 7 at the time. The idea was that she would marry her uncle, Miguel, when she came of age and, in the meantime, if he would agree to uphold the new constitution, Miguel would act as regent. Miguel readily agreed to do this, but as he had already tried to overthrow John VI several times, it was optimistic of Pedro to believe he could trust his brother. He must have known the situation was still volatile because there had been a minor absolutist uprising in 1826–27.

The Times had reported on 16 January 1827 that as many as 3,000 men and ships had been dispatched from Britain under Sir W. H. Clinton to help the constitutional government. Maria's army included a first-class general called Vila Flor, who would be rewarded for his efforts by being elevated to the Dukedom of Terceira. By 21 January the rebels were retreating and on 6 February they were routed.

Pedro's government asked Britain to keep a permanent garrison in Lisbon to help in any future emergency, and Canning agreed to this. Meanwhile the French had decided to support Miguel. The possibility of a unified France, Spain and Portugal under French suzerainty had long been a French dream.

Nevertheless, Miguel's return had the support of Wellington, who was prime minister in Britain at the time. Abroad, Wellington was not averse to a degree of absolutism. His years in control of France after 1815 had hardly been constitutional. At home he opposed the reform of the distribution of parliamentary seats, better to reflect the shifts in population in the country. Wellington's support for Miguel was a decision that spelt death and destruction for much of Portugal in the next few years.

Miguel married his child-bride, Maria, by proxy in October 1826. He was 24 and she was 7, and, as soon as he came back from exile in Vienna in February 1828, instead of announcing his allegiance to the charter as he had promised, he had himself proclaimed king by his supporters. They included all those who hated the tenets of the French Revolution, plus the church fighting for its ancient hegemony, the nobles who wanted to run the country, and most of the peasantry, who suspected change and did what the local clergy and notables told them. Even the army didn't support the legitimate king. Miguel certainly had a popular majority in the country. The excuse for rejecting Pedro was that he was not Portuguese, but born in Brazil, and therefore not qualified to succeed to the throne. It must also have been remembered that not long before, as Emperor of Brazil, he had declared war on Portugal, and that the parlous state of the Portuguese economy was largely due to the loss of the Brazilian revenues.

So, with such a large popular mandate, Miguel dissolved the Chambers of Peers and Deputies a month after he returned and summoned the traditional Cortes. They confirmed his accession and nullified the constitutional charter, while Maria delegated her authority to her uncle, leaving him with absolute power as Miguel I.

The new king was very much influenced by his mother, Queen Colota, as Palmerston, the British Secretary at the War Office, reported in his journal for 8 March 1828: 'The Queen Mother had got entire possession of Don Miguel; had persuaded him that the Freemasons threatened his life. He never goes out, walks from room to room with two guards, lest he should be assassinated, and eats nothing but what has been prepared by a particular person (an old nurse), for fear of being poisoned.'

When Miguel took over, Colota was in her element, having made a miraculous recovery from the ailments she had said made it impossible for her to live abroad. Soon she was firing governors and military commanders wholesale, with the result that radicals and moderates started fleeing the country in droves.

The only Portuguese military element which objected strongly to Miguel breaking his word to uphold the constitution was the garrison of Porto, whose governor was Joâo de Saldanha. He was Pedro's man. He may have effectively destroyed the 1822 constitution with his 1823 mutiny but that didn't mean he would stand by and see the same thing happen to the 1826 version. He could see a royal dictatorship looming as well as the next man and that wasn't his idea of a good way to run the country. Miguel was out to destroy Pedro's constitution and Saldanha was going to try to stop him. An army of 8,000 was quickly raised, which could have defeated the Miguelite forces, but Saldanha waited too long and fell back when he was attacked. As a consequence he felt that it might be wise to retreat and regroup at this point, so in 1828 he and Palmela, the former president of the council, withdrew to London to see what support could be raised for a counter-attack.

The revolt spread a little but the Miguelite masses gathered and the liberals were eventually hopelessly outnumbered. The Porto revolt collapsed and 'Miguel claimed the crown for himself, driving thousands of Liberals into exile in their turn.'[6] Fourteen thousand were said to have been arrested and many were tortured and executed. As *The Times* reported: 'Hardly any person of political importance is in safety, or out of prison.' Three thousand of the Porto army had fled to Spain and were then allowed to buy their own passages to England. Together with the liberal refugees, they were so numerous that when they arrived at the port of Plymouth in 1828, warehouses had to be turned into refugee camps.

They were the lucky ones. If they had been arrested and tried for taking part in the Porto uprising, the penalties were severe. One of those eventually released at the end of the war was a Mr Socres, whose brother, a London merchant, told the story to *The Times*.[7] Socres was condemned to death for his contribution to the uprising but managed to have this commuted to transportation for life to Africa by paying a vast seven *contos* as a fine. Miguel was, of course, as rapacious as any other dictator when dealing with his enemies; 800,000 families had property confiscated: 10 per cent of the kingdom.

Many of those fleeing ended up in Gibraltar, and Pedro looked for help for his friends. By this time he must have known David Pacifico, either personally or by reputation. Pacifico had two houses on the Rock and Pedro asked him to put up the refugee Portuguese Archbishop Ataite and his entourage in one of them, and many of the other liberal refugees in another. Pacifico, as a loyal supporter of both the king and the constitution, was happy to oblige. The rent was settled but, as money was tight, Pacifico agreed to be paid when – and if – Pedro's side had overthrown the usurper. The loyalty to Maria of the Portuguese refugees in Gibraltar never wavered. When she left Brazil, Miguel refused to allow her to land in Portugal and so she arrived in the colony aboard a British warship on 2 September 1828, where she was given a rousing welcome before continuing to London.

In his capital George IV gave her all the honours of a visiting monarch, but she was, naturally, a pawn in the game. When the king made a farewell speech hoping that Maria would be restored to her throne, the child threw her arms round his neck and kissed him, which completely captivated the old rake. There still seemed little chance of overthrowing her uncle and husband.

NOTES

1 *Freemasons Magazine & Masonic Mirror*, 4 November 1865, vol. XIII, no. 331, p 370.
2 *The Times*, 26 July 1821.
3 Stanley G. Payne, *A History of Spain & Portugal* (The Library of Iberian Resources online).
4 *The Times*, 13 October 1823.
5 H. V. Livermore, *A New History of Portugal* (Cambridge: Cambridge University Press, 1977).
6 David Barraclough, *A Concise History of Portugal* (Cambridge: Cambridge University Press, 1993).
7 *The Times*, 7 July 1833.

5 The War of the Two Brothers

There was no need for Pacifico's initial support for the Liberal Party to have been kept secret. When Miguel seized power, however, Pacifico's only protection was his British passport, which he kept with his new Portuguese one. He might also have hoped that his business base, a long way from Lisbon in the south of the country, might enable him to be overlooked, but the long arm of Miguel still did him as much harm as possible. Pacifico had four *commanderies* in the Alentejo. He must have made a lot of money over the years to have been able to afford these four small manor houses. Owning a *commanderie* made anyone a minor aristocrat and Pacifico probably bought his four properties before 1821. The Cortes had abolished the feudal dues that tenant farmers on the estates formerly had to pay, but only after the death of the present owner. So Pacifico would have had the benefit of the rents if he bought the *commanderies* before the law came into being. Miguel confiscated them in 1831. Pacifico had also owned *commendams*, which were the revenues of dissolved monasteries. He had sold these locally but the purchaser was a Miguelite who now refused to pay the bill.

As Miguel's forces harassed the liberals during the early years of his rule, the resistance movement shrank to Porto and the island of Terceira in the Azores. Terceira is about 1,500 kilometres off the coast of Portugal in the North Atlantic. The liberals were led by the Marquis of Palmela while the island garrison was commanded by Vila Flor, who had fought under Wellington and had a distinguished record as a commander. He had been made a marquis for his services to Pedro in January 1828 and was to be given the honour of reviewing British troops in London that June. Now he was back again on what had become the somewhat distant Pedroite front line in Terceira. The possibility of regaining Portugal from such a remote base bristled with difficulties.

Miguel didn't intend to leave the planning of such an operation to be carried out at Flor's leisure. In August 1829 he took the war to his enemy and mounted a full-scale invasion of Terceira, raising a fleet capable of carrying over 2,500 troops. The Miguelites would have expected an easy ride with their superior numbers and Flor, apparently spineless, allowed the first wave of infantry to reach the shore. Then he opened up on them with his coastal batteries and it was slaughter on the open beach. Of Miguel's army, over 1,300 drowned and a further 700 were killed on the shoreline. The battle was soon over, with the last 500 surrendering rather than be massacred. That ended Miguel's efforts to suppress the rearguard of Pedro's forces, but any invasion of the mainland would still have to be initiated from nearly 1,000 miles away.

Miguel had blatantly gone back on his word in 1828 and, initially, the nations of Europe withdrew their ambassadors in protest at the usurper's lack of integrity and accession to the throne. After they had made their point, however, most relented and normal relations were resumed. After all, this was an internal Portuguese matter and Metternich, the Austrian Chancellor, was just one of the European statesmen advising the tyrant. Only the British and French remained, nominally, on Pedro's side.

By 1830 the Miguelites were winning hands down. The opposition consisted, primarily, of the remnants of the professional and middle classes, the academics and the intellectuals in the main towns. These were strong on political philosophy, but not normally to be numbered among the ranks of potential cannon fodder. The end of the liberals seemed nigh. In fairness, if they were going to be defeated, the will of the majority would prevail.

Britain, the European power which most disliked autocratic government, appeared to be in a cleft stick. Wellington, as prime minister in 1828, had not been very interested. He had substantial holdings in Portugal, and if liberal principles were the creed of the French Revolution, then he'd spent a lot of his life fighting them tooth and nail. Wellington, to that extent, was an absolutist.

In power in 1829, Wellington refused Pedro's plea for help and instead allowed the British navy to aid Miguel against the liberals. A policy of neutrality was agreed with his Foreign Secretary, the Earl of Aberdeen. Miguel was good-looking, and charming when he wanted to be, and a good courtier. He was also very popular with George IV, had been the king's guest at Windsor and proved himself adept in the hunting field. There had been an army division of British troops stationed in Portugal to safeguard the succession, just in case of foreign interference, but this was now withdrawn.

When the British government changed in 1830, Palmerston, the new British Foreign Secretary, hated both Miguel's atrocities and his politics. Nevertheless he had to recognize that Portugal was an independent nation and so he couldn't do more militarily than maintain Britain's small fleet at the mouth of the Tagus to look after her interests. Otherwise the government had to appear even-handed between the belligerents, even if Palmerston was mortified. He realized very well that if the liberals were beaten in Portugal, the absolutist cause might recover lost ground in nearby Spain. Palmerston would probably have liked to forget what he had said about non-intervention when he was in opposition in 1829: 'That principle is sound. It ought to be sacred.' It could easily have been thrown back in his face in the future. He did attempt to have it both ways, though:

> If by interference is meant interference by force of arms, the Government are right in saying, general principles and our own practice forbade us to exert. But if by interference is meant intermeddling, and intermeddling in every way, and to every extent, short of actual military force; then I must affirm that there is nothing in such interference which the law of nations may not in certain cases permit.

The question was whether 'certain cases' included instances where the illegitimate ruler had the support of the majority of the citizens in the country, or whether all that mattered was the interests of a foreign government. It was also easy enough for an opposition politician to advocate extreme policies. Handling the realities of foreign policy decisions when in power might change the perspective, although in Palmerston's case it seldom seemed to. For the time being he had to content himself on the opposition benches with attacking Miguel verbally, with considerable vigour and scoring political points against the government:

> The civilized world rings with execrations upon Miguel and yet this destroyer of constitutional freedom – this breaker of solemn oaths – this faithless usurper – this enslaver of his country – this trampler upon public law – this violator of private rights – this attempter of the life of helpless and defenceless women ... is ... mainly indebted for his success ... that the cabinet of England looks upon his usurpation with no unfriendly eye.[1]

Miguel went on to institute a reign of terror to try to suppress the remaining liberals, and everybody knew that his ambition, as far as the foreign merchants were concerned, was to nationalise their assets and expel them from the country. That would have been easy enough without the annoying presence of Britain's naval squadron, which was under the command of Rear Admiral William Parker and firmly anchored just outside Lisbon. Parker also still had 700 marines located at Fort St Julien and these could be used in an emergency, but not otherwise. The British forces were present in accordance with the terms of the Methuen Treaty between Portugal and Britain, signed in 1703, so the presence of the squadron could not be designated an aggressive move.

Parker was just 12 when he joined the senior service in 1793. By the time he was 18 he was a lieutenant; he was acting captain at 19 and a full captain at 20. Even if an illustrious relative, Admiral Jervis, had eased his path at the outset of his career, nobody could deny that Parker was a first-rate officer. He commanded HMS *Amazon* throughout his 20s, mainly along the coast of Spain and Portugal between 1806 and 1812. Part of the responsibility of ships like the *Amazon* was to protect cargoes of precious grain on its way to feed Britain. The possibility must be on the cards that, at that early stage, he met Pacifico in the port of Lagos, where Parker would have anchored on many occasions.

Certainly he learned a great deal about the Portuguese, including their politics. After stints as senior officer on the coast of Greece and commander of the royal yacht, *Prince Regent*, he was appointed rear admiral in 1828, at the age of 48, and sent off to do what he could for the expats in Portugal. It was an independent command, so the Admiralty was relying on him to use his initiative, but with caution. Whatever happened, nobody should be able to blame the Admiralty – that is, the British government – and the brief gave Parker considerable scope.

Like a lot of military leaders, he hated to see the suffering war brought. He sent 100 *cruzados* for the poor and encouraged his officers to be charitable as well. Sometimes this could be difficult for officers serving with the Portuguese navy, as their pay was often as much as eighteen months in arrears. Many of them then offered to serve without pay, including Sir John Milly Doyle, son of a former governor of Gibraltar, who had been imprisoned by Miguel in Lisbon and was released only after Palmerston had issued dire threats of what would happen if he wasn't. Palmerston also insisted on massive compensation for Doyle from the Portuguese for wrongful arrest.

In April 1831 Pedro, by now an increasingly unpopular Brazilian emperor – he had just lost Uruguay – abdicated the throne in South

America in favour of his son and sailed for Britain. He was determined to raise an army to free Portugal from his brother. It was a considerable sacrifice as he never saw his children again. The Liberal Party supporters in Britain were more than willing to help, but raising armies is an expensive business. There was a court case in London in 1835 when a London Portuguese merchant sued a French banker for the commission he was due for helping to raise a massive loan of £600,000 for Pedro (£37 million in today's money). The commission was 0.75 per cent which came to £15,000 (now equivalent to £915,000) and the Paris banker got 2.5 per cent for his work (which would now be over £3 million). The case was settled out of court but it was mentioned that the original agreement was with Pedro's emissaries, who included Vila Flor.[2] The resulting war would ruin Portugal's finances all over again.

When he had the money, Pedro went off to Terceira to set up a government in exile. He was welcomed like a hero, took over from Palmela, and in July 1832 sailed from Terceira to Porto to carry the fight to his brother. Porto was under Miguelite control but Pedro knew that he still had a large body of supporters in the city.

The Pedroite forces landed without opposition some way up the coast and then marched on the city. The Miguelites abandoned their positions and Pedro's forces entered in triumph. About 10 per cent of them were mercenaries from all over Europe. These tough soldiers were better trained and disciplined than the Miguelites and it would show when the hard pounding eventually began. In a battle around Porto in September 1832, the British contingent had ten officers and sixty-nine other ranks killed or wounded, the French eleven officers and 114 other ranks, but Portuguese casualties were only twenty-seven; the main body of the Portuguese army still supported Miguel.

Pedro now held Porto, but the Miguelites besieged the city and it had to be provisioned entirely from the Atlantic. Food was often in short supply and there was also the threat of isolated cases of cholera turning into an epidemic. Admiral Parker, however, could at least keep the sea lanes open without difficulty, because his powerful squadron on the Tagus included some of the pride of the British fleet: the *Caledonia, Britannia, Revenge, Briton, Leveret* and *Viper*. The winter weather still created problems, however, often preventing the badly-needed food from being landed. The Miguelite troops had the advantage of shore batteries capable of firing on anything that moved, but their morale was poor; they were really in a bad way, short of clothing and shoes and unpaid for months at a time. Basically, most of them were peasant draftees, but there were a lot of them, and Pedro's forces also had their own share of peasant volunteers.

In Porto, Pedro decided to assume full control of the armed forces, at which point Vila Flor, not surprisingly, resigned. The relationship between Flor and the king was always volatile. Flor could rightly have considered that it was he who had defeated the Miguelites when they invaded Terceira, and not the king, who was comfortably in Brazil. Flor would also be very conscious that Pedro had no track record as a general. He was king, however, so he could act as he wished. To soften the blow, Pedro made Flor the Duke of Terceira and gave him a very large pension in perpetuity.

The new duke wasn't out of the picture for long, though. By February 1833 Pedro had reorganized the army into three fighting divisions, and Terceira accepted the command of the first. Marshall Saldanha had the second. Saldanha was now a great hero to the liberal refugees who had fled to France, and he had been elected Grand Master of their Grand Lodge in exile. There was a second Grand Master in José da Silva Carvalho and there would be a third created in Porto – Passos Manuel. The liberals and freemasonry remained very closely linked.

General Sir Thomas Stubbs commanded the third division which had a British brigade and two regiments of the Queen's Light Infantry. One was entirely French and the other had all the other mercenaries, primarily from Belgium and Germany. The overall commander in the field was Marshall Solignac, so there were enough chiefs but a distinct shortage of Indians.

Back on the Tagus, there was little that Miguel's fleet could do to escape Parker's eagle eye. The question was to whom to pass the information, so that it would do the most good. Parker had broken the Miguelite telegraph cypher but Pedro's Portuguese navy was as second-rate as Miguel's. All agreed, therefore, that a decent commander could make all the difference. Here the British could help because they had exactly the man Pedro needed: a senior naval officer with a fine record and out of work.

Captain Charles 'Mad Charley' Napier was two years younger than Parker and had become a full captain by the time he was 23. Temporarily without a ship and on half pay in 1810, he had gone to Portugal on holiday and decided to join its army. Napier had fought well in the Napoleonic Wars and was ideal for the job. He was a friend of Palmerston, and he readily accepted the offer of command of Pedro's fledgling navy. So it was that, in February 1833, complete with entourage and the alias of Carlos de Ponza, Mad Charley sailed out of Falmouth with Pedro's commission as vice-admiral of the liberal fleet.

If that took care of the navy, the next question was how to defeat the numerically vastly superior Miguelite forces on land. It wasn't going to be easy. It was quite normal for armies in Europe at the time to be divided into three distinct segments. There were those soldiers who would be recruited locally and used to defend their area if it was attacked. This didn't disturb their day job unless there was an emergency. The next element was the soldiery who defended the key points: the garrisons of towns and the defenders of castles. These were permanently employed, but also didn't usually move from their appointed positions. The third section was made up of those who took the field and went off to fight battles. That was where you'd find Terceira, Saldanha and Stubbs and it was the most dangerous place to be.

Besieged by the Miguelites, Terceira had been recalled to help the defence of the city and managed to hold his own against massively larger Miguelite forces. Pedro was bottled up in Porto for almost a year, though, and he wasn't making any progress, while the expenses mounted. British public opinion was convinced that his position was hopeless and Palmerston was almost ready to admit defeat. In desperation it was decided to try to break the deadlock by invading the country's south coast. It was a ludicrously high-risk decision; Pedro could spare a meagre 2,500 men against about 60,000 Miguelites in potentially hostile territory.

It was, nevertheless, agreed that Terceira's division would be transported by Mad Charley Napier, and during the forthcoming campaign it would obviously have to be fed and paid. That was the job of the commissary, and the duke's commissary was – David Pacifico. What was the future president of the Athens Jewish community doing on a battlefield, with all the formidable problems that would entail?

Pacifico wrote nothing about this period of his life, from the age of 48 to 50, except to ask for his back pay and expenses. Fortunately, A. L. F. Schaumann, a commissary for Wellington during the Peninsular War in Portugal, did. In his book he laments the lot of commissaries: 'to expose themselves to the dangers of meeting enemy forces, to shoulder the greatest responsibilities, to be constantly threatened with assassination by enraged natives and to be treated shabbily by the generals'.[3] The reason the natives were going to be enraged was if their produce was bought for a price they thought unfair, or if it was simply confiscated.

What made things worse for the commissary was that the natives always blamed him for the looting, which was invariably carried out by the rest of the army. Particularly if the troops weren't paid – and the pay on both sides was usually many months in arrears in the War of the Two Brothers – the soldiers would steal everything that wasn't nailed down and a lot of things that were. The generals were not concerned with the problems this made for the commissary – even if they could have restrained their forces, which they usually couldn't. To the generals, the commissaries were just the army's controllers of the kitchen, but not the equivalent of fighting troops.

How Pacifico got the job of commissary is conjecture. Pedro might have met him in London when the king came to Britain to try to raise money for the expedition. He obviously knew Pacifico because of the Archbishop Ataite–Gibraltar connection. Pacifico would have been accepted as an enthusiastic and dedicated supporter of the liberal cause, and so pro-Portuguese that he had become naturalized in 1822. Pedro would also know that Pacifico was very well connected at home in Gibraltar where many Jewish merchants had given succour to refugees fighting the Spanish absolutists. In 1822: 'The inhabitants of Gibraltar treated the ill-fated exiles with great hospitality; numbers of the Constitutionalists resided on visits at the houses of their friends, both in the town and at Europa Point beyond the Almeda. At the mansion of [Aaron] Cardozo about twenty found refuge: among his guests were Sir Robert Wilson and General Quiroga.'[4]

Pacifico could also have relied on a line of credit from his family in Britain. David Pacifico, the Elder, had a brother, Asher, who had two sons, Isaac and Emanuel. Isaac finished up in Jamaica but Emanuel practised as a doctor in London. He was also an early director of the Atlas Assurance Company, who publicly boasted of William IV as one of their clients. Emanuel would have known, or could have found out, who was prepared to help Pedro's cause in Portugal. Pacifico also had his brother, Aaron, on hand. When Aaron returned to Gibraltar, he set up again as a merchant.

The Jews were well known as good commissaries:

> Their favourite and most important quasi-military profession, however, was contracting supplies to the armies, a business which several of them had developed and learnt while in Spain and Portugal. It relied on quick and good communications and good international credit links so that bands of bakers and huge trains of bread wagons could be readily marshalled at a given

date and spot to feed the hungry troops. At this they were great experts.[5]

Commissaries were 'civilians who combined the responsibility of treasury officials, paymasters and purveyors. They bought, stored, transported and issued rations for men and animals and issued cash for the pay of officers and men.'[6]

In this war, however, behind the bald job specification, there was even more than the usual amount of worry for a commissary. To begin with, the whole initial idea of conquering Portugal with an army of 7,500 men could only be described as a suicide mission. Miguel had the best part of 100,000 men; Pacifico would have known the peasantry was apathetic about Pedro, and that the church and nobility were against him. If Pedro and Pacifico began negotiating in London in 1831, the chances of eventual success for the king at the time were slim indeed.

Potentially, it was also a dreadful job. The only certainty was that you would be fired at the end of the campaign; commissaries were only needed in time of war. In addition you could easily be killed in the fighting; commissaries had to work near the front where the men they were feeding actually bivouacked. That was where the meals were needed and the shorter your lines of communication, the better.

War is terrible anywhere and at any time, but early nineteenth-century war had its own horrors. During a retreat nobody had time to bury the dead, and the stench of putrefaction was made worse when the bodies were those of horses and mules. Cholera, dysentery and typhoid could do more damage than the fighting. The working conditions for the commissaries were appalling: a different head-quarters every night as the army advanced or retreated, extremely long hours and trying to get a few hours sleep on the floor if you were lucky, with lice, fleas and bedbugs for your constant companions. When the soldiery settled down for the night, the commissary still had to do the books, accounting minutely for the supplies he had received and handed out. The troops had to be fed in all weathers and the commissary would often find himself scouring the countryside looking for supplies in dreadful climatic conditions.

The combatants in the War of the Two Brothers hated each other with a passion, and so atrocities were frequent. When an army was advancing, there would be some sort of order and discipline in the supply routes, but if it was retreating, discipline could easily break down. Then it would be every man for himself, and the plight of the old, and of the women and children caught up in the melee, was always heartbreaking, with long columns of helpless refugees fleeing the slaughter on foot, having lost all their possessions. The troops could be in danger of starving as well: as Schaumann wrote 'I was the deity to whom men prayed: Give us this day our daily bread.'

Pacifico had no need to volunteer. He could have taken the family back to Gibraltar and escaped the whole mess. Why should a middle-aged man, accustomed to the normal comforts of home, risk his life and leave his loved ones, with the real possibility that Clara could end up a widow trying to bring up his two young daughters? The only logical answer is that Pacifico believed passionately in the cause. He was prepared to make the sacrifices because of his patriotism. Alright, it was certainly possible for a commissary to make a lot of money; the pay for the soldiers was carried with the army and accounting for it provided any number of opportunities for graft.

There were also enemy stores and possessions to capture of every sort – auctions were held in the aftermath of battles. But to profit from the conditions you had to be on the winning side and you had to survive the gunfire. Terceira's force was going to be outnumbered many times over by the Miguelites. There were definitely easier ways of making a living. Furthermore, in a large army, the commissary had assistants who did a lot of the dirty work. In a small battle group, like Terceira's, Pacifico would have had to undertake most of the chores himself. He deserved well of his adopted country.

Pedro would have been told that Pacifico had a strong track record as a merchant in the Algarve, dating back to those early days in 1812 in Mertola. If the invasion was going to be in the south, Pacifico knew the territory. Indeed, he was still operating the business and he also had the qualification of ship's agent. So he was well equipped to be Terceira's commissary. To make the necessary arrangements Pacifico might well have had to travel to Gibraltar, Terceira and London, but he could still use his British nationality when it suited him. He was certainly in Gibraltar on 1 March 1833, a couple of months before Terceira set out, because he got a new British passport from the lieutenant governor on that date. He was probably taking precautions before rejoining his division. If you were captured by the Miguelites, a British passport might be some protection from the consequences.

Pacifico had told the Gibraltar authorities that he had been born in 1789 and the question arises of why he had reduced his age by five years. One possible explanation was that a commissary obviously had to be a man in prime condition and 44 might have sounded better than 49, the expectation of life being that much lower than it is today.

Although the Miguelites should have been able to count on local support, money talked. Pacifico was a very experienced trader in Portugal, with massive contacts. His main suppliers would also have considered the advantage of a record of supporting Pedro if he actually won. Backing both sides in a war can have its advantages. Pacifico was obviously able to use his passport as a means of travelling safely in hostile territory. He had to be in Porto with Pedro's forces to do the planning of the commissariat. Then he would have needed to be in contact with the suppliers who could be counted on when Terceira's forces landed; his friends among the corn producers in the Mertola area would have come in useful there. Finally, he had to be in Gibraltar to talk to the liberal supporters about financial support for the Pedroite cause. To get all the pieces in place at the right time would have been a major achievement.

The most likely reason for choosing Pacifico was probably that nobody else had the same qualifications as those he offered. He could even have been headhunted – 'Can anybody recommend a decent commissary?' The record of the Portuguese, on the last occasion they had gone into the field seriously, had not been good; Beresford's chief of staff, Sir Benjamin d'Urban, wrote about the 1808 period: 'The Marshall is arranging with Lord Wellington some certain means of subsisting the Portuguese troops when their supplies fail ... This is absolutely requisite or the troops will often starve, for such is the poverty, imbecility and total want of arrangements of the Portuguese government that any regular system of supply is not to be expected.'[7] When considering how the commissaries for the Miguelite troops measured up to their tasks, not a great deal seemed to have changed over the intervening twenty-five years.

From Pacifico's point of view, the only way he was going to get compensation for his lost *commanderies* was if Pedro won. Well, that would have been the game plan anyway. When Pedro came back to Portugal, Miguel spun the story that the Pedroites would plunder the country, but the king's information machine was able to report: 'Horses, mules, oxen, sheep and provisions of all sorts have been purchased and paid for with ready money.'

The grapevine was optimistically suggesting that Miguel might be losing support at a massive rate. In foreign affairs he supported Carlos, King Ferdinand of Spain's brother, who was trying to usurp the Spanish throne. This upset the liberal governments in Europe.

Domestically, Miguel had also had to find money. He did this by asking for voluntary contributions – which everybody knew were 100 per cent compulsory – and from heavy taxation. The investors had no option about whether or how much they contributed. This was decided for them by the Miguelites and, if they resisted, the figure was doubled. The rich were mulcted and they resented it. These impositions, together with the damage to trade and the atrocities of war, soon made the people very tired of hostilities. Miguel became as unpopular as his brother had been at the outset of the conflict. He may have had numerical superiority but, as far as the war was concerned, the hearts of most of his troops weren't usually in it.

Mad Charley's arrival made it possible for Pedro's flotilla to sail from Porto on 21 June 1833. It consisted of three frigates, two corvettes and a brig, and there were said to be more than 3,000 troops on board.[8] Mad Charley was in charge of the ships and Terceira of the military. It was assumed that the fleet was bound for Lisbon to make an attempt on the capital. In fact, the army landed at the small harbour of Cacela Velha on Portugal's Costa del Sol. The town's current tourist board literature records the arrival of the fighting troops: 'Nothing happens in the hamlet of Cacela Velha but... it was here in June 1833 that the English Admiral Charles Napier put 2,500 Portuguese troops ashore... The only remnant of war in Cacela Velha today is a tiny fort... with a peaceful panoramic view over a lagoon and the broad, sandy strand.'

The Times on 10 July 1833 provided the additional information that 'the small fort at Cacela struck its flag within 5 minutes after the first 100 men had stepped on shore, and a fine brass 12-pounder fell into our hands on landing'.

So the crazy idea was now launched. Just one third of an already numerically inadequate army had been landed in the south of the country, hundreds of miles from the Porto headquarters, to take on the massive Miguelite forces. As an 'eminent correspondent' wrote in *The Times* on 13 July 1833: 'But who ever thought of performing a military movement by land in the Algarve? What empty head ever conceived the Quixotic idea of conquering a kingdom with 2,500 men?' The liberal leaders hoped the people would rise spontaneously in favour of the young queen. If they were wrong, it would be a disaster waiting to happen.

When the king's fleet had finally sailed, it included a number of senior British officers. The flagship was the *Rainha de Portugal*, with Captain Reeves on the bridge. The *Donna Maria* had Captain

Henry; the *Pedro*, Captain Goblet; and the corvette, *Portense*, Captain Balkeston. There were also five steamers and a number of store ships, with the 2,500 men on board. They were all carefully watched by Parker's accompanying naval squadron. As Parker would have had to be kept fully informed of the plans for the invasion, he would have come into contact with all the senior liberals and would have encountered Pacifico, whom he had probably met before. In later years Pacifico would benefit a lot from the connection.

Mad Charley was a fast worker and he had Parker to spy on the enemy for him. Having landed Terceira he turned back, and on 2 July Miguel's fleet was sighted off Cape St Vincent. Mad Charley attacked without hesitation. It was said of Napier that he was 'not to be trusted except in the hour of danger, and then he performs prodigies far beyond all calculations'. Miguel's captains knew little of premier league naval warfare, and Mad Charley was soon able to send a dispatch to the Portuguese: 'I have taken all the Miguelite squadron, with the exception of two corvettes and two brigs. I shall go off to Lisbon the moment I can get a few ships ready.' He had put out of action two battleships, two frigates and a corvette.[9] The absolutist fleet was never a real threat again and Mad Charley, now raised by a grateful Pedro to Admiral of the Royal Armada of Portugal and Viscount Cape St Vincent, joined the Portuguese nobility. As Terceira drove north to Lisbon, so Napier sailed round the coast to meet him.

In the event, the Miguelites in the south proved to be broken reeds. They had the numbers but they had lost heart. Their pay and conditions had been neglected for months, the support of the locals had been lost through the harsh taxation and most of those involved just wanted the whole thing to be over. The defence of Tavira was typical: 'our troops marched early to Tavira, outside of which they met 300 Miguelites, who fired one volley and fled'.[10] The Miguelite army simply ran away and the people proclaimed their allegiance to the queen even before Terceira arrived.

There were few casualties on the Pedroite side but the Miguelites suffered badly. As *The Times* reported from the front on one occasion: 'Charles Duveirin lost his left arm but very few men. 48 of the Miguelites were put to the bayonet.'[11] The alternative for the Miguelite forces was, of course, desertion and a large number went that route. If, however, they were found and recaptured, the penalty, at the very least, was to be beaten unmercifully with the flat of a sword, which could well kill them.[12]

The relief that the war was likely to end gave rise to great civil celebrations. One night *The Times'* correspondent reported: 'the last batch of men have just gone off and about 90 farmers and townspeople have come down to the boats with skyrockets, which they are now discharging on the beach amidst the music of the bands of the different regiments'. Of course, the opportunity for looting was still popular. Because of the 'ungovernable misconduct on shore' of some of the French soldiers, 112 of them were sent back to Porto. Three were killed in riots because they didn't want to leave.

Although Pacifico was on the liberal side, there was nothing he could do to stop the soldiers pillaging his home and looting his corn warehouse when they reached Mertola on their march to Lisbon. Nobody was hurt and he contented himself with getting a judge in Faro, on 13 February 1834, to confirm that his claim for damages was correct. Logically, he would have told Terceira, his commander in the field, what had happened and they would have agreed on the correct course of action in the circumstances. The question was whether Terceira would have a sufficiently good memory.

The whole success seemed too good to be true. Mad Charley himself went round to each of the steamers carrying supplies 'to prevail upon the masters to bring their vehicles close to the shore, assuring them that they should be entirely covered by the frigates from the enemy's fire, which they were disinclined to endanger their owner's property by approaching'.[13]

The triumphant little army marched 100 miles north to Lisbon in one short month and faced its last great challenge. Miguel had raised the siege of Porto and brought his army to face the liberals in a final battle for the capital. The Miguelite force was under the command of the dreaded General Telles Jordao who had 6,000 Miguelite troops to Terceira's 1,500. Jordao had been responsible for many outrages but this was his last stand. He was killed on the banks of the river and his men fled again. Jordao's head and hands were cut off to display to the multitude and the rest of the body was buried in the sand. This wasn't enough for those who hated him; they dug up the body again and cut it into pieces.

Terceira's army entered Lisbon on 26 July and freed 5,000 captives, many of whom had been imprisoned for many years under appalling conditions. The British flag was raised over the citadel alongside the Portuguese banner. Parker, in the bay, fired a twenty-one-gun salute as his part of the celebrations. Mad Charley was lionised as well: 'Admiral Parker intends to receive him with every honour he can bestow, manning yards, saluting and cheering him as he passes. We have a guard on the *Maitland*'s poop and the rest of the men arranged along the ship's gangways with the drummers to play "see the conquering hero comes" as he passes'.[14]

The campaign had taken a month thus far: 'Really the success of this expedition has been astonishing: those who had planned it never dreamed that it would do more than create a diversion of the enemy's force: but in one short month it has overthrown, it is hoped for ever, a Government.'[15]

The war wasn't over. The Miguelite forces retreated north from Lisbon and the struggle dragged on for another nine months. At the end of September, however, Ferdinand VII of Spain died and most of the senior Spanish officers serving in the Miguelite army resigned and went home to Madrid in case there was a civil war.

Relations between Terceira and Pedro continued to be explosive. In January 1834 the king wanted Terceira to go to Porto which would enable him to start a second front against Miguel. Terceira didn't like the idea of being subordinate to Marshall Saldanha. It was customary for the army to be the province of the nobility, and Terceira hadn't been born to the purple. When he had originally been given a title, it was rejected by the nobility because Pedro hadn't consulted them. Terceira's excellent fighting qualities tended to be dismissed: 'The general opinion respecting the Duke of Terceira is that he is a brave soldier, very fortunate in his undertakings, a most gentleman like and honourable man, very much beloved by his troops, but not possessing any very great talents.'[16] This was to underestimate Terceira, who might well have commented that the harder he worked the more fortunate he became. He was by far the best of the Portuguese generals and 'though always decried and often opposed by the extreme Liberals'[17] he went on winning.

So, in February 1834, Terceira resigned again and this time General Stubbs was appointed to replace him. When tempers had cooled, Terceira agreed to take up the military cudgels once more, but as joint commander with Saldanha. It must have been difficult for his officers, including Pacifico, who had to operate in such an uncertain atmosphere.

The Miguelite army raised their siege of Porto and gave battle in February at Altmoster instead; they lost. They tried again at Asseiteira in May with the same result. They went in for the last time in early June in defence of their headquarters in Santoram and they lost again. The battle of Evora-Monte was the last in the civil war. Pacifico could go home to Clara and the children. As an army travels on its stomach, that had been filled the entire year by Pacifico's efforts and, like the rest of Terceira's team, he had performed nobly in the Pedroite cause.

Pedro and Miguel finally met to settle the terms of the peace, not in some grand palace but in a one-storied house. Terceira and Saldanha negotiated for Pedro and General Lemos spoke for the absolutists. It was apposite that the British were still involved, as John Grant from the British Embassy was in the chair.[18] A Regency Council was proclaimed for Maria, with Palmela as president, and Terceira and Mad Charley as the other members. When the two sides finally settled the last points, Pedro was back in power, but in fact Miguel, tricky to the last, never ratified the agreement. In Britain, Pedro was considered, potentially, to be equally unreliable. His promises to his people were met with suspicion in many quarters; as Lord John Russell, a future prime minister, put it: 'I feel that they have exchanged one set of robbers for another.'

If that background goes some way to explain Pacifico's claims against the Portuguese, what about the situation in Greece?

NOTES

1 Evelyn Ashley, *The Life and Correspondence of Viscount Palmerston* (Richard Bentley, 1879).
2 *The Times*, 10 July 1835.
3 A. L. F. Schaumann, *On the Road with Wellington* (Greenhill Books, 1999).
4 Thomas Steele, *Notes of the War in Spain* (London: 1824).
5 Richard D. Barnett, *The Western Sephardim: The Sephardim of England* (Gibraltar Books 1989).
6 *Encyclopaedia Britannica*, vol. 11, p. 78.
7 I. Rousseau (ed.), *The Peninsular War Journal of Sir Benjamin D'Urban* (London: 1930).
8 *The Times*, 6 July 1833.
9 Ibid., 5 August 1833.
10 Ibid., 10 July 1833.
11 Ibid., 18 June 1833.
12 Ibid., 18 February 1833.
13 Ibid., 10 July 1833.
14 Ibid., 25 July 1833.
15 Ibid., 5 August 1833.
16 Ibid., 12 January 1834.
17 Ibid., 3 May 1834.
18 José Saramago, *Journey to Portugal* (Harcourt Inc. 1990).

6 The birth of Greece

Frankly, if there had been only one Greece, early nineteenth-century European foreign policy would have been that much simpler to manage. Unfortunately, there were two of them.

One was the ancient world of classical Greece. The Greece of Socrates, Euclid, Plato and Aristophanes. The birthplace of democracy and of the glory of some of the seven wonders of the ancient world. Olympian Greece, with all the beauty of its sculpture and its language, its heroic cast of gods in works by epic writers like Homer, and the great deeds of warriors like Alexander the Great. The culture that was taught in Britain at Eton, Harrow and Winchester, held up to admiration by the greatest west European scholars and whose columns, pediments and sheer mass were the architectural antecedents of the finest buildings of the Regency period.

Then there was the reality of the Greece that actually existed in 1820, the core to be found in a poverty-stricken province of the Turkish Empire, but an additional population dispersed in pockets all over the north east of the Mediterranean. Most of them were backward and the great movements of western Europe over the centuries had passed them by; the Renaissance, Reformation, science, the Enlightenment and the Industrial Revolution didn't travel well into the lands ruled from Constantinople.

Greece was still a nation of seafarers, still populated almost entirely by members of the Greek Orthodox Church, but with the great days when Athens dominated the Western world, a distant, if powerful, memory. As the poet, Lord Byron, wrote at the time: 'Fair Greece! sad relic of departed worth! Immortal, though no more; though fallen, great.'[1] Even Castlereagh, the British Foreign Secretary at the Congress of Vienna, which was held to tidy up after the Napoleonic Wars, went on record on the subject: must 'those, in admiration of whom we have been educated, be doomed... to drag out, for all time to come, the miserable existence to which circumstances have reduced them'. It was generally agreed that 'the great mass of their people are in a semi-barbarous state'.

The Turks had finally conquered Greece in 1456. The Greek Orthodox Church still remained separated from the Roman Catholic Church and wanted to stay that way. Catholic Europe had a tendency to demand papal supremacy as the price of military help, but the Turks didn't interfere much in other people's religious practices.

The Turks had indeed placed a Greek Orthodox patriarch over all the other Christian religious leaders in their empire and given the clergy considerable legal authority. There were, of course, limits to the Turks' tolerance; for example, the word of a Christian was not accepted in court against that of a Muslim, but at least you could remain a Christian. The Turks were forbidden by the *Sheriat*, the Holy Law of Islam, from forcibly converting anybody. They could encourage conversion, but they couldn't use force.

Because of their mercantile abilities, the Greeks made a major economic contribution to the economy of the Ottoman Empire. The Turks were really happiest when they could just sit back and collect taxes from their provinces; they realised that the richer the provinces, the greater the tax revenue, so their main objective was to try to keep everything on an even keel. The Greeks were allowed a considerable amount of local autonomy and a small class of rich merchants emerged, who were often ship owners: 'Muslims regarded trade as an unbecoming occupation.'[2]

For a civilized, law-abiding society to be created in Greece, the main problem was who would keep order? The countryside was full of gangs of brigands, who were called klephts. Sometimes, the local leaders adopted a policy of 'if you can't beat them, join them'. They bribed the gang leaders to act as their police force. In return for protection money, the klephts kept order in the district. Sometimes the leaders produced their own local force to oppose the klephts. These were called *armataloi*. The klephts might even regain their place in legitimate society by becoming *armataloi*; poachers turned gamekeepers. It was not surprising that most Greeks continued to have little confidence in the rule of law. It was considered a more prudent course of survival practice to ally yourself to a powerful local figure and leave him to sort out your problems. It might cost in terms of money, service and eventually votes, but it offered you your best chance in times of trouble. It was widely held within the widespread rural communities that the only people you could really trust were your family.

That was the real Greece in 1820 and in any war of independence against the Turks, it would be the klephts and the *armataloi* who would provide the muscle. In the popular imagination, they came to symbolize a national resistance movement. As a consequence, those Greek nationalists who, with British, French and Russian aid, finally succeeded in getting rid of the Turkish hegemony, were some of the nastiest pirates who ever sailed under false colours.

As there weren't enough Turks to colonise their vast empire, some form of delegation was essential. If, however, within the provinces, any of their appointees became too powerful in the eyes of Constantinople, they were removed and often executed as well. The system worked well enough for the sultan until Napoleon upset autocratic apple carts all over Europe. The burning question, for the lovers of Ancient Greece, had always been whether Byron's 'departed worth' could be restored. The trigger to believe that it could be was the French Revolution: the overthrow of old regimes and the successful blossoming of a philosophy of freedom, equality and fraternity.

Isolated as the Greeks were within the Turkish Empire, far from the influences of the West, the Napoleonic ideals did slowly filter through to a small number of dissidents. At any attempt to throw off the Turkish yoke and to restore at least some of the old boundaries of the country, the romantics would gather round the flag; foreign romantics would not be far behind.

When the revolt began in 1821 it went on for ten years of bloodshed. Among the casualties were memorable volunteers like Byron – who succumbed to illness – as well as innumerable forgotten Greeks, cut down in the resulting slaughter. One philhelline who survived was a Scottish historian named George Finlay, who arrived in Greece in 1821 and eventually settled in Athens. Finlay, like Pacifico, was to become a claimant against the future Greek government.

The Greek independence movement was supported financially by successful fund-raising in Europe, by personal contributions from Greeks within the country and, to some extent, by the ubiquitous Rothschilds. The French people quickly donated £50,000 but the British government was a lot more cautious about supporting the insurgents. If they showed little enthusiasm themselves, however, funds for the revolution still arrived from philhellines from all over the world. In London the Quaker community raised more money than the local Greek community and support also arrived in the form of mercenaries, technical advisers and funds for humanitarian relief. Whether everything reached its prescribed destination, however, is very doubtful; not much change there then.

No revolt was ever likely to be officially encouraged by the Greek Orthodox Church leaders. They were content to be in charge of the religious and much secular activity for their communities. All the Turks demanded in return was the payment of the levies and loyalty to the Porte, the central Turkish government in Constantinople, the capital.

The Porte appointed various Greek representatives to do the job for them. These were called the *phanariots*, and other senior officials under that heading could come from the mercantile class and important provincial figures. The majority of these could be relied upon: 'The elites of pre-independence Greek society – the Phanariots, the higher clergy, the wealthy merchants and the provincial notables...were for the most part too comfortably locked into the Ottoman status quo to identify with the national movement.'[3]

So if Greece was to become an independent nation again, there needed to be a trigger. As with the liberals in Portugal, this was to be a secret society. In Greece it was called the *Philiki Etaireia* – the Friendly Society. Well, friendly to Greek nationalists, but hell-bent on a serious revolution as far as the Turks were concerned. The *eterists* formed freemasons' lodges – again, just like the Portuguese liberals – to keep their secret membership unidentified. There were elaborate rituals, clandestine meetings and a slow growth in their numbers. Like the Portuguese, once more, this society had strong backing among the intelligentsia, although the merchant membership had the largest single group of supporters.

One of the early opportunities to test the revolutionary water came in 1821 when the Turks were distracted by their efforts to put down a local warlord. Seeing the Turks otherwise engaged, the *eterists*, led by the Ypsilanti brothers, issued a call to arms and a war of independence spluttered into life. It received very little support, however, and the revolutionary light went out as quickly as it had emerged. Still, from the *eterists'* point of view, it had been a start.

Among those who had condemned the *eterists* was the Greek Archbishop Gregorios V, who had loyally supported the Porte. Unfortunately, as his support had not prevented the outbreak, the Porte felt that he had fallen down on the job. In 1821 the patriarch was summoned to Constantinople, for what was announced as a routine visit, and then summarily murdered, together with other senior members of his delegation. When the story of this atrocity reached Greece it had become slightly embellished. Now it was said that the Turks had got the local Jewish community in

Constantinople to kill the archbishop and throw his body into the river Bosporus. All the *phanariots* knew that the murders were, in reality, a Turkish reprisal, but they didn't like the Jews anyway. A bloodbath quickly followed.

The Jews had always got on well with the Turks. That religious toleration which characterized Turkish rule applied to them as well. When they had been expelled from Spain in 1492, Sultan Bayezid II had encouraged them to settle in his empire. Over 20,000 availed themselves of the opportunity and the sultan was well pleased to have bolstered his economic base. The Jews had, of course, been living in Greece since biblical times and those communities were called *Romaniote* Jews. Indeed, the Jews had a much longer lineage in the country than most of the inhabitants, but they were still hated for not accepting Christianity. When asked by the sultan centuries before, the Athenians had said they didn't want Jews living in their area, and Athens was off-limits for hundreds of years as a consequence. As usual, a small number of Jews did come to the town but there was no real community.

When the death of Gregorios was reported, the Greeks were prepared to believe the rumours and were determined to avenge their beloved archbishop. They decided to do this by destroying many of the ancient Jewish communities. These were eliminated by the simple process of murdering anyone who didn't run away fast enough. The congregations of Patras, Vrachori, Corinth, Kalamata, Tripolitza, Mistras, Modon, Thebes, and Livadia were totally destroyed after thousands of years. More than 5,000 Jews died or fled north into areas such as Chalcis and Corfu which were still held by the Ottomans.[4] 'After the bloodbath of 1821, no Jews were left in the areas liberated by the Hellenic revolution.'[5] This was the kind of prejudice that Don Pacifico could unsafely expect if he ever came to Greece, and yet many Jews fought and died on the Greek side between 1821 and 1829.

Indeed, as early as 1822, the revolutionary Greek National Assembly recognized Jews as equal citizens. While a number of Jews benefited from this, there was usually a substantial gap between theory and practice at the time. The Greek Jews would not be legally organized until 1885 and not given an official charter until 1889. There was no synagogue in Athens until 1904.

The geographical location of Greece made it potentially very important to a number of countries. He who controlled Greece would have a major say in the free flow of trade throughout the eastern Mediterranean. The trade routes from Britain to India led through the area, and anything or anybody who could threaten the communications with India was always a prime object for the British Foreign Office to eliminate.

Greece was, therefore, equally important to those who were, potentially, Britain's enemies. The French were great traders as well and the Russians wanted to dominate the Balkans and replace the Turks wherever possible. Trade relations between Russia and Greece were so close that Greek ships were allowed to sail under the Russian flag. As the Greek Orthodox Church and the Russian Orthodox Church were as one, it was always possible for the Russians to intervene in Greek affairs on the grounds that their co-religionists were involved. The Russian was, in fact, the only Greek Orthodox community which wasn't controlled by the Turks, and Russia and Greece would remain close for a very long time. France would claim the same role internationally on behalf of the Catholics, and Britain on behalf of the Protestants – which left the Jews as the only religious body without a powerful nation to protect them.

The Jews did have one secret weapon at the time: the House of Rothschild. Increasingly, after the Napoleonic Wars, it was the Rothschilds who were best placed to raise money for European governments. The British government was at least prepared to try to help Jewish communities in trouble overseas, as they received an enormous amount of help from the banking house, and as their own Jewish community had always been a good commercial asset. The accusations of persecution had to be well founded and the persecutors relatively weak, however, and even then it was a strictly limited and unofficial commitment, but it helped quite a lot on a number of occasions.

The Greek war against the Turks was marked by remarkable savagery on both sides. The Turks had modern weapons but the Greeks were experts in guerilla warfare. The Portuguese had needed to learn. In Greece it was part of the culture. Their understanding of guerilla techniques was based on the tactics of the klephts, even if the gangs were seldom prepared to move far from their own districts.

Meanwhile, the Greeks had recognized that they needed a commander-in-chief, and an admiral if they were to put together any sort of navy. The commander-in-chief was needed to draw their regional forces together and most agreed that a suitably qualified Brit would be the best choice. After all, British military prowess had beaten Napoleon, and their reputation as philhellenes was very high in Greece. The choice fell on Richard Church, who was involved in fighting in Greece as early as 1809. Church had pleaded the cause of Greek independence at the Congress of Vienna in 1815 and he went back to Greece in March 1827, where he was made commander-in-chief within a month. Church stayed in the country after the war as a councillor of state and the governor of the district of Rumeli. He would remain an important figure in the background because he tutored his British successors – particularly the new British minister, Sir Edmund Lyons – in how Greece worked.

For their admiral the Greeks chose another of the great British Napoleonic War heroes: Lord Cochrane, a true individualist. Cochrane was captain of the brig *Speedy* by the time he was 25 in 1800, and he then had an astonishing career sinking French and Spanish ships, far larger, more powerful and more numerous than the warships he commanded. He was very unpopular with the Admiralty because he objected to having the resulting prize money diverted into the pockets of chair-bound warriors in London, which happened all the time. As his victories were usually achieved against overwhelming odds, he felt he deserved something more concrete than his reputation as a naval hero. Indeed he was so good in battle that Napoleon himself called him the Sea Wolf.

Cochrane retired from the navy to become an MP and everything was going fine until 1814, when his uncle involved him in a Stock Exchange fraud. His Lordship was imprisoned, ceremonially deprived of the Order of the Bath he had won for his wartime exploits and lost his seat in the House of Commons. When he was released, he became one of those very senior mercenaries who were much in demand in countries seeking independence. He served as admiral for the Chileans from 1817 to 1822 and then took the same position for the Brazilians from 1823 to 1825. Neither paid him for the great work he did for them and he was then headhunted by the Greeks. They at least gave him £150,000 to fit out a suitable navy and £37,000 (over £2 million in today's money) for giving up what the Brazilians owed him. It was a great price for what was, effectively, a bad debt. As a sailor, Cochrane went on to do an excellent job.

Unfortunately for his already tarnished commercial reputation, Cochrane was also involved in London in raising the money the Greeks needed for ships. There was a lot of cash involved. The first Greek war loan had been reasonably controlled but then, in 1825, a loan of £2 million was floated and the job was given to a firm of stockbrokers called Ricardo. As the nominal stock had to be sold at a massive 45 per cent discount, only £1.1 million of the £2 million was actually available for financing the war, but the fund was then plundered; a number of Greek politicians made sure they benefited personally. As Colonel Stanhope, one of the investors, said at a committee of enquiry meeting later in London: 'for how highly soever he might value the exertions of the Greeks in defence of their liberty, he was of opinion that any money transmitted to them or left to their management, without keeping in this country some check on its application, was like throwing so much money into the sea'.[6] Not much change there then either with many charities.

Cochrane was involved in the shenanigans. Charles Greville, the great diarist, wrote: 'He has made £100,000 by the Greek bonds.'[7] Ricardo charged £64,000 as a fee for raising the money, but said in his defence that nobody had to accept the terms he offered for doing the job. When it came out that the final contract with him involved a payment to some of those who had to make the final choice of agent, tongues wagged furiously. Ricardo also spent some of the fund on a contract with a shipbuilder who was certainly known to Cochrane, but the ships were delivered either terribly late or not at all. Cochrane's reputation attracted more mud-slingers. To make matters worse, when in Greek waters during the war, there was the usual difficulty for some contestants in distinguishing between fighting the enemy and piracy. Cochrane was accused of giving the pirates the official papers they needed to escape retribution if they were caught, much like the Gibraltarian ships during the Napoleonic Wars.

On the admiral's behalf, Lady Cochrane wrote indignantly to the papers to deny everything, insisting that that her husband was acting strictly as a Greek patriot, and unpaid at that. Critics might have raised the question of the £37,000 in the 1825 contract and the profits on the Greek bonds, but there was a defence in both cases and for a few years the admiral did live on expenses.

The British and Russians were asked by the Greeks to mediate when the war developed into a stalemate in 1825. They weren't all that keen, but their trading interests could be affected by the outcome of the conflict. They got involved, but there were limits. The British Foreign Secretary, George Canning, would have nothing to do with one suggestion from a number of Greeks, called the Act of Submission, that he should agree to make Greece a British protectorate; the sentimental appeal would stretch only so far. The powers finally came up with proposals for making peace, which the Turks initially rejected. They agreed to settle only after the Battle of Navarino in 1827, when a combined Anglo–French fleet, under

Admiral Sir Edward Codrington, badly defeated a Turko–Egyptian force. The Porte was then forced right onto the back foot.

When both sides had had enough, a treaty was signed in London in 1830, guaranteeing Greek independence and defining the boundaries of the new country. The treaty was agreed by Russia, France, Britain and Bavaria, who became the protecting powers, and the Greeks and Turks weren't invited to help in settling their own future. The chair of the conference was Lord Palmerston, the newly-appointed British Foreign Secretary, whose handling of the negotiations was commended by all.

The reason for the inclusion of Bavaria in the discussions was that the powers felt that Greece would need to become a constitutional monarchy. They touted the job round the courts of Europe to try to find a suitable aristocrat, who would agree to spend the rest of his life in a Mediterranean backwater. The 17-year-old Prince Otho of Bavaria, son of King Ludwig I and Therese of Saxe-Altenburg, fancied the idea; the powers breathed a sigh of relief. After all Ludwig was a well-known philhelline and the Greek assembly readily approved the candidature of Otho in 1832. The guarantee of Greek independence was signed by Ludwig and the protecting powers. Palmerston gave the whole arrangement his full support, but he was later to regret it.

Aboard a British battleship, Otho arrived in Greece to popular acclaim in February 1833. He came with a retinue of advisers – many of whom were Jewish businessmen and financiers – and 3,500 Bavarian troops to look after him. All of this was backed up by a Greek loan of FF60 million, about £2.4 million. Greece was now effectively a protectorate, run by Bavaria on behalf of the guarantor powers.

It would have been nice if the Bavarians could have created a national Greek army to back up the new government. After all there were plenty of demobilized soldiers available. Unfortunately the pay and conditions in an army officered by foreigners did not appeal to most of the heroes of the war. They preferred to go back to brigandage in the klephts, and plunder the population as before. Even the king's personal Greek Household Regiment was full of Bavarians. The other side of the coin was that an unhappy army is a gift to potential revolutionaries. Stratford Canning, George Canning's cousin and the British minister in Constantinople, had warned Palmerston back in 1831 that trouble was imminent. He suggested that an immediate injection of £15,000 to £20,000 was essential if piracy and looting were not to break out; the guaranteeing powers reluctantly came up with the money.

As Otho was only 17, it was decided that it would be better to set up a Regency Council until he had the necessary time to get his feet properly under the table. The man selected as regent was the successful Minister of Finance and leader of the Bavarian Constitutional Party, Count Joseph von Armansperg. He was backed up by two other regents, Professor Ludwig von Maurer, formerly the Bavarian Minister of Justice, and General Karl Wilhelm von Heideck – a board of directors guaranteed to reassure any city investor, but definitely not Greek.

There was an executive body of eight ministers in addition, but the regents were not obliged to pay any attention to them or to the members of the new Greek Parliament, and they often didn't. Then again, while a constitution might have been part of the treaty and ratified by King Ludwig on behalf of his son, the Bavarians were still not keen on any such thing. They excused their reluctance to have a constitution enacted by saying that Greece wasn't ready for it.

Otho and Armansperg had also promised to set up democratic local councils but there were frequent reports of definitely undemocratic activities, like arbitrary arrests and torture. Palmerston defended Otho in debates in the House of Commons but, at the same time, wrote impatient despatches to Athens and the King of Bavaria, asking him when the situation would improve:

> On England, therefore, fell the burden of remonstrance against the evils of a constitution without free government, the fruit of which was licence without liberty...Justice could not be expected where the judges were at the mercy of the advisers of the Crown. The finances could not be in any order where there was no public responsibility on the part of those who were to collect or to spend the revenue. Every sort of abuse was practised, from brigandage in the country to 'compulsory appropriation' in the capital itself and the tyranny of the police was almost unbearable.[8]

Palmerston was quite right but the majority of those involved didn't care. There were, however, some areas of concern which affected all the protecting powers – the most important of which was money.

It had been necessary to pay the Turks for the territory they were giving up to the new Greek nation. The financing of the loan came from the Rothschilds, and the guarantors were the protecting powers. The customs duties of several ports were, in theory, set aside to pay the annual £40,000 interest, but the money wasn't easy to collect. To protect their own reputation, the Rothschilds found themselves, for a couple of years, paying the interest for the Greeks to the bond owners. This, they felt strongly, was not in any merchant bank association code of practice. When the Rothschilds decided they'd had enough, Britain, France and Russia had to take on the burden. Yet it was the Rothschilds who had insisted on Armansperg and, to do justice to the regent's efforts, the Greeks were soon taxed more heavily than they had been under the Turks. This did not improve Armansperg's popularity.

Britain, France and Russia each wanted the country to develop according to their own lights. The instrument they used to achieve their objectives was the minister they appointed to Greece, and in the British case it was Edmund Lyons. His job was made very clear to him from the outset: 'Sir Edmund Lyons went to Athens as wet nurse of the youthful monarch'.[9]

Lyons was another member of that successful family of British Napoleonic War naval veterans. He was a bit younger than Parker and Napier, but he reached captain's rank by 1814 and was at the Battle of Navarino against the Turks. To that extent, he was regarded as a friend in Greece and respected as a winning member of the British armed forces. When his ship was withdrawn from service in 1835, he was knighted and decided to change careers. He was sent to Athens as the appointed British minister:

> The naval profession at that time did not seem likely to offer those chances of distinction which the heroic in Captain Lyons' character would have preferred to any other. It struck him, then, that to be British Minister at a Court which was certain to concentrate on itself much of the attention of Europe, would be a desirable post; and with this idea before his mind, it is easy to conceive how he insinuated into the mind of King Otho the idea that he was precisely the man who, in such a situation, would be most agreeable and useful to him.[10]

The problem was that Otho didn't turn out to be the docile pupil that Lyons had anticipated, and Lyons didn't give Otho the consistent support that the king wanted for all his ideas. By nature, the king was slow and cautious, where Lyons was hasty and impetuous. An eventual clash of personalities was almost inevitable. Then there was Armansperg, who had to try to build a nation when the normal Greek loyalties were, primarily, to the family, and then to the village or the region. In this he was not helped by the local warlords, the klepht leaders, who preferred the old status quo. He did get a lot of support from Lyons who, in return, was able to obtain for Britain a preferential position in the setting up of the Bank of Greece. Finlay, when writing his *History of Greece* later, was sure that Lyons and Armansperg ran the country between them. Fundamentally, however, the traditional absolutist views of the Bavarian Armansperg were always going to run counter to the constitutional beliefs of Lyons.

Lyons was said to breathe the air of Greek intrigue and he got involved in it with enthusiasm. In theory, the British, Russian and French ministers were in Greece to act in accord to protect Greek independence. In reality, they all fought each other to establish the greatest level of influence for their individual nations. The Russians curried favour with the Greeks by refusing to press for the servicing of the loan. Lyons built up his own supporters among the parliamentarians, and gave the British party's leader in Parliament, Aléxandros Mavrokordátos, a permanent bodyguard, paid for out of British secret service funds. Lyons viewpoint was always crystal clear: 'Greece is either Russian or English, and since she *must* not be Russian, she *must* be English'. The result of all this infighting, however, was that the diplomats ceased to just be representatives of their countries. They became the enemies of whichever faction was in power if it didn't support their position. As a consequence, when Kolettis eventually became Otho's principal ally, Lyons was seen as the leader of the opposition rather than as the English minister.

It was not the diplomatic approach, but then: 'Captain Lyons was an active, able, ambitious, astute man; a man of the world too: but he wanted experience in the business he had been plunged into, and consequently he was often firing off very big guns at very small affairs.'[11]

Soon after he arrived, Lyons went to work on Armansperg. He encouraged him to wrest control back from the Greek parliamentarians who were sabotaging his efforts. Many were undemocratically prepared to stir up their gangs in the countryside to show Armansperg that they were not to be ignored. For his part, Armansperg responded by shifting one of the chief culprits, Ionnis Kolettis, to be ambassador to France. He would stay there for the next eight years.

Kolettis would be back, however. He was born in 1774, so he was a mature leader. He had been a warlord's doctor and had been able to watch the machinations of that brigand at close quarters. It was a useful education in all manner of sharp practices, but he was always a patriot and was one of the earliest members of *Etaireia*.

Kolettis set up as a leader of the independence movement and was effective in the field: 'the adventurous chief of the half-savage insurgents in Epirus'.[12] He mixed his fighting, however, with brigandage in his stronghold. The public image of Kolettis was as one of the old breed; he continued to dress in the Turkish style, and played on his respectability as a doctor.

For Kolettis, the existing boundaries of Greece were not enough. He was passionately in favour of the Great Idea. As he said in 1844: 'the Greek kingdom is not the whole of Greece, but only a part, the smallest and poorest part. A native is not only someone who lives within this kingdom, but also one who lives in any land associated with Greek history or the Greek race.' Nevertheless, it became official Greek policy under Otho to seek ways of expanding the size of the country. At one time Otho tried to prise Crete out of the hands of Turkey, but Palmerston supported the sultan and this came to nothing.

Kolettis had always been keen on France and led the pro-French party in the assembly. He never wavered in his Gallic support, which didn't make him any more popular with the British minister. British foreign policy had swung towards supporting Turkey within a few years of the fighting over Greece. In 1838 they concluded an important trade agreement with the Porte, who gave Britain a very privileged position in the Ottoman Empire. The sultan always tried to play one great power off against another, but British interests were best served by propping up a weak Turkey in the eastern Mediterranean rather than have it replaced by a strong Russia or France. Another important grouping were the Napists. Constantine Colocotroni, who became Foreign Minister later, was one of their number. So the protecting powers competed to see who could obtain the most parliamentarians to vote for their programmes.

To ease the financial problem, Armansperg managed to persuade Lyons to lend the country a million francs, to which Palmerston gave his approval. The influence of Lyons at court was naturally increased thereby, and when Otho went home on holiday to Bavaria in 1836, Armansperg took the opportunity to introduce constitutional reforms. When Otho heard of these changes on his way back to Greece, his reaction was exactly what Armansperg should have expected. Before the king even set foot on shore, he dismissed Armansperg and revoked the new laws. It was back to absolutism. In December 1837 Otho decided to appoint himself prime minister and in 1838 felt his position sufficiently secure to send the Bavarian troops home.

Now the Napists became very influential. The all-important power of patronage came to rest with Glarikis, who was the Minister of the Interior, and Paikos, who was the Minister of Justice. With help from the Russians, the Napists started to get appointed to all the important positions. Although Otho disliked this pro-Russian influence, the alternative was the constitutional liberals whom he disliked even more. The Napists seemed the best of a bad bunch.

Another concern for the king was where to set up the capital of the new nation. Everybody, naturally, wanted the final capital to be Athens. Unfortunately, the fabled ancient city was no more than a dusty village in 1832. There were, admittedly, good property bargains to be picked up as the Turkish owners fled back to Constantinople. George Finlay was just one investor who had £500 and bought land all over Athens for peanuts. He then waited confidently for house prices to rise.

To encourage Otho to agree to Athens as the capital, work was started on restoring the great symbols of ancient Greek democracy; from 1835 to 1845, for example, the Athena Nike on the Acropolis was saved from crumbling into ruins. In addition a large number of merchants, who owned property in the city, offered the king land for a palace, which was built in front of what is now known as Constitution Square. Finlay's land was not taken at this time. It was requisitioned afterwards in 1836, without the land being officially scheduled for the development, which it had to be. There were also rules that the agreement had to be set out in six months, but the Finlay transfer wasn't settled in that time frame. In fact Finlay complained that he didn't get a farthing (0.1p) in six years.

Finlay could afford to wait; he had paid Noukh Effendi £11 for the land and turned down an offer from the Greeks of £100. The Greeks said it was a 'miserable champ' and wasn't worth more. Finlay said that if the land was so useless, why was it needed for a royal palace? He added that his incidental expenses in the original purchase had been very high. He was very much in the position of the owner of a small piece of property needed to complete the site for a major development. The owner can hold the developer to ransom if the work cannot start without his land. The developer can complain to high heaven but the owner would say that this was his land and his price: take it or leave it. It has always been a game played for high stakes.

The original 1830 game plan, which had been to put Otho on the throne and then to draw up a democratic constitution, was constantly delayed by the Palace. Everybody agreed except Otho, but he was adamantly against a reduction in his power. In addition he refused to change from Catholic to Greek Orthodox, which upset a large proportion of the religious section of the community. It was nevertheless agreed that he would become the head of the Greek church, and this would enable it to split from the ecumenical patriarch's suzerainty in Constantinople. The archbishop was understandably displeased and refused to accept the decision. From that moment the Greek church was regarded as schismatic and the patriarch refused to supply it with the sacred oil which was needed to consecrate new bishops. As both sides agreed the oil had to come from the prelate, it followed that, as Greek bishops died, there could be no authentically recognized replacements. Eventually, whether the Greek government liked the consequences or not, this problem would have to be sorted.

In 1836 Otho had departed for Bavaria and resurfaced late in the year as a married man. He had married Amélie of Oldenburg, and the Greek government was neither consulted, nor invited to the wedding. Amélie was a stout philhellene who decided to dress like a Greek and was careful to take a major interest in the veterans of the War of Independence. The royal pair were, however, to commit two faux pas; they didn't manage to produce an heir, and the queen interfered far more than she should have done in state affairs, often influencing the somewhat weak-willed Otho. As Lord Normanby, the British ambassador to France, reflected in 1848:

> Unfortunately it has happened that the King of Greece, ever since his majority, has pursued a system of policy diametrically at variance with the attainment of all these ends. Endowed by nature with a very limited capacity, he has nevertheless persuaded himself, or has been persuaded by others, that he is capable of managing alone all the affairs, great and small, of his kingdom, and though he is slow at making up his mind upon any thing, and is sometimes unable on some things to make up his mind at all, he looks upon any interference with his own personal will as a personal offence to himself. The consequence has been that he has excluded from the service of the State all men of liberal political opinions, of self respect, and of independence of mind, and has surrounded himself with ministers who have been either so pliant in character as to be always ready to submit their opinions to his will, or who have been so deficient in the qualities required for the government of a state that they had scarcely any opinions for him to overrule.

You hear so little of the communications of members of the
Foreign Office that it is difficult to appreciate just how caustic,
sarcastic and downright rude they often are. On this occasion,
Normanby went on:

> For many years past King Otho has been encouraged in his
> vicious system of government by all the powers of Europe with
> which he has diplomatic relations, with the single exception of
> England; Russia, Austria and Prussia entertaining strong
> adversion to, and great dread of, constitutional principles,
> backed up King Otho in all his schemes, for at first evading to
> grant a constitution, and for afterwards practically tendering
> that constitution a nullity. The government of France might
> indeed have been looked to for support for the constitutional
> liberty of the Greeks, but the French government, under the late
> Monarchy, abetted in Greece the same system of corruption and
> illegality which in France has brought the Monarchy to the
> ground.

When Otho returned to Athens there was obviously a need for a
suitable home for the king. Otho was both ostentatious and
extravagant, which might be excused if he was using his own money,
but was hardly appropriate when his adopted country was
desperately short of funds.

Having decided on a large central site to include appropriate
gardens, the landowners were asked to sell their property at an
especially reasonable price: 'Mr Finlay was one of more than 100
persons who thus sold land to the Greek Government; that is
admitted by all parties in the correspondence.'[13] At this time Athens
was described as little better than a village of huts. The problem was
that the work started before a definite price had been fixed for the
ground. Eventually all the Greek landowners 'signed an engagement
with the commune or principality of Athens to furnish land for
erecting public buildings upon, the price fixed being equivalent to
about 3¼d to 3½d per square yard' (now about 2p).[14] The hidden
agenda for the landowners was the increase in the value of their
property and businesses if Athens became the capital of Greece.

Nevertheless, the signatories did not include George Finlay. He
considered that 3¼d was the equivalent of confiscation and he asked
for the help of the British government in getting a more equitable
settlement. Lyons duly took the matter up with the Foreign
Secretary, who was at the time Lord Aberdeen. After some argument
'all the other proprietors of these lands, without exception, agreed to

the terms'. Finlay still refused to take the money. Pacifico also had some land which was needed later as Amélie expanded the size of the grounds but he did accept the offer. Only he wasn't paid either.

This was the country to which Pacifico would travel as the new representative of the Portuguese government. It had been created through a combination of heroic sacrifice, the generosity of well-wishers – a large number of whom saw the country through rose-coloured glasses – and the machinations of many European powers with trade interests to protect.

Although it possessed the trappings of a European democracy, the reality was that Greece was a conglomerate of many dictatorships. The major centre of power lay with Otho, but he was constrained by the fact that he needed the support of the regional warlords to keep the whole show on the road. He couldn't rely on the rule of law and neither did he want to do so, if it got in the way of his objectives. Whatever Pacifico might be told by the Portuguese, that was the reality of the situation and he would have to operate in a mixture of a banana republic and the wild west.

NOTES

1   Byron, *Bride of Abydos*.
2   Roni Waterfield, *History of Athens* (Macmillan, 2004).
3   Richard Clogg, *A Concise History of Greece* (Cambridge: Cambridge University Press, 1992).
4   Nicholas Stavroulakis, *The Jews of Greece* (Talos Press, 1990).
5   J. Nehama, *The Western Sephardim: Jews of Salonika in the Ottoman Period* (1936).
6   *The Times*, 25 October 1826.
7   Edward Pearce (ed.), *The Diaries of Charles Greville* (Pimlico, 2005: 26 March 1830).
8   Evelyn Ashley, *Lord Palmerston* (Richard Bentley, 1879).
9   *The Times*, 2 February 1850.
10 Ashley, *Lord Palmerston*.
11 Ibid.
12 Ibid.
13 Richard Cobden, MP, in his speech in the House of Commons on 28 June 1850.
14 Ibid.

7 Where's the money coming from?

The war was over. The heroes were the three great Portuguese generals: João Carlos, now the Duke of Saldanha; Vila Flor, now the Duke of Terceira; and Sá Nogueìra, now the Viscount Sá da Bandeira. They had vanquished Pedro's enemies and the legitimate king was back on the throne. It was at last time for the country to try to build on the wreckage a war leaves behind. First, there had to be punishment of the Miguelites for their many atrocities, although in fairness the brutality had certainly not been confined to one side. Then, the enemy having been destroyed, it was considered appropriate to get the armed forces totally back under Portuguese control. Napier's expertise might have been necessary to defeat the Miguelite navy and transport Terceira's army, but he wasn't Portuguese, so he wasn't wanted any more. His plans for reorganising the Portuguese navy were quietly sabotaged and by 1836 he had resigned and rejoined the British navy. Saldanha, Terceira and Sá da Bandeira set out to achieve and retain political power and each served as prime minister, often several times.

Pacifico would have returned home a hero: one of the small, intrepid band of patriots who had overthrown the despot, in spite of their numerical inferiority. A man of courage, prepared to risk his life for the liberal cause. No longer just a local corn merchant and trader, but a friend of generals, a man on good terms with the highest in the land, and – best of all – a winner. Pacifico wasn't a mercenary like Napier. He had lived in Portugal for over twenty years and he had supported the Liberal Party through and through. As a key member of Terceira's force, he would have been well known to Saldanha and Sá de Bandeira. In due course, it would have been agreed that he should get a reasonable reward for his efforts. He was a success in Portugal and the prospects of returning to Gibraltar were certainly far less attractive. There had been another outbreak of cholera in the colony which killed nearly 400 on the Rock and drove many more away. With the growth in the importance of Malta, the Gibraltarian economy began to decline and the wisest solution for Pacifico seemed to be to keep a foot in both camps.

The cost of the war had been tremendous. The country was bankrupt, the economy was sluggish, with the continuing diminution of the revenues from Brazil, and unemployment was high. Apart from the casualties on both sides, the war had been financed by loans bearing, on average, a crippling 20 per cent interest. The war cost 6,000 *contos* – six billion *reis* – and, at the finish, the national debt had risen to £18 million.

Now, if Portugal wanted to raise loans, the terms demanded by the bankers on behalf of the investing public had to take into account the risks involved. An investor had alternatives; he could put his money in gilt-edged British government bonds (Consols) and get 3.5 per cent interest, without the slightest chance of his capital being lost or the government defaulting on the annual payments. Or he could invest in a country like Portugal, where the currency might depreciate over the years, so that his original investment stock certificates became worth less. Even worse, the Portuguese might also fail to pay the interest charges, sending the nominal value of the bonds through the floor. To invest in Portugal you needed substantially better terms than the British government would offer if you were thinking of buying Consols.

The Rothschilds did manage to raise £4 million for the country in 1835. The bonds were in £100 units but you had to pay only £67.50 for them when they were issued, and you got 3 per cent interest as well on the nominal £100 value. Which made the interest – if it got paid – over 4.5 per cent. If the Portuguese government ever paid you the face value of the stock – and if their currency remained stable – you would make a lot of money.

It soon became clear, however, that the Portuguese couldn't afford to pay the interest. The government's expenditure in the ten years after the war averaged 10,000 *contos* a year but their income was only 8,000 *contos*, so every year their debt grew alarmingly. This was a severe embarrassment to the Rothschilds. They were well aware that a charge of mis-selling the bonds had no legal force, but a default would hardly encourage their investors to retain confidence in the bank's offerings in the future. So the Rothschilds reluctantly lent the Portuguese sufficient capital to pay the interest for 1835 and 1836. After that the Portuguese and the investors were on their own, with disastrous results. By 1839 the £100 stock had fallen to £25.

None of this surprised the Rothschilds. As James wrote to Nathaniel: 'We have a great many asses who have been buying this shit.'[1] By then the Portuguese economy had got into an even worse mess and successive governments twisted and turned to escape their obligations. In the City of London the reputation of Portugal as a safe home for your money sank without trace. 'The government borrowed money from every available source, both internally and abroad...England was the main source and required prompt and honest payment...Regarding other sources, the usual solution was not to pay and periodically to declare bankruptcy.'[2] As early as July 1836 the Minister of Finance found it necessary to try to borrow 800 *contos* (about £200,000 then) for just three months from the Portuguese tobacco contractors. He was turned down. The parliamentary opposition then tried to engineer a run on the *reis* to undermine the government, which was as suicidal as it was unpatriotic.

The British government was, of course, well aware of all this financial turmoil. If Palmerston were asked in the future whether he could trust the Portuguese government as the defendant in any monetary dispute, he would have been more inclined from the beginning to believe the account of the plaintiff. As James de Rothschild said at the time: 'We are dealing here with thoroughly disreputable people.'[3] If Pacifico said he had a case against the Portuguese for non-payment of moneys owed to him, no one who knew the dramatis personae would dismiss the statement out of hand.

Rothschild's criticism was accurate but, in defence of the Portuguese, they were faced with truly insuperable difficulties. They tried to raise money internally and attempted to kill two birds with one stone, when they dissolved the hated monasteries and nunneries in May 1834. This was in order to get hold of their wealth but the rewards were meagre in relation to the massive debts.

The supporters of Pedro had fought for constitutional monarchy and they had won. Pedro's 1826 charter had, however, given the monarch a good deal more power than the 1822 version and, as Maria grew up, she would defend her father's political legacy against the constitutionalists who had wanted the nation – that is, the government – to be sovereign. The major problem successive governments faced was how to go about exercising power. They were totally unaccustomed to it and their traditional society had given them little training for how to approach the difficulties. Agreed, there was a constitution, but it was untested and there were plenty of politicians with hidden agendas.

After all his efforts, Pedro survived the end of the war for only six months. Even in that short time he managed to lose a lot of his popularity by acting in a dictatorial manner and allowing Miguel to retire to Italy rather than suffer in any way for his excesses. He even gave his brother sixty *contos* a year as a kind of pension, but Miguel lost this when he disavowed the agreement he had signed before going into exile. Never a well man, Pedro died of tuberculosis in September 1834 at the age of 36.

Maria turned to the Count de Palmela, her former ambassador in London, to lead her government. This was, basically, the old guard who now accepted the 1826 constitution which Pedro had originally produced. Palmela was the safe pair of hands, the man with the experience, but his administration lasted less than twelve months, although that was going to be a quite respectable period of office as governments came and went over the next few years.

As the 1826 constitution gave the Crown, the nobility and the church a greater say in the running of the country, there was a strong argument for a nasty split in the Liberal Party ranks, which duly appeared. The liberals now split into three sections. We call them parties today but in post-war Portugal they were more 'currents of opinion, ideological groups, political forces... but hardly parties in the sense of duly organized bodies'.[4] If you could characterise the three groups: there were, first, the Ventistas, who stood by the 1820 uprising and the 1822 constitution which emerged from it. Then, second, the conservatives, who aimed for a compromise between the absolutists and the liberal positions. The third group were the bourgeoisie who tried to find a third way. Like so many others, Pacifico's task was to keep abreast of the constantly shifting political fortunes and do the best he could for himself and his family.

When the victory parades and the street parties were over, the job of creating a less absolutist regime had to be addressed. The fact of the matter was that the country's finances, poor as they were, depended very much on agricultural produce. The land was owned by the nobles – either those who had supported Pedro or those allies who had been rewarded with titles and land after the war was won. No matter how much the liberal intelligentsia – the civil servants, the academics and the merchants – wanted to create a democracy, the resident landowners could not be ignored and it was in their best interests to be absolutist. Their view was that it might make good sense discussing policy with intellectuals, but with the great mass of the rural peasantry, it was local leadership that was needed to avoid chaos.

It wasn't even that difficult to make the case for giving the clergy and the nobility a major role in the running of the country. The illiteracy rate in 1834 was 90 per cent and even at the end of the decade, only half the male children in the country would have any schooling at all. In such a country, an educated and sophisticated, middle-aged trader like Pacifico was not likely to find the local competition too difficult.

When the dust settled, the Miguelites still remained a force outside government. One cavalry colonel, told to take his regiment to Spain, refused to do so unless the officer corps was purged of Miguelites, which would have meant dismissing about half of them. The differing points of view led to schism within the Liberal Party. Men who had fought the good fight together during the war found it more difficult to work together to win the peace. In spite of all the fine words, the top posts were still going to be in the hands of the nobility for many years: 'Up to the 1870s more than one fourth of the cabinet ministers and 80 per cent of the prime ministers were title-bearers, all of constitutional stock.'[5]

Among them, of course, were Saldanha, Sá da Bandeira and Terceira. Like Wellington in England, they were popular heroes with their networks of followers, and large numbers would rally round their flags. All three were thirsty for power, wealth and permanent status. They had, however, been through dreadful times together and they were keen to avoid another outbreak of civil war. There might be old scores to settle; bandits might account for hundreds of victims over the next few years, and there would be many assassinations when there were arguments over spheres of influence and past wrongs, but actual civil war was usually avoided. It would often be touch and go though. Even with the coming of peace, Portugal was not a safe place to be, and Pacifico was soon thinking that the time had come to move on again.

Pedro's victory had not been the ambition of many of the absolutist regimes in Europe. The possibility of an attempt to overthrow the government and revert to absolutism was taken very seriously by the constitutional countries. As far as Palmerston in London was concerned, this was a straight fight between constitutionalism and absolutism and he was going to make sure that the constitutionalists remained in power in Portugal. As a consequence a Quadruple Alliance was created to safeguard the independence of Portugal, consisting of Spain, France, Britain and Portugal itself. If there were rebellions, the other countries would come to Portugal's aid. Palmerston decided he deserved all the credit: 'the treaty was a capital hit and all my own doing'.[6]

Maria was now 15 years old and rather than have another regency
– as far as the liberals were concerned, Miguel's had not worked out
all that brilliantly – the government had asked her to take the
throne, twelve days before her father's death. Maria II ruled until her
own death in 1853. As she matured, she unfortunately developed a
taste for meddling in political waters, often to the ruling
administration's annoyance.

Maria had, of course, been married to Miguel but that marriage
had been annulled and her next husband was Prince Augustus of
Leuchtenberg. They married in January 1835. Unfortunately he died
after only two months, of diphtheria. Her third marriage was to
Prince Ferdinand of Saxe-Coburg-Gotha, in January 1836, by whom
she had eleven children. She was now a relation by marriage of the
King of the Belgians and of his nephew, Albert, who would become
Queen Victoria's prince consort. Ferdinand was soon elevated to the
title of King Fernando II in 1837.

When the war was over, a lot of people hoped to enjoy the spoils
of victory. 'The military and all those who had fought for the Liberal
cause now wanted a reward for their services.'[7] A large number of
wartime scores were settled. If the courts took too long or if the
accused could buy themselves out of trouble, assassination was
always a possible alternative and up to a thousand died as a consequence. In material ways the liberals took revenge on their richer
opponents as well: 'Land and other goods were auctioned off and
promptly acquired by the wealthy victors, most of them traders or
industrialists.'[8] To that extent, the bourgeoisie had triumphed and
about one quarter of the cultivated land in Portugal changed
ownership.

This could well account, of course, for the richness of the
furniture, linen and china in Don Pacifico's house in Athens. Those
auctions would have been a treasure trove for the traders; with
nobody caring what the items brought – after all, they had been
confiscated and cost the government nothing – there must have been
any number of terrific bargains. It was a version of war surplus sales
which make fortunes for second-hand dealers after conflicts end. As
a senior liberal supporter, Pacifico would have been welcome to bid,
and with the line of credit he had needed for the feeding and paying
of the troops still intact, he could lay his hands on ready money.

It wouldn't have mattered if Pacifico didn't know who would buy
the goods at a better price afterwards. The important thing about
trading is to have enough quality stock, and the finer possessions of
the defeated absolutist leaders would certainly come under that

heading. As many of the items were likely to be antiques, Don Pacifico could use them in his own house until an opportunity came to cash in.

So Pacifico divided his time between Gibraltar and Portugal. He had houses in Gibraltar, and Aaron and many of his old friends were still on the Rock. The Jewish community in Gibraltar was far better established than in Portugal, and Pacifico would have been happy worshipping in the synagogues of his childhood and taking part in their activities. He would also have wanted to continue his links with the merchants in the colony whom he could serve in Portugal. There was a great demand for textiles and the normal route for their import was from the merchants in Manchester, shipping first to Gibraltar and then moving the goods to the Portuguese mainland from there. A reliable merchant, a member in good standing of the Jewish community, with bases in both countries, would have been an asset to the Gibraltar-based traders. Certainly, Pacifico's core cereal business wasn't what it had been. Exports had naturally declined with the ending of the Continental Blockade and Pacifico needed a new field of enterprise to replace it.

From the Portuguese government's point of view, there was the serious problem that they owed supporters like Pacifico small fortunes which they simply couldn't afford to pay. The state was bankrupt, it was almost impossible to raise finance and Queen Maria herself was reduced to going round her aristocratic friends and asking if they could lend her some money.

All the Portuguese government could really offer as compensation was land, titles and jobs. By 1836 its debts had reached £247 million. Pacifico didn't want land; Jews were not farmers before the State of Israel. He certainly was very willing to accept titles and had well earned both the Don he was normally known by, and the 'Chevalier' he liked to use personally. Between 1831 and 1840 at least 100 titles a year were bestowed on grateful recipients. A title, however, was certainly not full compensation for what he had lost over the years in supporting Pedro.

Meanwhile the new Portuguese governments changed with bewildering speed and each faction tried to gain and keep its supporters rather than alienate its influential and fervent backers. The key question, however, was how much did they really owe those who demanded money? Claims were pouring in from people the authorities didn't know, for expenditure they didn't think they'd authorised. If you could manufacture a claim in 1834, relating to wartime events, and then make it difficult to disprove, you could defraud the government far too easily for its liking.

The Times' correspondent in Lisbon explained what happened next, in a report sent to the paper at the height of the Pacifico affair in March 1850:

> Don Pacifico...is the veritable David Pacifico who, 20 years ago, resided partly at Gibraltar and partly in the Algarves, engaged in the trade which supplies the inhabitants of that province with many foreign productions at one-half their cost in this capital...all my researches have been fruitless until 1822, when he did Portugal the honour of naturalising himself as one of its subjects. This fact is, however, fully established by letters and documents written and signed by the Don himself...For the due appreciation of this matter [the Portuguese claim] it is necessary to explain that after the expulsion of Don Miguel and the restoration of the Queen of Portugal, her father, Don Pedro, named in 1834 a commission to investigate all claims for losses caused by the civil war, and to pass certificates admissible in the purchase of national property for such as were proved to be valid.
>
> It was subsequently decreed in 1835 that in consequence of the appearance of numerous spurious claims, none of the certificates should be held good until confirmed by the sentence of another tribunal, and that no claim would be entertained after the year 1837.
>
> Now if Don Pacifico had any claims of the nature referred to, his modesty and generosity led him to forego them and accept the honour of being named a Portuguese Consul rather than trouble the commission and tribunal with their investigation. Upon his application, he was named Consul at Morocco, and in 1835, wishing to be transferred to Athens, he made several petition to the Viscount Sa da Bandeira, as minister of Foreign Affairs, stating 'that the Morocco Consulate had been given to him in remuneration for his losses and services in the Queen's cause.'

The Lisbon correspondent was either well informed or was acting as a mouthpiece for the Portuguese government. The latter is more likely because Pacifico was appointed Portuguese consul in Morocco in 1835 and asked for Athens only in 1837.

Pacifico had moved a long way up in the world by this time. In an impecunious country he had the connections to the Gibraltar movers and shakers. As a Don, a chevalier and one of Terceira's fighting 2,500, he was accepted now in the great houses and major government offices. As a man who could get you what you wanted, he would be a useful contact to know, even if he was still going to be considered by some as a nouveau riche Jew in a society where the nobility still considered trade an undignified pursuit for a gentleman. Behind his back the nobility might talk of him with disdain, but in public he was acceptable.

It was a heady new world for anybody to deal with, but Pacifico now had a new objective. He had decided to try to take one further step up the social ladder and become a diplomat. Discussions would have been held in the palatial accommodation of the Foreign Office with Pacifico treated as an old friend of the state and a valued ally within the Liberal Party. A key member of the Foreign Ministry from 1835 to 1836 was the Marquis of Loulé. The marquis was a very young man at the time, only in his early 30s, but among his perceived qualifications was the fact that he was the the former king's brother-in-law. Loulé's father had been in John VI's entourage as Master of the Horse when John returned from Brazil, but in the violent internal squabbling of the time, he unexpectedly died. Nobody was surprised and a British coroner's jury would have returned a verdict of murder by person or persons unknown. His son learned the lesson. When he reached the top of the tree, he was inclined for years to keep a low profile and make his mark as a wirepuller.

The second marquis was a force in Portuguese politics for the next thirty years. Elegant and very handsome, with impressive moustaches, Loulé was the perfect courtier and well able to charm the birds off the trees. As part of Pedro's court, he was likely to have met Pacifico during the war, and he must have been impressed, because he would shortly offer the former Gibraltarian a position in the Portuguese foreign service. In these negotiations Pacifico would find himself dealing with a highly professional diplomat. In the opulent surroundings of ministries and great houses, treated with charm and respect, he would have been no match for Loulé, who would go on to eventually become the Duke of Loulé in 1862, and prime minister. The negotiations were undoubtedly very amicable, but here Pacifico was in uncharted waters. He was dealing with a heavyweight courtier who knew how to persuade and cajole, flatter and charm a newcomer to the corridors of power. Pacifico was way out of his depth.

Morocco and Portugal had been closely linked for centuries. Indeed, the Portuguese had colonial control of the coastal village of Casablanca until towards the end of the eighteenth century. It was all very delicate, however – imperial power and former colony – and whoever got the job of Portuguese consul in the capital, Rabat, was going to have to be an able diplomat.

Pacifico could obviously point to the family's track record, created by his father, Jacob, when he held the post for the British fifty years before. Being Jewish himself, Pacifico could point to the advantage of his ability to work with the Moroccan Jewish community. He probably still had relatives in Morocco, and languages like French and Ladino would not present him with a problem. He was a very good candidate and he was known to be loyal to the government and well connected. The Portuguese, however, had to be careful to make the right choice. They might fob off some countries with incompetents, just to clear a part of the ever-pressing national debt, but that couldn't apply to a near neighbour like Morocco.

The emperors of Morocco had always needed careful and diplomatic handling. To complicate the matter further, Portugal's financial problems were sufficiently grave for the consul to be an important cog in the national trade wheel. It was, therefore, hardly likely that the government would choose Pacifico if they considered that he could't be trusted or had a shady past. That court case, for instance, over the forged bill in 1817, would have been disinterred, even if it had occurred twenty years before, but obviously it wasn't considered an obstacle to Pacifico's appointment.

So the case in favour of Pacifico was strong enough for Loulé to try to kill two birds with one stone: to get himself a minister who might improve trade between the countries, and to avoid the necessity for the government to pay that minister what he was owed. The problem, it turned out, was the Emperor of Morocco himself, Moulay Abderrahmane bin Moulay Hicham bin Moulay Abdullah ben Moulay Ismael. He was the descendent of that same Moulay Ismael who had told the British that if they were going to throw the Jews out of Gibraltar, at Spanish insistence in 1718, he would cut off all trade with the colony.

Abderrahmane was not so much the ruler as the senior warlord in Morocco. He controlled the country's capital, because the capital was wherever he happened to be at the time. Outside the capital he controlled the coast but not the inland provinces. He could claim descent from the prophet, Mohammed, but that didn't cut enough ice with the other warlords to gain their allegiance. His financial problems were exacerbated by the fact that, according to Moslem law, he couldn't raise taxes on anything except livestock and the harvest. He was, therefore, seriously dependent on foreign trade.

This created problems in itself because the Moroccans hated the export of grain. If the harvest failed and the surplus grain from past years had been exported, they could and did starve. In 1820 there was an uprising in Fez as a result, which nearly brought down Abderrahmane's predecessor.

The Jews were still major players in Moroccan trade, and the connection with Gibraltar remained intact. The first Portuguese consul had been appointed in 1823 when Abderrahmane announced his intention of increasing Morocco's trade with the rest of the world. It was, he hoped, trade of which he had personally approved. He didn't want the other warlords in the interior to benefit from the increasing commerce. If they had more money, they could spend it on guns, which were just as likely to be turned on Abderrahmane as on anybody else. The emperor lowered taxes on exporting wheat and allowed the export of wool. Pacifico was an expert in corn exports, and commissions on future Portuguese trade could produce rich pickings. It was a real chance to get back the money he was owed. Moroccan exports had nearly doubled in value between 1833 and 1834 and would go up another 50 per cent by 1836.

Unfortunately for Pacifico, Abderrahmane also recognized the possibilities. He preferred to use his own Moroccan Jews as his agents: 'So he barred European traders from the ports without his permission and forbade them completely from living in the interior.'[9] An experienced corn merchant consul from a major trading partner could prove difficult to control.

The political situation in North Africa at the time was even more fraught than usual. Apart from tribal warfare, which was endemic, the French had decided to increase their empire by creating North African colonies. One of their earlier efforts had produced the desired effect. The ruling Dey of Algeria was talking to the French consul in the casbah in 1827 and there was a disagreement. The dey was unwise enough to tap the cheek of the consul with a fly whisk in aggravation. This massive insult to the French was duly reported to Paris, and Louis-Philippe immediately set out to avenge the honour of France. An armed force of 37,000 men was embarked for Algiers in 1830. They captured the city, dethroned the dey and absorbed Algeria as a colony. It was true that their hegemony didn't extend beyond the outskirts of the city, but Algiers was a good trading and naval port. Abderrahmane was unwise enough to go to the aid of the Algerians through a local intermediary, and risked the invasion of Morocco as well.

If such an apparently minor incident could have such catastrophic effects for a neighbour, Abderrahmane would have been keen to carry on working with diplomats he knew. He wouldn't want to give any country an excuse to invade Morocco as his neighbour had been assailed. Moreover, the emperor did like to throw his weight about. He had, for example, declared war on Naples and grandiloquently threatened its Mediterranean shipping. *The Times'* correspondent wrote drily: 'If by prodigious efforts the government of Morocco should succeed in sending these armed vessels out to sea, they would amount to 10–12 . . . in bad condition.'[10] The correspondent thought that Moroccan pirates were more likely to be used to harry the Neapolitans. They certainly had been plundering British merchant shipping, but when the British consul complained, the emperor virtually challenged the British to do anything about it. He asked the consul: 'Does my good brother, the king of England, want any tigers?'

It wasn't even as if the Portuguese incumbent was doing a very good job. A number of Miguelite soldiers had left the Cape Verde Islands after the end of the war and taken refuge in Morocco. It was a similar situation to Nazis fleeing to South America after 1945. The Portuguese consul had made the case for the Miguelites to be extradited but the emperor decided they could stay. He also refused to accept Pacifico. He preferred the man he had, irrespective of whether he belonged to the party which had now gained power. The incumbent probably couldn't claim such membership, because it is highly likely that the job was vacant only because Sá da Bandeira was busy firing all the appointees of the previous government, in order to put his own cronies in their places. One prime minister, entering office at the time, told a colleague that his 'arm was weary from signing notices of dismissal'.[11]

The Times' Lisbon correspondent returned to the subject of Pacifico's appointment many years later:

> Now setting aside the peculiar circumstances of Don Pacifico's case, he, like some of the present claimants, had certificates of certain amounts liquidated by the commission of 1834, but never applied for the confirmatory sentence . . . if it should now be decided . . . that any claim he might have had upon Portugal is invalidated for want of that formality, it would tend to support this Government in resisting, as it appears disposed to resist, all claims of the same nature which were not put in a legal train of settlement during the ample time conceded by the decree of 1835.[12]

In fact it says much for Pacifico's standing with the government after the war ended that he was considered for the Portuguese diplomatic service in the first place. His title might have been consul-general but he was, in reality, the country's ambassador. Pacifico had come a long way from buying and selling corn twenty years before, and membership of the diplomatic corps was a feather of considerable proportions in his cap. He wasn't out of the top drawer, however, and the permanent diplomats looked down on the Johnny-Come-Latelys, from what they perceived to be the sordid face of trade, not to mention his Judaism. Pacifico did what he could to conform. Like many other Jews living in a Christian society, he adopted a less biblical name than David in his commercial life. He was known as Boniface, but to professional diplomats, he would remain the unacceptable face of the amateur, in spite of his good connections in the corridors of power.

With the diplomatic role in Morocco closed to Pacifico, he and Loulé went back to the drawing board. What post could now be offered instead, which would still be acceptable to Pacifico and settle the Portuguese government's debt to him? It was now 1837, the last year in which claims could be made for losses during the war. The commission's law had been designed to eliminate fraudulent claims, but the government was still unable to pay the genuine ones. So there had to be negotiations and these were particularly difficult when the government was dealing with its best and most loyal supporters. No one could deny that among this group was Don David (Boniface) Pacifico.

There was no doubt at the time that he had put up the refugees in Gibraltar for years, having been asked to do so by Pedro. The destruction of Pacifico's possessions in Mertola were confirmed by the judge, and Terceira would have known this. Pacifico was obviously owed for acting as commissary to the duke's division. There could be no justification for denying him what he was due.

Not, in fairness, that Pacifico had, in fact, lost everything, as he subsequently claimed. He still had two houses in Gibraltar. If he chose to forget those, he might well have omitted other assets which could have been carefully salted away during the troubles. On the other hand, as Rothschild had pointed out, Pacifico was well aware that he was dealing with thoroughly disreputable people. As far as Pacifico was concerned in 1837, however, the government was still trying to settle its obligations in difficult times.

Loulé came up with the consul's job in Greece. Pacifico had no previous experience of the country but Loulé would have assured him that this was a new nation with a great maritime commercial tradition and ripe for a major increase in Graeco–Portuguese trade. The opportunities for the Portuguese consul to make money would have been painted in glowing colours. Pacifico accepted the position, again in settlement of his claims.

Pacifico was 54 now, with a growing family to support in an uncertain economic and political climate in Portugal. He could see that being a member of the Liberal Party was no longer enough. It now also depended on which wing of the party you supported. If he could get away from it all to a diplomatic post in Athens, he should be able to keep his head below the political parapet very easily, and with the glowing references Loulé had given the Greek posting, it would have seemed the perfect solution.

The Times' Lisbon correspondent had continued: 'After he had been transferred, he, in 1837, applied for the advance of a year's salary to enable him to take his family to Greece, upon the ground "that he had lost all he possessed during the civil war without making any claims upon the Queen's government." '[13] If this was an exaggeration, it was certainly true that he had lost a great deal. The problem for Pacifico in Athens was that he soon discovered that Loulé had sold him a pup. There was no meaningful trade between Portugal and Greece, and where foreign vessels carried Moroccan exports, Greek boats carried Greek exports.

The consul's job was not a fair exchange for the government's debts to Pacifico and, by 1839, he would be pointing out in no uncertain terms that he had been cheated. In the future, however, the Portuguese would ignore the fraudulent deal Loulé had done and concentrate on the fact that by the end of 1837, Pacifico had not provided the necessary documentation for his original claim. On a technicality of that flimsy kind, the Portuguese government would try for years to get out of its liabilities to one of its most devoted servants.

In 1836, supporters of the 1822 version of the constitution – the Septembrists – won power. Loulé had no difficulty in switching sides and was elected to the new constitutional Parliament where he was appointed a senator, which accounts for the fact that he was still capable of influencing appointments within the diplomatic corps. Loulé was not Foreign Secretary, but Pacifico said that it was he who had offered the position and discussed the terms.

The Septembrist leader, Passos Manuel, soldiered on for only eight months before handing back power to the moderates. In 1838 there emerged 'a new centre more related to the right than the left' which realigned its forces as the Order Party. The Liberal government remained in power until 1842 under a series of prime ministers. There were eleven in all between September 1834 and June 1841, but they were mostly influenced by the head of the party, which often meant one of the three generals.

Another major player was António Bernardo da Costa Cabral, who was the power behind the scenes for many years. The radicals didn't believe that Maria should have any real authority, and Cabral held on to the reins of power until June 1841. As Pacifico was an 1822 constitution man and a trader, he could rely on the support of his wing as long as it stayed in control. Within six months of Cabral losing office, Pacifico's tenure in Athens would come under fire.

For Pacifico the new die was cast. It was agreed he would go to Athens as the Portuguese consul-general. The appointment was made in 1837, but it was to be well over a year before David and Clara set sail for the Greek capital. A lot had to be arranged. Greece was a comparatively new nation state and Pacifico would not have expected to spend all his time on consular duties. There would be plenty of opportunity to carry on as a trader, so he would need to pack up not only his household possessions but also all his merchant's stock. His lines of communication with Gibraltar from his new base would also need to be established, and a reputable captain to transfer both the family and the precious cargo across the Mediterranean. It all took time and Pacifico must have hoped he was making the right decision; Greece had seldom been a bed of roses for the Jews; it wouldn't be for Pacifico either.

NOTES

1 Niall Ferguson, *The World's Banker* (Weidenfeld & Nicolson, 1998).
2 A. H. de Oliveira Marques, *History of Portugal* (Columbia University Press, 1972).
3 Ferguson, *The World's Banker*.
4 de Oliveira Marques, *History of Portugal*.
5 Ibid.
6 Evelyn Ashley, *Lord Palmerston* (Richard Bentley, 1879).
7 de Oliveira Marques, *History of Portugal*.
8 Ibid.
9 C. R. Pennell, *Morocco since 1830* (Hurst & Co., 2000).
10 *The Times*, 28 April 1834.

11 Manuel da Silva Passos quoted in de Oliveira Marques, *History of Portugal.*
12 *The Times,* 15 November 1850.
13 Ibid.

Duque da Terceira,
Biblioteca Nacional,
Portugal, courtesy
Aurora Machado,
National Library of
Lisbon

Admiral William Parker,
copyright National Portrait Gallery

Admiral Charles 'Mad Charlie' Napier
copyright Hulton Archive

Ionnis Kolettis,
from S. Markezinis,
*Politiki Istoria tis
Neoteras Ellados
1818–1862*
(Athens, 1966),
courtesy Papyros
Publications

Otho, courtesy http://stores.ebay.com/juliesantiquesprints?refid+store

Sir Edmund Lyons, Rear-Admiral of the British Fleet,
Illustrated London News, 1854

Lord Palmerston,
copyright Hulton Archive

John Thaddeus Delane,
copyright National Portrait Gallery

8　The prelude to the riot

When Don Pacifico was born, the Jews weren't officially allowed to live in Athens. This had been the rule agreed by the Christian inhabitants for hundreds of years, although a seventeenth-century French traveller had reported fifteen to twenty Jewish families in the town. The Pacificos finally arrived in Athens in 1839. If the prospects were nothing like as good as for the post in Morocco, the sultan showed no sign of changing his mind and Pacifico couldn't wait for ever. He was in his 50s now and the Marquis of Loulé had encouraged him to accept the position, and authorised him to spend whatever was necessary to get his family to the Greek capital and set himself up in suitable style as the Portuguese consul. As the Portuguese were still in serious financial difficulties, Pacifico should surely have smelt a rat when the arrangement was made that he'd spend the money up front and get reimbursed later.

If Loulé was impressive at home in Portugal, his reputation in international diplomatic circles was far less brilliant. Palmerston had written to his ambassador in Paris on the subject in April 1836: 'In Portugal they [the French] succeeded in ousting Cavalho and got Loulé appointed instead; and a pretty mess Loulé and his colleagues made of it.'[1] The professional and cultured diplomat was still quite suave enough, however, to take in a less sophisticated merchant such as Pacifico.

Athens in 1839 was a squalid, dusty city. Life was still dangerous and difficult because it was so hard to keep the streets safe. The inhabitants were hardly more secure than those in Prohibition Chicago under Al Capone. The unpainted wooden shacks that huddled at the base of the ruins of the Acropolis were in stark contrast to the glory that had been Ancient Greece. In the centre of the city, Otho ruled in what was considered brash and vulgar splendour, but in what was, by European standards, a pretty small palace. Amélie devoted her time to the planning and planting of the royal gardens. Pacifico hoped that the palace, which had been begun in 1836, could become the home for many of the objets d'art he had brought from the homes of those Portuguese nobles who had not backed Pedro.

The Pacifico family had arrived in Athens complete with their three daughters. The youngest was Esther, who was born in 1836. She would have been a typical post-war baby, as Pacifico was away from home between 1832 and 1834 with Terceira. Clara might have gone back to Gibraltar during the War of the Two Brothers, but there is no reference to her in the 1833 census. David, of course, had to visit the colony to get his British passport, but he moved on almost immediately as well.

David and Clara Pacifico also had two older daughters, both of whom were married by 1847. The likelihood is that they were born before the War of the Two Brothers broke out in 1828, since starting babies during wartime in a primitive country only complicates matters. The oldest daughter was called Clara and she would have been born after 1823, when Aaron, David's brother, and his wife, Rachel, had their son, Jacob. For the first time in over 100 years, a new member of the Pacifico family was not named according to the normal Sephardic tradition; the daughter was named after the mother. It wasn't against any Jewish law, but it was extremely unusual. One well-known precedent was recorded when Josephus, the Roman Jewish author, was listing the Zadokite high priests; one was Onias, the son of Onias. Nearer Pacifico's time, Abraham and Abigail Ricardo, the parents of economist David Ricardo, named two of their children Abraham and Abigail.[2] The Pacificos may have adopted the practice from the Portuguese community because, while it was known amongst them, it was not a custom among the Gibraltar Jews.

Aaron's son, Jacob, was, of course, named after his paternal grandfather, as was usual. Jacob would grow up to marry Clara and would move to Athens to join the family. There are three possible reasons for this: perhaps he didn't get on with his father, who was back in Gibraltar; Don Pacifico might have offered him a place in his business; or Clara didn't want to be separated from her parents. The family had travelled to Athens in high hopes of a successful and profitable stay, and trade in Gibraltar was going through a bad patch. As Pacifico arrived in Athens when Jacob was only 16, the wedding was likely to have been an arranged one some years later. Otherwise, it is difficult to see how the young couple could have met as adults, with Jacob's family still living in Gibraltar.

We don't even know the name of the second daughter, except that she became Mrs Lante. When she grew up, she fell in love with a

Greek army officer of that name and married him against the wishes
of her parents. When he heard the news of her betrothal, Don
Pacifico reacted by throwing her out of the house.[2] The vehemence
of such a rejection – which Pacifico admitted was because she had
married a Christian – needs some explaining. With Orthodox Jews
there is naturally a deep desire for the children to carry on family
traditions, which do not include marrying out of the faith. Catholic
and Muslim families take a similar view.

Pacifico bought a fine house across the road from the palace. It
had formerly belonged to Count Armansperg, the regent. Loulé had
surely told him that all he needed to do was to submit the accounts
to the Lisbon Foreign Office and the cheque would soon be in the
post. As the bill for the War of the Two Brothers five years before
was somewhat overdue, to believe this promise involved a
substantial risk, but the Marquis was obviously a smooth talker. The
golden prospects Pacifico had been spun were worthy of Barnum
and Bailey. Stories of fees on Portuguese trade in Greece had made
the job look attractive and, in truth, there was also ample time for
Pacifico's own commercial activities, as it transpired that apparently,
no Portuguese ship ever came into a Greek harbour. Pacifico
certainly said at the end of his tenure of office that not one had
arrived during his years there. Portuguese shipping headed north to
Europe, south to Africa and west to Brazil. It did not head east
beyond Italy.

Pacifico was, however, able to find the money for the house from
his own resources, so he obviously had substantial capital at the
time. David and Clara set up home with their three daughters in the
dilapidated capital. Pacifico had chosen one of the very few fine
houses available. It was a three-storied building, constructed in what
was known as the Constantinople style. It was a landmark in
Athens, and Otho had attended balls there in Armansperg's time.
Part of Pacifico's land overlooked the royal palace garden and when
Queen Amélie wanted to extend the estate, Pacifico readily agreed to
sell his ground for what he'd paid for it. Doing a favour for the
queen might well improve the relationship, and help when it came to
selling his high-quality stock of Portuguese goods to the
Establishment.

Of course, whilst Pacifico wanted only to be reimbursed for the
cost of the land, Finlay was still trying to settle with the Greek
government at a substantial profit. The whole claim had been
studied by the Foreign Office in London, and in 1842 the Foreign
Secretary, Lord Aberdeen, told Lyons to press for Finlay to be paid.

The Greeks offered a commission of enquiry but when they announced the make-up of the tribunal, Finlay rejected its proposed members – not for the last time. The arguments dragged on and Finlay was proved right when another commission was proposed. This time Finlay accepted the nominees, who sat for three years but came to no conclusion. They didn't question that there was a valid bill to be paid; only the total.

The Greek government didn't pay, the Portuguese government didn't pay, but Pacifico lived in hope. He was welcomed by both the Jewish and the English communities. Both were small and would have been happy to see newcomers – particularly the Sephardic community, who acquired an observant and knowledgeable congregant. Pacifico had also progressed to a highly prestigious diplomatic position and basked in the recognition it brought. He was now persona grata everywhere. It was a proud transformation.

Over the years Pacifico grew to be an important member of the Sephardic community and eventually became its president. This obviously meant that he was a learned and observant Jew, ready to spend the considerable amount of time involved in carrying out the dictates of the faith. The president of a community is, above all, an example to the rest of the congregation. He also acts as an ambassador to the country at large. The Jews might not even have a synagogue but they lived in hopes of permission to build one and of gathering the funds to pay for it.

Pacifico was well aware that the level of toleration in Athens could change without warning. No Jewish community on the European Continent or in the Middle East was immune from outbreaks of virulent anti-Semitism. In 1840 there was an incident which not only illustrated this, but also strongly influenced British policy towards Jews outside the country for many years.

It is now known as the Damascus Blood Libel. Syria, which had been under Turkish rule since 1515, had rebelled. It came to be ruled by a new power in the Middle East, one Mehemet Ali, who had defeated the Turks in 1832 in Egypt and had then decided to expand his Nile territory. France supported Ali, and Britain supported Sultan Machmud II of Turkey, because it wanted to limit French influence in the Mediterranean. Austria and Russia were also at the time on the Turkish side.

On 5 February 1840, a monk, Tomaso de Comangiano, the superior of a Capuchin cloister, disappeared in Damascus with his servant. It was rumoured he had argued with a Turkish mule driver and insulted Mohammed. The driver had said: 'That dog of a

Christian shall die by no other hand than mine.' Pure rumour, but he was never seen again and his disappearance became a cause célèbre. It soon also became an embarrassment for the Turkish authorities and another rumour started that he had been murdered by local Jews in order for his blood to be used to make matzo for the Passover festival. For bigoted anti-Semites, such fantasies have always been perfectly plausible. Jews were then arrested and tortured to make them confess, which one did. Two others died from the torture they endured. The French consul in Damascus, Count Ulysse de Ratti-Menton, who was himself a rabid anti-Semite, supported the allegations and drummed up support for them. Many Jews fled and sixty Jewish children were kidnapped, so that their mothers could be threatened with their death if they didn't disclose the whereabouts of the fathers.

To make matters worse, bones were found and proclaimed to be those of Thomas, even though a doctor tried to point out that the bones weren't human. The Vatican supported Ratti-Menton, 'contending that the blood libel accusations were justified in the light of many previous similar "crimes" committed by Jews'. As alleged Catholic victims had even been beatified on occasions in the past, the totally implausible nature of the accusations could not be admitted. It is, of course, a fact, that one of the intrinsic rules in making food kosher is that all the blood must be totally eliminated from any carcass used. Ancient religions in biblical times used to indulge in human sacrifices, offering the victim's blood to the pagan gods. Judaism, uniquely for the time, abhorred such abominations and removing even traces of blood became a symbol of that revulsion. Matzo simply cannot be made from a recipe including blood.

Matters were going from bad to worse; the British consul wrote to Palmerston to support the Syrians, although Palmerston ignored his views. *The Times* reported that the Jews were guilty and it seemed that this preposterous accusation would run and run. Fortunately for the Jewish community, the Damascus authorities decided to arrest an Austrian Jew who had a cast-iron alibi. Austria demanded civilized court procedures on his behalf. The Austrian ambassador in Constantinople described the situation as 'inhuman excesses by the Arab who anyhow were known for their brutalities and disregard for truth and Justice'.

Little of this was known in Europe until the Austrian consul in Egypt, without asking permission, informed the Austrian consul in Paris. That French worthy was none other than James de Rothschild, and for Ratti-Menton the fat was now in the fire. The French might not help Rothschild, wishing instead to support their own man, Ratti-Menton, but Rothschild asked Metternich, the Austrian Chancellor, to order his ambassadors in Egypt and Turkey to intervene on behalf of the Jews. Lionel Rothschild in London also went to work to persuade the government that protecting Jews abroad would help them to get involved in the affairs of other countries, in the political as well as religious arenas.

In the end Rothschild financed a mission by his cousin, Sir Moses Montefiore, and the French Jewish leader, Adolph Cremieux, to intervene in Alexandria with Mehemet Ali. It was officially a joint Austro–British delegation which went to the Middle East. No less than thirteen European countries signed a petition for the release of the prisoners.

Mehemet Ali disliked Britain, but he realised that war was imminent between Egypt and Turkey and he needed friends. Knowing where the political and human bodies were buried, neither he nor the French wanted the conduct of the Blood Libel affair properly investigated. Ali agreed to free the imprisoned Jews in Damascus and retract the accusations. It didn't do him much good. He had been told to get out of Syria by Austria, Russia, Prussia and Turkey, but he refused to go. Palmerston, in London, threatened to resign if he were prevented by the Cabinet from using force to throw Mehemet Ali out. Some of his colleagues immediately threatened to resign if he was allowed to do so. Stalemate was on the cards, but the position was complicated by the fact that Queen Victoria was having her first baby at the time. The queen particularly wanted the Whig government, of which Palmerston was a member, to remain in office. She relied heavily on the support and advice of its leader, Lord Melbourne. Risking upsetting Her Majesty, when she was about to give birth to the heir to the throne, was considered unwise. The government reluctantly agreed to support Palmerston. Once again, it was evident that besting the Foreign Secretary was an intractable problem for his opponents.

So it was the British who acted. In September, Mad Charley Napier was sent to the Levant in HMS *Powerful* and then put in charge of the British land forces in the area, because of the illness of the commander-in-chief, General Sir Charles Smith. Napier did a competent job but when Smith was better, Napier was instructed to hand back the command. Instead he decided he could do a better job than Smith, and successfully attacked the Egyptian land forces. In quick succession he captured Acre, Beirut and Sidon. That was not according to instructions and the Admiralty in London tore their hair, deciding to send him to Alexandria to get him out of the way. At the same time, they really had no alternative but to award him a KCB (Knight Commander of the Order of the Bath) in recognition of his victories. Napier then decided to try his own diplomacy on Ali and agreed with the de facto ruler that he could be hereditary pasha of Egypt if he left Syria. Ali agreed to this and ordered the withdrawal of Egyptian forces, who were then brought home in British ships.

Palmerston was delighted, although other nations rejected the terms of the agreement. It illustrates the almost unavoidable independence of military commanders a long way from London in early Victorian times. When Leopold of the Belgians and Queen Victoria – no doubt leaned on by her uncle – tried to get for France at least some of the credit for the withdrawal, Palmerston wasn't having any of it.

For his part, the sultan in Constantinople was happy as well and issued a firman denouncing the Blood Libel; the Jews were still being well treated by the Turks. For years afterwards, however, the Catholics in Damascus continued to tell tourists of 'the saint who had been tortured and murdered by the Jews and how the Jews had been saved from the gallows by the intrigues of Jewish notables from abroad'.[3]

To protect the Yemenite Jewish community, Britain now occupied Aden to stop any Egyptian advance in that direction. Furthermore, it was agreed to set up a Protestant bishopric in Jerusalem for the first time. The new incumbent was taken in a British warship to the port of Jaffa. He was Michael Alexander, who as Solomon Alexander before his conversion to Christianity, had been the rabbi of the Plymouth community.

If it could get that bad out of nowhere in Syria in 1840, it was also true that the Jews were still only barely tolerated in Greece. The law may have said that citizens must have the freedom to practice their religion, but the Jewish community couldn't afford a synagogue and had no permission from the authorities to build one. Although there were no attacks of any importance on the community as a whole, it would be difficult to forget the tragic fate of so many Jewish congregations, slaughtered in the war against the Turks only twenty years before. Pacifico took no chances. He had gone to the British Embassy in Athens when he arrived and got another British passport for himself. He ignored the fact that he had become a Portuguese citizen in 1822 and was the accredited Portuguese minister, although this latter position did not necessarily mean that he had to be a citizen of the nation he represented. James de Rothschild might have been the Austrian minister in Paris, but he was still French.

As a fluent English speaker and a recognized diplomat, Pacifico would have been welcomed by Lyons. They were of a similar age and both had been involved in the war against Napoleon. They must have got on very well because Lyons remained his friend when Pacifico fell foul of the new Portuguese government who succeeded the Septembrists, when Sá da Bandeira fell from office in 1839. This time it was not Pacifico's sector of the Liberal Party who gained power, and the eventual list of jobs for the boys did not include his name.

The official Portuguese version of events was sent by their Foreign Minister, Count de Tojal, to a new Portuguese vice-consul in Athens, M. E. Petychalis, in early 1850 and extracts were reprinted in *The Times* on 3 May that year. The Portuguese government was commenting on one of their most loyal supporters during the War of the Two Brothers:

> This individual, a naturalised subject of Portugal in 1822, was appointed Consul for Portugal in Greece on the 5th January 1837; he immediately set out for Athens but the complaints raised against him became so numerous that Her Majesty the Queen deemed it expedient to recall him by a decree of the 21st January 1842. On the 26th January in the same year his dismissal was communicated to him in the shape of an order requiring him to remit without delay the archives and other objects appertaining to the consulate into the hands of his successor as soon as the latter should have obtained the necessary fiat from the Greek Government.
>
> David Pacifico refused to obey the orders of Her Majesty and complained of the injustice of his dismissal, threatening at the same time that he would present a considerable claim as an indemnity for the losses which he asserted he had experienced in the service of the august Sovereign aforesaid. On the 31st December 1844, the aforesaid Pacifico presented an account of his supposed losses, which he reckoned at 94,645,915 reis, a sum which he afterwards reduced of his own accord to 80 contos. But her Majesty's Government had no cognizance of any such account, no part of which was supported by the necessary documents and, moreover, it is necessary to take into consideration that a term was fixed by law within which the liquidation of similar indemnities should be effected, which

terms were extended two years more by another law of the 25th of April 1835 and that the said David Pacifico, though certainly not ignorant of this, did not prefer his claim until 1844, and in the manner aforesaid.

The Foreign Minister then had second thoughts and wrote to Petychalis again:

> It is my duty to announce to you that additional documents have been found signed by the said Pacifico, dated at the time when he solicited the post of consul in Morocco, and from which it became apparent that he held himself sufficiently indemnified for his losses by this appointment which Her Majesty granted to him by a decree of the 28th February 1835. In one of these documents he declares that, although the usurper had confiscated and robbed him of his property, he did not exact from the legitimate Government any indemnity for these losses.

The Portuguese were confirming Pacifico's position. As they couldn't pay him what he was owed in 1835, he had agreed to settle for a remunerative consulship, which the Portuguese then couldn't deliver. Although Tojal referred to numerous complaints against Pacifico, at no time did he ever specify what these were, so that others might judge their seriousness and validity. If Pacifico had performed his duties badly, surely some description of the type of complaints would have been forthcoming, which, if true, would have strengthened the Portuguese case immensely. In such a quiet backwater, whatever passed for a Portuguese Official Secrets Act would hardly have needed to be invoked. Pacifico always denied the accusations and the Portuguese never produced any evidence to justify them.

Five years is a very long time in politics, however, and Pacifico was now easily expendable. If he was going to kick up a fuss about what he was owed, then he would become a nuisance, and Loulé had made sure the Portuguese government had at least a technicality for avoiding its obligations to one of its most senior veterans. Ironically, the leader of the government in Portugal at the time was Pacifico's former comrade-in-arms, the Duke of Terceira.

It was to be the beginning of eight lean years for Pacifico. *The Times'* Lisbon correspondent explained the event to his readers in March 1850: 'At Athens Senhor Pacifico must... have been a prosperous man and consequently subject to envious and malicious reports, which, having made their way to Lisbon, and being accompanied by complaints from the Greek Ministry, caused this Government to dismiss him from the consulate in 1842.' It was possible to do this discreetly, and Pacifico's dismissal was not well known in Athens, but what exactly were the Greeks complaining about? What was Pacifico supposed to have done? For their part, the Greeks never elaborated either. The Portuguese government obviously preferred the whole story to be brushed under the carpet, rather than made the subject of an examination of the evidence. Pacifico's appeal in Portugal disappeared into committee, while a case for his replacement in Athens was built up. If the complaints were justified, as the Portuguese stated, why were they never specified?

Pacifico did not go quietly and the Portuguese had to get a judgement from the Greek courts that he must give up the consular archive. With so many outstanding bills owed by the Portuguese, Pacifico tried to keep as many bargaining counters as he could. He had obviously found that the job didn't produce a living wage and so he tried once again to get payment for his past services. At the end of 1839 – not in 1844 as Tojal had suggested – he had submitted his claims against the Portuguese to the Chamber of Deputies, using the good offices of Deputy Paul Midosi; he still had some friends in the Portuguese corridors of power. As *The Times'* correspondent in Lisbon reported some years later: 'It was then that his patience and forbearance became exhausted, and he threatened Portugal with his claims if he were not maintained in his office, and ultimately, being compelled to give it up, he, in 1844, preferred his claim for 91 contos or £21,300.'

Loulé remained a power in the land in Portugal. He was a vice-secretary in 1845 and he was made the civil governor of the university town of Coimbra in 1846. He was publicly amiable and a popular character. Loulé was never going to be sent into exile if he could help it.

Meanwhile, the Greek political picture remained in turmoil. Otho was determined to rule as an absolutist king and was supported by Russia. Lyons was still equally determined that there should be a constitution. In July 1841 Otho tried to placate Lyons by appointing, as Prime Minister, Aléxandros Mavrokordátos, who still led the party favourable to Britain. There was, however, an obvious necessity for Mavrokordátos to have wider support than the English party could provide, and he soon discovered that to obtain a majority of the deputies was impossible. To make matters worse, he suggested that the ruling Cabinet should be shorn of its Bavarian representatives, which upset the king, and then tried to lessen the influence of the army, which upset the liberals. Nothing worked but, even more discouraging, Mavrokordátos also found that corruption was all-pervasive, to such an extent that he threw in the sponge after only six weeks.

In July 1843 the three great power guarantors had had enough. They had been paying the interest on the original Greek loan ever since the country came into being. Now they called a meeting in London and set the figures for interest and repayments which they expected the Greeks to honour in future. What was more, they specified which Greek government revenues would be set aside for those purposes and even installed an agency to collect them.

Faced with a fait accompli, Otho had to find savings in the national budget. He proposed to reduce the size of the standing army, but the cuts were to be in the Greek contingents and not the Bavarian. This didn't go down at all well and within a few months a major conspiracy was forming to move the king's thinking in a different direction. On 14 September 1843 the palace was surrounded and Otho was asked to accept a constitution. The king rushed for advice and Lyons, naturally, told him to agree to the proposal. As the second request would have been for his abdication, Otho decided that the best thing was to accept, and wait to fight another day. On 15 September Greece finally became a constitutional monarchy, albeit without a constitution.

Britain and France were particularly keen for Otho to stay because the alternative they foresaw was that the country would switch to Greek Orthodoxy without him. If that happened, they believed the Russians would claim that they had a responsibility to defend their co-religionists, and they would be likely to assume a predominant role among the guarantors.

Twenty of the Greek good and great settled down to frame the constitution. The Greek church was granted permission to appoint its own head. It was further agreed that if Otho and Amélie didn't produce an heir, then the next king would have to be Greek Orthodox.

Meanwhile, Pacifico was continuing to press his claim against the Portuguese. In December 1844 he made a formal protest, before a notary in Athens, that the Portuguese government: 'not according to his reasonable claim for £21,295... which it owed him, abandoned him to want far from his country and in a foreign land'.[4] 'Want' is, of course, relative. 'Want', for a very rich man, may involve being reduced to only one helicopter. He hadn't retreated from Greece, which must have been an embarrassment for his successor. It was also in 1844 that Pacifico asked Lyons to help him with his Portuguese claim and Lyons wrote to Admiral Parker, who was on the Tagus, on his behalf. Parker was back in Portuguese waters after a stint in China. The admiral replied that the time was inopportune; the British knew very well how strapped for money the Portuguese were, and Portugal was heading towards a civil war in the immediate future.

The Greek finances remained in a dreadful state, through incompetence and corruption. The Finance Minister reported to the Greek Parliament in 1846:

> Gentlemen, – some days ago you sent for me to give you some account of the state of our finances; and I excused myself on the plea of just having taken office. I now come down to this House to tell you that the finance department is in a complete state of disorganization and paralysis: that no accounts exist either as to revenue or the expenditure, and that it will be utterly impossible to furnish you with anything in the shape of a correct budget. In consequence of the dishonesty and incapacity of the public functionaries, the public accounts are in a state of chaos. All that M. Provilegio and others have told you respecting every honest man having been dismissed, and of the spoliation of the public money at Syra and elsewhere, is perfectly true. Millions are due to the State; and we do not know our debtors, as the revenue books have disappeared. This is the financial statement I have to make.[5]

The news could hardly have been gloomier and the chances of getting paid the interest on the Greek loan were now getting slimmer by the day. Moreover, the lawlessness and corruption in the countryside was affecting British nationals. These included the citizens of the Ionian Isles.

At the Treaty of Paris in 1815, the British agreed to act as the protectors of the islanders. Geographically, the Ionian Isles were usefully placed for a naval base and provided another way of guarding the route to India. Sir Thomas Maitland was appointed Lord High Commissioner and given both the islands and Malta as his bailiwicks. The British kept order on the islands, sometimes harshly, but they were also concerned to establish that the inhabitants should not be treated as unimportant Greek peasants if they got into trouble on the mainland.

There were a number of cases over the years where Ionians, living in Greece, complained of being badly treated. Lyons had the greatest difficulty in getting these resolved, as charge and countercharge crossed the diplomatic table. The cases remained irritants between the two countries for many years. In addition, there was the problem of who should control two small islands, Cervi and Sapienza. The question was whether or not they were part of the Ionian Islands. The Greeks ran them, but was this right? The British wanted the Greeks out. Arguments on the subject dragged on for years and further undermined the relations between Britain and Greece.

If the political situation in Greece was unsatisfactory, the same could be said of Portugal, where Pacifico's claim was not top of the list of the government's priorities. In 1839 the infighting within the Liberal Party was getting so heated that Maria started deporting dissident politicians to Angola in the wilds of Africa. This alienated public opinion in constitutional countries like Britain, because the expectation of life in Angola was nothing to write home about. As Palmerston leaned on Queen Maria, she looked to Spain to intervene on her behalf and the Foreign Secretary had to warn off the Spanish. He knew how to deal with the situation, but he was concerned about how he would justify to Parliament the extent of his interference in the affairs of an ally. The behaviour of the Portuguese, however, was not unique. In 1834 an Ionian was very severely ill-treated by a great favourite of the Turkish sultan. Palmerston was told by his man on the spot that it would be unwise to interfere, and he accepted this.

Matters in Portugal deteriorated. In 1847 the dissident branches of the liberals were in revolt against Costa Cabral. Once again the junta in Porto were manning the barricades. Maria was being ever more arbitrary and taking sides, but neither government nor opposition could defeat the other. The French and Spanish were concerned at a centre of unrest so near their borders; these things could easily become contagious. So they sent their navies to bring about an amnesty. Palmerston's main concern was to prevent Maria turning into an absolutist monarch, maintained in that role by the Spanish. His advice to the queen was to summon the Cortes and promise an acceptable constitution.

Peace was restored, but then the problem of public finances immediately cropped up again. To get the loan they desperately needed, the Portuguese had to find a guarantor who would be acceptable to the bankers. Palmerston didn't want to know. He instructed the British minister in Lisbon to 'tell them as to our guaranteeing a loan, they might as well ask us to give them a slice of the moon.' This was the country and the government that Pacifico was trying to get to settle his claims from nearly twenty years before.

Some people in Greece did have money. One of them was Sophie Berbe Marboise, the Duchess of Plaisance. The duchess was an American heiress whose father was very important in Pennsylvania. She had been married to a French lawyer and she was left very well provided for when her father and husband passed away, so she went to Palestine for some years in the 1820s. As so much else had changed during Napoleonic times, there was a belief among some that it was even possible the Jews might return to the land of Israel from their centuries-old wanderings. The duchess must have been influenced by this thought and, as she travelled round the ancient ruins, was very much affected by the tragedy of the Holy Land which had sunk into torpor and decay. She eventually moved on to Athens in 1831, where she was equally affected by the glory that was Greece. So she settled down as a strong supporter of both ancient cultures. She also bought a great deal of land speculatively in the city. As Finlay had worked out, it was very cheap at the time.

The duchess became a well-known local character. She announced that she followed the faith of Moses and dressed in flowing robes and heavy veils. She ate no pork, studied the Bible at great length and befriended the small Jewish community. It is likely that the duchess' mother was Jewish which, according to Jewish law, would have made the duchess Jewish too, even if she was brought up as a Christian.

As a rich and aristocratic widow, the duchess soon became friends with Queen Amélie and also with Don Pacifico, whose house overlooked the garden of her winter home. He could see the duchess, on occasion, dressed in her flowing white tunic which imitated antique statuary, keeping vigil by the glass casket which contained the body of a daughter who had died at an early age. Pacifico was an accredited diplomat when they first met, an experienced traveller and a cultured man. They got on very well and both regretted that there was no proper synagogue in Athens. Pacifico told her that if she would give him some land, he would set about raising the necessary funds from the international Jewish communities to pay for the building.

The duchess was happy to help the local Jewish community and in 1843 made Pacifico a gift of 3,200 square metres of land near Constitution Square, by the palace. Her only condition was that the synagogue had to be completed within five years or the gift would be cancelled.

Pacifico spread his net widely and not in vain. Money came from the Rothschilds, from Italian Jewish communities and from individual Jews. A synagogue, however, is not the most vital element in a Jewish assembly called to prayer. That distinction belongs to the first five books of the Bible, which are written on parchment and bound into a scroll. A portion of the narrative is read every Sabbath and this book of the law is called the Sefer Torah. Pacifico wrote to the rabbi in Corfu and asked if he could spare one. The rabbi replied that he would be happy to do so if the community was going to be Orthodox and abide by their rules. The letter from Pacifico was in the Corfu synagogue archives until the Second World War, when it was destroyed, together with 86 per cent of the 80,000 Jews in the country.

The duchess was living near the Pacificos and the two families became good friends. Indeed, the friendship was so close that when Pacifico's oldest daughter fell in love with Captain Lante and had to leave home, it was the duchess who took her in.

After 1843 Otho continued to appoint all the ministers, but now in cahoots with Ionnis Kolettis as Prime Minister, although neither of them had much real parliamentary support. Kolettis had come back from running the Greek Embassy in Paris when Otho accepted the constitution, and the two of them made a formidable team of despots, constitution or no constitution. Palmerston's view of the Greek government at the time – and of the Kolettis' pro-French bias – was made clear to the British ambassador in Paris in April 1847:

> I have no doubt that Coletti would, as Wallenstein says, prefer France to the gallows, but I do not see why he should be reduced to that alternative. To be sure, St Aulaire [French diplomat] said to me the other day that Coletti was a necessary Minister, for that he is the chief and leader of all the robbers and scamps in Greece, and that if he was turned out of office, he would put himself at their head ... To this I replied that it seemed an odd qualification for a Minister that a man was a robber by profession ... Otho loves him as a second self, because he is as despotic as Otho himself; and as long as a majority can be had for Coletti in the Chambers, by corruption and intimidation, by the personal influence of the King, and by money from France, Coletti will remain Minister.

As the acceptance of corruption and intimidation continued to undermine the democratic process in Athens, the British vice-consul in Greece commented gloomily in 1846: 'It was useless to attempt to disguise the fact that there no longer existed in these parts the slightest security for either life or property.' It did not augur well for private citizens in the future.

In 1847 the Greeks had a general election and, by a combination of fraud and terror, the nominees of Otho and Kolettis topped the polls. Palmerston sent a strong protest to both the Greek and Bavarian governments, complaining of the way the election had been conducted. There had been many cases where opposition candidates had been assaulted and their supporters prevented by threats and violence from going to the polls. He expanded on the situation in a damning letter to the Bavarian prime minister in May of that year:

> That M. Coletti should hate a constitutional Greek government is not surprising. He was brought up as a boy in the land of Ali Pacha of Iannina, one of the most cruel and ferocious tyrants to have appeared in late times even in a Turkish province... his time was spent in irregular war. Part of his manhood in the amusements of Paris, and now at a more advanced Time of Life he finds himself devoid of the acquirements, the knowledge or the parliamentary faculties which are necessary for a Constitutional Minister. It can be no wonder that Coletti should think that it would be more convenient and agreeable to be the Minister of a despotic Sovereign and to govern by making or breaking laws as it might suit his purpose of the moment. But it was certainly not to be expected that King Otho should imbibe a fixed aversion of Constitutional government. He was chosen to be King of Greece especially because it was hoped that a son of the wise and enlightened Sovereign of Constitutional Bavaria would have been early imbued with such notions in Principles of government and would have had imbued in his mind just feelings of respect for the rights of his Grecian Subjects. It might also have been expected that King Otho would have been impressed with the consciousness that Greece was not detached from Turkey and erected into a separate and independent State, merely to the personal Benefit and Advantage of a Younger Prince of the house of Bavaria.

This didn't stop the three powers committed to ensuring the independence of Greece – Britain, France and Russia – from continuing to try to gain the upper hand in controlling the country's political policy. As Palmerston continued:

> As to Lyons, there has been a standing conspiracy against him for several years past among all his diplomatic colleagues

headed by the Greek Government. Lyons has been looked upon as the only advocate of constitutional government. Otho and Coletti wish it at the devil. Piscatory detests it, because the French Government think they can exercise more influence over ministers and Courts than over popular assemblies; the Bavarian Minister has, like his King, been hitherto all for despotism; Prokesch, obeying Metternich, goes into convulsions at the very notion of popular institutions; the Prussian Minister has been told implicitly to follow the Austrian; and the Russian only dares support the Constitutional party when there is a chance of Otho being frightened away and of his making room for the Grand Duke of Oldenburg. All these gentlemen, therefore, combined to suppress all information as to the disorder and abuses going on in Greece, and united to run down Lyons.[6]

Palmerston wasn't satisfied with grumbling to his staff. He told Lord Normanby in Paris to make his views clear to the French that England and France shouldn't quarrel over who had the most influence over the government of Greece. Which was a bit rich as the struggle had been going on for years.

When the Russians complained that the British claims against the Greeks were unreasonable, Palmerston gave the British ambassador in St Petersburg another very clear order: 'Tell Nesselrode [the Russian Foreign Minister] and the Emperor that if they think the enforcement of our demands would be injurious to the stability of Greece, an opinion which we in no degree share, the only way of preventing it is to persuade Coletti to do what we require, as the Greeks have ample means to pay us if they choose.'[7]

In spite of the efforts of the Russian and French ministers, Lyons was still on station in Athens when the riot broke out at Easter that year. The question was whether he was prepared to help Pacifico in any meaningful way and if he would be allowed to do so by his chief in London, the ever-present Foreign Secretary, Lord Palmerston.

NOTES

1   Evelyn Ashley, *Lord Palmerston* (Richard Bentley, 1879).
2   Edgar Samuel, *At the End of the Earth* (Jewish Historical Society of England, 2004).
3   The circumstances were explained by Don Pacifico's lawyer in court as reported in *The Times* on 19 November 1850.

4   *Gates to Jewish Heritage* – Internet: www.jewishgates.com/
     file.asp.
5   *The Examiner*, June 1850.
6   Palmerston to Lord Normanby, 20 April 1847.
7   Ashley, *Lord Palmerston*.

9 Palmerston: Lords Cupid, Pumicestone and Firebrand

It had been one of the wettest Februarys on record and it was still raining. In that spring of 1847, Harry Temple, Viscount, Lord Palmerston, sat at his impressive desk in the Foreign Office in London as the continuing grey skies threatened a dismal summer. The department's headquarters were in Lord Sheffield's old house in Downing Street but the rest was spread over several buildings in the vicinity, most of which were dilapidated and subject to flooding. Palmerston was 62 years old, with grey hair brushed forward and balanced by large crops of side whiskers. He was only of medium height but he stood out in a crowd because he went in for floppy bow ties They were one of his trademarks and Winston Churchill might well have recognized their effectiveness in this respect when he adopted them himself in future years.

The long days at the department didn't faze the Foreign Secretary; he could put in seven-day weeks, often working past midnight, without affecting his excellent health. He was a poor delegator at the best of times and wrote most of his despatches by hand, standing up at his desk. On a number of occasions he wrote private letters to colleagues overseas, en clair. It was a good way to menace other countries unofficially, because he knew that his letters would always be opened if they were not in the secure diplomatic bag, and their deliberately alarming contents would consequently be uncomfortably absorbed by those at whom the threats were aimed.

Things were getting back to normal. When he had lost his parliamentary office in 1841, his successor, in his opinion, had let things slide. Palmerston had kept everybody's noses to the grindstone and, indeed, in 1840 Lord Granville had said: 'The clerks detest Palmerston and have an absurd idea that he takes a pleasure in bullying them.' Palmerston felt that working at the ministry, under Lord Aberdeen, had become something of a sinecure again. The junior staff seemed to have reacquired the habit of arriving late and leaving early. When he had once again become Foreign Secretary in

1846, his nickname of Lord Pumicestone had soon been well earned. Overseas he was known as Lord Firebrand, which further emphasised the fact that he was not a man with whom to trifle. There was now a new work ethic at the Foreign Office, which was just as well, as a major international power such as Britain was heavily involved in foreign affairs all over the world. The clerks were not short of files.

Harry Temple had become Lord Palmerston when he was 17 years old, when his father died in 1802. Born into an extremely rich and noble Irish family in October 1784, Palmerston never had any real money problems. The family owned over 10,000 acres of land in farming country in County Sligo. He was almost the same age as David Pacifico, but their worlds could hardly have been more different.

Palmerston's father had been a great traveller and Harry spent some years as a child with the family in Switzerland and Italy. He had an Italian tutor and soon spoke good Italian and French.

At the age of 10, in 1795, he was sent to Harrow, which was a tough apprenticeship. The cream of the aristocratic crop went to Eton and Harrow, though, and they made friendships which would last them throughout their public lives. When the old boys gathered in later years to reminisce about their schooldays, Harry was always remembered as a chap who would take on the largest bully, no matter what the consequences were. That combative determination to succeed never deserted him, for he also knew how uncertain and transient life could be; when he was young, his father had insisted on his sister having one of the newfangled smallpox inoculations, and it killed her.

After Harrow, Harry went on to Edinburgh University, where 'I lived with Dugald Stewart and attended his lectures (on political economy) at the University. In these three years, I laid the foundation of whatever useful knowledge and habits of mind I possess.'[1]

It was while he was at Edinburgh that his father died. As the new Viscount Palmerston, he continued his education at Cambridge and benefited from both universities. So it was a well-rounded mind which had to decide what to do with his adult life. Palmerston chose politics, although he was not at all keen on work getting in the way of sowing his sizeable crop of wild oats.

Harry Temple was definitely a ladies' man – he was known then as Lord Cupid – and a hard-playing man about town. He particularly enjoyed the very exclusive balls at Almacks on a Wednesday evening, where he made many lifelong friends. These included Leopold of Saxe-Coburg, a minor German prince who would play an important role in the future, behind the scenes, in the life of the British royal family. He gambled at Watiers, where the stakes were very high and the host was Beau Brummell – until 1812 a favourite of the prince regent and the supreme arbiter of Regency fashion. Naturally, the viscount was also a member of all the best political clubs. Running the country, however, was not a well-paid career. MPs received no salary and government was considered a social duty rather than a way of paying your bills. This naturally meant that only the rich or very dedicated could really afford to devote their lives to it.

Palmerston was in his 20s during the Regency period of George IV, and he was a very typical Regency buck. His racing colours of green with an orange cap – which became the Irish colours – were to be seen at Epsom and Newmarket. He became a very good billiards player and his charm and high spirits put him high on the list of eligible bachelors to be invited to the soirées of the great society hostesses. In all this he was following in the footsteps of his parents who had, in their time, been equally involved in the social whirl.

One of Palmerston's favourite woman friends was Lady Cowper, who was the first Lord Melbourne's daughter. Her mother had taught her that a husband was entitled to his first son being his progeny, but if he didn't keep his wife happy after that, she should be free to look elsewhere. At least one subsequent child of Lady Cowper looked very much like Palmerston. He was discreet about his affairs, however, and the gossipmongers very seldom had any hard evidence.

Palmerston stood as a Tory in Cambridge in 1806, and lost. In quick succession he also lost in Horsham and then in Cambridge again. After those setbacks, however, he was adopted for the pocket borough of Newport, Isle of Wight, and won an uncontested election, entering the House of Commons in May 1807 at the age of 22. As he was an Irish peer, he sat in the Commons. As a well-connected nobleman he had been made a Junior Lord of Admiralty even before he became an MP. Amazingly, within a year of his successful election, he was offered the position of Chancellor of the Exchequer by Spencer Perceval, the Prime Minister, who was another Old Harrovian. Perceval's problem was that the previous administration had been so fraught with dissension that the Cabinet ministers refused to serve together in the next government. All kinds of youngsters got a flying start to their parliamentary careers but the Exchequer, Palmerston thought, might be just slightly beyond his capabilities. So he opted for the position of Secretary at the War Office without, of course, knowing that he would spend the next eighteen years there.

The main job of the secretary was supposed to be acting as the government's auditor when it came to spending the money allocated by Parliament for the army. The job specification had changed over the years, however, and who was actually responsible for what, in the War Office in 1809, was often clouded in uncertainty. The result was the 'perfect camouflage for corruption and incompetence'.[2] If Palmerston found himself dealing with foreign powers with the same doubtful standards in the future, he would have been thoroughly prepared by his earlier experiences.

Palmerston arrived at the War Office at the height of the Napoleonic Wars, when the emperor was carrying all before him. The only blot on Napoleon's war record was at sea, where the British navy had proved far superior to the French fleet on many occasions. After Napoleon lost at Trafalgar he, naturally, hoped to get his warships replaced by the next largest navy in Europe, that of Denmark. George Canning, then Foreign Secretary, had, however, foreseen this, and decided in 1807 to send a British fleet to Copenhagen. The idea was either to get the Danes to agree to an alliance with Britain, or to surrender their ships.

The Danes indignantly refused to do either of these, which was foolhardy as their fleet had been caught in harbour. The British peppered the Danish flotilla, and Copenhagen itself, with volleys and salvos which eventually resulted in the Scandinavians surrendering. They abandoned the vessels which remained afloat, and British crews were put on board to tow them away. It was a major victory, but many members of the House of Commons condemned the action as against international law and as a big power bullying a small, neutral one. Such ethical attitudes were becoming increasingly popular. They sprang simplistically from a reaction to being bullied at public school and from the growing popularity of romantic historical novels, in which the hero would refuse to destroy even the most villainous of opponents if he had him at an unfair disadvantage. It was considered unsporting, and the treatment with honour of wounded and captured senior enemy officers in the Napoleonic Wars was a reflection of this.

In February 1808 a motion in the House of Commons enabled the subject of the treatment of the Danes to be thoroughly aired. Palmerston, as a Lord of Admiralty, spoke in the debate and made clear what his position was going to be throughout his lifetime. He defended his guru, Canning: 'In the case before the House, the law of nature is stronger even than the law of nations. It is to the law of self-preservation that England appeals for the justification of her proceedings.' If there was no alternative, Palmerston believed in Gunboat Diplomacy.

The truth was that if Napoleon could have enrolled the Danish fleet, he wouldn't have hesitated to do so. International law meant very little to Bonaparte, as would be the case with many other aggressors and dictators with whom Palmerston would have to deal in the future. Pragmatically, if Palmerston had decided to keep to the Marquis of Queensberry's rules when his opponents were prepared to tear up the instruction manual altogether, Britain would have stood an excellent chance of being beaten. That was the reality of the situation. That was the basis on which Palmerston would usually decide what to do in the future when it came to the crunch. Only if it was unrealistic to try to use force, when diplomacy had initially been tried and failed, would he reluctantly accept the inevitable loss of his objectives.

As a minister, applying meticulous attention to detail, Palmerston sorted out the mess which had been the War Office accounts. He pushed the clerks to regularly achieve a level of hard work which reduced the outstanding bills from over 4,000 to a negligible number. As a consequence, he was not popular in his department, but he was respected. Haughty and light-hearted in equal measure, it was best to be on the right side of him.

As a disciple of George Canning, Palmerston soon learned once more the importance of standing his ground. Sometimes this was necessary to protect his own role. The commander-in-chief of the army was the prince regent's brother, the Duke of York. It was he who had 10,000 men in the old rhyme, and led them up to the top of the hill before he led them down again: a reference to a disastrous expedition to Holland at the beginning of the wars against the French, when no battle ensued but a large proportion of the 10,000 British soldiers succumbed to disease.

If the prince regent died, the duke, Frederick Augustus, was next in line to the throne. With only one short pause he was commander-in-chief from 1798 until he died in 1827. The duke was 46 in 1809 and certainly didn't intend to take orders from some 25-year-old whippersnapper at the War Office. Palmerston, however, had equally no intention of allowing the army to control the politicians. Establish that as the norm and parliamentary democracy would be under serious threat. The pre-eminence of Parliament was written in blood and set in stone. In years to come Queen Victoria and Prince Albert would be treated by Palmerston no differently from the duke.

This meant that Perceval had to umpire, and to reiterate that the Secretary at War was not subordinate to the commander-in-chief. If the two couldn't agree, the necessary compromise was that they would have to come to him for a final decision. With that the duke had to be satisfied. After Perceval had, unhappily, been assassinated – the only British Prime Minister to suffer in that way – his successor, Lord Liverpool, had the same unenviable task.

If Palmerston's job was to look after the army budget, a substantial part of it had to go to pay the troops, many of whom were with another Irishman, Arthur Wellesley, the future Duke of Wellington, who was in the middle of the Peninsular War in Spain and Portugal. As we've seen much of the pay came through Gibraltar, and the support of Jewish merchants oiled the wheels of transportation. Palmerston would have needed to know a lot about what was going on in the area during the Peninsular War years, so he may well have heard of the activities of a fast privateer called the *Pacifico*.

When the Napoleonic Wars finally ended, Palmerston soldiered on at the War Office, although not for lack of encouragement to move. Lord Liverpool and his successors offered him everything from the Home Office and the Exchequer to the post of governor of Jamaica, but he regularly decided in the end that he was perfectly happy where he was. On the very few occasions when he wanted a change, the infighting and internal politics of the powers that be frustrated him; George IV refused to accept him at the Exchequer in the short-lived Canning and Goderich administrations in 1827. Usually, though, the crucial point to Palmerston was that the War Office job in peacetime wasn't overtaxing, now that he'd cleared out the Augean stable, and it didn't get in the way of his social life. His spare time continued to be happily and fully occupied.

In 1828, he at last fell out with the Tories. The Cabinet had promised to disenfranchise a constituency with very few voters and give the seat to the under-represented new town of Birmingham. They went back on their word and Palmerston resigned along with other senior members. He joined the Whigs and, when they gained power in 1830, he was offered the Foreign Office by the new Prime Minister, Earl Grey. At 46 years of age he was now happy to take it.

The post of Foreign Secretary was a comparatively new one; foreign affairs had been delegated to a single man only when Charles James Fox took on the responsibility in 1782. In his high office Palmerston was, above all, a patriotic British gentleman. He believed

Britain knew best, particularly when it came to the best system of government. After 1815 much of Europe disagreed with him. Britain found itself back in its traditional position as one of the few flag bearers for constitutional monarchy, albeit without a written constitution. Palmerston was passionately involved in the struggle. He was never able to take a detached view of foreign policy. He believed strongly in whatever he was doing.

Palmerston's French opposite number was Talleyrand, the great French statesman, who was a survivor and pragmatic. He said of Palmerston: 'He is so impassioned in public affairs that he will sacrifice the greatest interests to his resentments; almost every political question is complicated in his case by a personal question.' Palmerston was also not afraid of brinkmanship. As a high-stakes card player that was a necessary skill, although gambling with foreign policy was putting up the stakes a great deal. To get his own way in the creation of Belgium, for example, he threatened the French with war if they didn't withdraw from land he wanted for the new kingdom.

When you talk about Britain's foreign policy in the next thirty years, there would often be occasions when it would be more correct to describe it as Palmerston's foreign policy. If he thought a course of action with a specific country was the right one for Britain, he was quite prepared to conceal any unwelcome facts from his Cabinet colleagues, who often showed little interest in the subject anyway. He took a similar attitude towards the court, and this was to lead to a lot of trouble with Queen Victoria and Prince Albert. Palmerston did his own thing.

Furthermore, he was quite prepared to bluff his way out of the trouble such a policy was almost bound to produce. When Parliament asked to see the despatches which referred to a foreign policy issue in 1834, Palmerston brushed the request aside:

> If, in the present case, they [Parliament] are not willing to trust us with the maintenance of the honour of the country, without calling upon us, from day to day, to come down to this House, and produce the last dispatches we have received, for the purpose of enabling them to judge whether our answers to those dispatches are right or wrong – if such, I say, be the opinion of the House, let them declare it, and let his Majesty's ministers retire . . .

The opposition didn't have enough votes to call his bluff.

So the first objective of British foreign policy, as Palmerston saw it, was to make sure that as many European countries as possible had constitutional governments. If there had been a European Parliament at the time, the leader of the Constitutional Party would have been Britain. The Absolutist Party would have included Russia, Austria–Hungary, Prussia and many Italian states. Countries like Spain, Portugal, Greece and Belgium were the arenas where supporters of the conflicting philosophies could try to gain ascendancy. Only the hard work that Palmerston put in during the 1830s saved these countries from finishing up under absolutist regimes. And there was always the danger of the domino effect; if Palmerston had failed in Portugal, Spain could well have gone the same way.

The fight for constitutional government was expensive. Many senior British politicians would have been quite happy with an isolationist agenda. Unless the national honour was clearly involved, they would have preferred to let the Europeans get on with it. Their position was that – then as now – there were more important things to worry about. To avoid upsetting many of his own backbenchers, Palmerston would resort to clandestine methods. Moreover, like so many ministers before and since, it was often Palmerston's view that what the public didn't know wouldn't worry them.

Another vital principle of the country's foreign policy was predicated on the need to sustain Britain's position as the foremost international trading nation. In 1850 Britain's production of iron was greater than all the other countries in the world put together. Half the world's manufactured cotton came from England. Two thirds of the world's coal was mined in Britain. There would come a time when Britain, as the world's number one exporter, sent more goods abroad than countries two and three – Germany and the United States – put together. To export the volume of goods that the country managed to send across the globe, you needed your companies at home to have offices in any number of foreign lands. If you wanted volunteers to man them, you needed to look after the expats thus involved. If you didn't ensure that British citizens could operate safely, no matter what the political complexions of the foreign government in which they lived, your trade was likely to be disrupted by desertions.

Now, of course, there might be occasions when it would be impossible to protect your overseas merchants. If they ran into trouble with one of the great European powers, you were unlikely to want to go to war with the likes of Russia or Prussia. Then again, if the countries were too remote, it was going to be difficult to bring pressure to bear in somewhere like the deepest interior of Asia. Two brave British spies, Colonel Stoddart and Captain Conolly, were captured and executed in Bokhara, a hopelessly remote, 85,000 square-mile state north of Afghanistan, in 1838. There was nothing Palmerston could do.

Britain had to try to intervene unless such considerations made it impossible. More than a century later, when there was considerable doubt whether they could recover the distant Falkland Islands from the Argentineans, the Prime Minister decided the effort had to be made on behalf of British citizens. If, on occasion, the Victorians appeared heavy-handed and dictatorial in dealing with small countries, the benefit to Britain was that the word would get round: that those countries who arbitrarily and unjustly mistreated their own citizens would treat expat British merchants in the same fashion only at their peril.

Palmerston was often belligerent. He protested vigourously on behalf of Maltese labourers in Constantinople and of Ionian peasants in Greece. He always impressed on British ambassadors and consuls the duty of protecting every British subject who was in difficulties. Government offices today do not have a particularly brilliant reputation for serving the citizenry. We are, perhaps, a long way from the rebuke Palmerston sent his minister in Belgium in 1840 when that worthy's staff had fallen down on the job of looking after one unfortunate British subject:

> It is the duty of a Consular officer to go immediately to any British Subject who from having been arrested or for any other difficulty in which he may find himself with the local Authorities, may request his aid; and such Consular Officer is not performing his duty when he rests satisfied with the statements made to him by Authorities who have arrested a British Subject as to the grounds on which they have done so; and who neglects to go and hear from the accused himself what he may have to say on his own behalf. A British Subject may be unjustly accused by the Officers of the Police. And a British Consular officer would very imperfectly perform his duty by sending him the name of a lawyer to be employed, instead of enquiring into the case and giving such assistance as might appear expedient and proper.

Furthermore, Palmerston expected foreign countries to treat British visitors with what he considered suitable deference. In Belgium, for example, there had been a number of cases of crooks

travelling on false papers. The Belgians wanted to stop this by
having some of the personal details of passport holders included in
the forms, such as the colour of their hair. Palmerston refused
outright. He insisted that 'no Englishman could be subjected to the
humiliation of having to give such personal details to government
officials'.[3] The Belgians responded angrily by turning back British
visitors at the customs posts. Palmerston shrugged and told them
that if they wanted to destroy their tourist trade, that was up to
them.

To police the world in British interests, Palmerston had the British
navy. He didn't have much of a mobile British army. There was no
need, after the Napoleonic Wars, for a large military force to defend
the island against invasion, with twenty miles of English Channel as
a virtually impassible barrier. So there was no conscription, and
where there were sizeable army detachments in the empire, they
were normally needed to control their own colonies. The overall
policy was not to waste troops.

The navy was a different matter. It was vast – over 250 ships in
mid-century – and it was highly professional, and its reach was as
far as the oceans covered. This led to the favourite weapon used
by the British to coerce other nations: making life extremely
difficult for the recalcitrant nation's shipping, with bombardment
always available to be carried out by highly professional gunnery
crews for good measure. It wasn't just the British, of course. The
French and Americans had sizeable fleets and used them in the
same way. When James Monroe and George Canning developed
the Monroe Doctrine, it was to stop Spain holding on to its
empire in South America. Those countries would, in the future, be
free to develop independently, but their defence depended on the
American and British navies, and the British were the major
partners. On one occasion Palmerston listed thirty-three separate
instances where major powers had used military force to defend
the interests of their nationals when they were in difficulties in
overseas countries.

The navy acted as Britain's bobby on the beat. If there was
trouble, there would soon be a British squadron on the spot. In
1839, for instance, the King of Naples granted a sulphur monopoly
to certain firms, freezing British merchants out of the markets.
Palmerston sent the navy to blockade Naples until the king changed
his mind – which he promptly did, because bringing a major port to
a halt is excessively disruptive to a nation's commerce.

International law and treaty rights were, of course, above the law of the foreign state, and Palmerston would, therefore, not permit a foreign government to enforce a law which violated Britain's negotiated position. If the British consul said that the court had been prejudiced against a British subject, Palmerston would take up the case with the foreign government, even if no question of international law or treaty rights was involved.

If, however, British subjects were guilty, then Palmerston believed they had to be punished. In 1838 the Turks asked Britain to relinquish its treaty rights on British criminals in Turkey. Palmerston wrote to Ponsonby: 'I feel equally with Your Excellency the importance of endeavouring without delay to remedy a state of things, which cannot continue to exist without reflecting serious discredit on the British name... Her Majesty's Government can never sanction the principle that British subjects are to be protected whether right or wrong'.⁴ He still insisted, however, that British observers be present at trials to see that justice was done. He was also sufficiently cautious, when international law issues were involved, to always refer to the Queen's Advocate in Parliament, and he accepted his decision.

The next plank of Palmerston's foreign policy often followed on from the first. It was to support almost any revolutionary movement which was prepared to do battle to introduce constitutional government, instead of suffer the rule of a dictatorial regime. Palmerston believed that in looking at a civil war overseas, it was necessary to answer two questions at the outset. Which side had the better case and was it in Britain's interests to support it? Those who opposed absolutist regimes fitted the bill as far as Palmerston was concerned.

As Foreign Secretary, he soon became determined to get rid of Don Miguel in Portugal and the Turks in Greece. When he arrived in 1830, he was pitched into taking over the chairmanship of the conference which settled Greek independence. He gained his spurs for the skill with which he carried through the negotiations. As a result, he got Greece far more territory than was on offer at the beginning of the talks. Palmerston would also support Italian independence from Austria and a democratic government in Spain. Everybody on the continent knew that was his position, so he was not at all popular in absolutist eastern Europe, Germany as a whole, or often in France.

Most European rulers owed a very great deal to Britain. The Continent owed its deliverance from Napoleon to Wellington and Nelson. Debts of that nature, however, are soon forgotten or rationalised away. The absolutists didn't want to give up their hegemony and looked for ways to change Britain's stance.

One possibility, they thought, was that their rulers were often related to members of the British royal family. Until Victoria came to the throne, the ruling British dynasty were also kings of Hanover; they had a definite place among the German aristocracy. Victoria had come to the throne as the great-niece of Hanoverians, George IV and William IV, because of the death of George's daughter, Charlotte, in childbirth, together with the baby, just before he came to the throne.

Charlotte was married to Leopold of Saxe-Coburg, Victoria's favourite uncle – the same Leopold who danced at Almacks and whom Palmerston made sure was placed firmly on the throne of the new European country, Belgium. He even blockaded the Scheldt, this time together with the French, to stop Holland trying to alter the treaty that had created Belgium in the first place. Leopold's brother was later married to the Queen of Portugal – and so it went on: dynastic connection after dynastic connection, as royal sibling married royal sibling. As a consequence, the rulers would often approach the sovereign in Britain, asking that the government's policy be changed through her intervention. They knew that, officially, the British monarch couldn't do anything except advise her ministers, but as they often didn't keep to the rules in their own country, they couldn't imagine a situation in which the British conscientiously adhered to the settlement of 1689 which had, effectively, settled the relationship between the Crown and Parliament.

It always has to be remembered, however, that Palmerston's belief in liberal principles did not extend to many of the aspects of the world he inhabited in the United Kingdom. He was a benevolent Irish landlord, but supported the often harsh status quo which applied over the Irish Sea. During the Irish potato famine in the 1840s, he shipped a lot of his suffering tenants to an inhospitable Canadian climate to get them out of the way. In the spring of 1847, conditions for the destitute in Ireland had become too terrible for words. There were 4,800 poor souls in the Cork workhouse and over 100 died every week. Mass graves were often necessary and, in eighteen months, 2,000 died in that institution alone. At the same time that Pacifico's house was being looted, the government suspended public works in Ireland, which was the only source of income for many in the country. Tens of thousands of people were left to literally starve to death, and they did.

In 1847 over 250,000 Irish crossed the Atlantic, as landlords got rid of their obligations to keep their impoverished tenants alive. The government in London watched all this happen with a degree of indifference which laid the foundation for the Home Rule movement in Ireland. In Europe, however, Palmerston's basic policy was always to try to combine with the weak against the strong. For the maintenance of the balance of power he wanted no permanent alliances – although Portugal was an exception. Otherwise he continued what had long been a key plank in British foreign policy; to maintain that balance of power in Europe, you never totally destroyed an enemy, because he might be needed in the future as a collaborator against your former allies. The traditional enemy was France, and the traditional ally Germany.

Domestically, it had been an important factor during Melbourne's time that a considerable number of the most important members of his Cabinet were with Palmerston at the same boarding house at Harrow, and he wouldn't have had it any other way; if politics was the art of the possible, your former school chums were more likely to extend the range of possibilities. He also invariably appointed Whigs to vacant embassies.

Once Palmerston was in the Foreign Office, he became a fixture. He was Foreign Secretary almost throughout the 1830s, from 1830 to 1834 and again from 1835 to 1841. He served in the Cabinet under Lord Melbourne and, as Palmerston's relationship with Lady Cowper, Melbourne's sister, was very well known, he was almost a member of the clan. Melbourne fell out with the king over church reform and was dismissed in 1834. Sir Robert Peel, the leader of the Tories, tried to form a government but it lasted less than three months. When Melbourne took up the reins again, he really didn't want Palmerston to go back to the Foreign Office in Downing Street. Foreign affairs were both extremely important and extremely delicate. The Prime Minister knew that Lord Liverpool hadn't trusted Palmerston even to keep the Cabinet informed of exactly what he was doing in his much less important position in the War Office.

Melbourne knew the viscount would be difficult to handle, but Palmerston was by now an extremely experienced and senior politician. He also had the support of the Radical Whigs, whom Melbourne needed to retain a majority in the House of Commons. They had been very impressed by his successful efforts to liberate countries like Spain, Portugal, Greece and Belgium from absolutist rulers and they were fully prepared to reward him with their votes.

There was also the family connection and that had to be taken into account as well. So Palmerston couldn't be left out, and wouldn't accept any other office. In a cleft stick, Melbourne reluctantly gave him his old job back.

William IV died in 1837 and was succeeded by Queen Victoria. The 18-year-old entranced a couple of old Regency bucks such as Melbourne and Palmerston. Melbourne coached her on most parliamentary subjects but left Palmerston to explain foreign affairs to her. She was well pleased and when he explained her Uncle Leopold's position in Belgium – the king was her mother's brother, as well as everything else – he did so 'in such a very pleasant, clear and agreeable manner, as to put me quite au fait of the whole thing'.

Palmerston was charmed and flattered to be invited to tutor Her Majesty, but that didn't mean that he was going to change his ways. He annoyed Victoria in the first few months of her reign by being late for a state dinner, and then properly blotted his copybook in 1839 when he was invited to stay overnight at Windsor Castle. Another of the guests was Lady Cowper, whose husband had died two years before, and Palmerston went searching for her room during the small hours. Unfortunately he wandered into the wrong bedroom, and Mrs Brand, a most respectable lady, shrieked the place down. It was all hushed up, of course, which meant that it was soon the talk of the town.

Victoria's austere approach to life was a reaction to the profligacy of the Regency years. She succeeded uncles who were both kings and fathers of strings of illegitimate children; gambling and debauchery had been the order of the day and night on all sides. Victoria's reign was the swing of the pendulum, but Palmerston had understood and enjoyed the old times. There was a serious generation gap here between the middle-aged minister and the young queen.

When Victoria married Albert in 1841, the situation only worsened. Albert was entirely in tune with the queen's feelings. Palmerston's jauntiness and insouciance soon grated on them both. What was more, Albert added more royal and noble relatives, spread all over the Continent and leaning on him for support whenever they felt it appropriate to do so. The preferred foreign policy of the royal couple was never likely to equate with that of the Foreign Secretary. For example, the Queen fully supported the absolutist Emperor of Austria and denounced the Hungarians as revolutionaries in 1849, even though they had been downtrodden by the Austrians for years. Palmerston dryly compared the Hungarians to the revolutionaries who had put her ancestors on the throne in 1688.

Victoria did, nevertheless, have the constitutional right to review foreign policy with Palmerston and to give him her advice. She wrote: 'Lord Palmerston has a perfect right to state to the Queen his reasons for disagreeing with her views, and will always have found her ready to listen to his reasons; but she cannot allow a servant of the Crown and her minister to act contrary to her orders, and this without her knowledge.'

Palmerston, in his turn, would have found it difficult to take her seriously. After all, thirty years ago, he had first crossed swords with her uncle, at the War Office; he had been a minister of the Crown longer than she had been alive, and indeed he was thirty-five years older than the queen. On occasion she exceeded her authority and instructed him to alter a despatch but he would often send it unchanged. The alternative was to send the draft of the message to Victoria and wait for the queen's comments, which might come after a substantial delay. Then, if she wanted changes, more time would elapse as he put his point of view in rebuttal. Then he had to wait until she had digested this and sent another memo. The proceedings could drag on for a fortnight and, on one memorable occasion, the French Foreign Minister was very vexed at not receiving a reply to his despatch for such a long period. Palmerston had to apologise without being able to explain that it was the Queen's fault.

The keenly observant Greville had written in his diary in 1839 that Palmerston 'is detested by the Corps Diplomatique, abhorred in his own office, unpopular in the House of Commons, liked by nobody, abused by everybody, still reigns in his little kingdom of the Foreign Office, and is impervious to any sense of shame'. In 1840 he returned to the subject: 'Palmerston, in fact, appears to exercise an absolute despotism at the Foreign Office and deals with all our vast and complicated questions of diplomacy according to his own views and opinions without the slightest control and scarcely any interference on the part of his colleagues...his letters so dashing, bold and confident in their tone.'

In December 1839, when he was 55 and she 48, Palmerston and Emily Cowper finally got married. Their home was Broadlands in Hampshire which covered three square miles. In 1841 Melbourne lost the general election to Peel, and Palmerston retired to the back benches for the next five years. He remained, however, a very influential voice in public opinion. Emily Cowper had been well taught by her mother and knew exactly what was necessary to bring the good and the great to the Palmerston hearth. In addition, while the expansive host was not the first parliamentary spin doctor, he was certainly one of the most able of the breed.

Palmerston didn't just invite leading editors and journalists to his home. He also wrote articles, sometimes in his own name and sometimes under pseudonyms. Like Winston Churchill nearly a hundred years later, he was in no need of help from ghostwriters. The public image Palmerston studiously set out to portray was some considerable distance from reality. When tackling a particularly thorny foreign policy problem later, it has been remarked of him: 'Palmerston's public image as a jovial bon vivant and blustering patriot...masked the deadly seriousness with which he had disciplined himself to master the various facets.' It was typical, however, of his theatrical persona that Palmerston summed up his contribution on that occasion by stating that only three people understood the 1848 Schleswig Holstein affair; one was dead, one was in an asylum, and he, Palmerston, had forgotten the details. But then it was generally agreed that Palmerston saw intricate questions of foreign policy more as 'challenges to a boxing match'.[5]

In the early 1840s the key domestic issue in Britain was the conflict of interest between the British landowners and the manufacturing and merchant classes, centred on the Corn Laws. The merchants' and manufacturers' group, of which Sir Robert Peel was a member, as well as being Prime Minister, wanted the Corn Laws abolished. Many countries insisted on substantial import duties on British goods because their corn exports were taxed when they entered Britain. The price of wheat was kept artificially high in this way, which benefited the landowners but made the cost of living higher than necessary for the poor. Eventually, with the help of the Whigs, the Corn Laws were repealed in 1846, but this hopelessly split the Tory party. The most able of their members left the fold and formed a substantial new grouping under Peel. The remainder were left with few parliamentary stars and were, effectively, out of office for the next twenty-five years.

After 1846 it took ten years for the Tory party to get the opportunity to form even a minority government. The rump of Peel's Tories protected the farmers and the established church. Then there were the Whigs – a tight group of aristocratic families well known for opposition to monarchical autocracy and a willingness to embrace reform and limited religious tolerance. In future they would usually be supported by the Radical Whigs – the Peelites. The Irish MPs were normally Whig or Radical and their main interests were land tenure in Ireland and Roman Catholicism.

The Peelites officially called themselves liberal-conservatives. They held the balance of power with about a hundred MPs who wouldn't go back to the Tories. MPs at the time were more loyal to their constituencies anyway than to their parties, and the constituencies were controlled by the most important people in the local communities.

In 1846 Lord John Russell, from the Duke of Bedford's family, formed the last Whig administration. The Bedfords had been Whigs for 100 years. Russell was short, (five feet, four-and-three-quarter inches), light (fifty kilograms), shy, delicate and bookish, but he was a bold operator. Bulwer Lytton, a noted politician, wit and author of the time, wrote of the duke's fourth son:

> How formed to lead, if not too proud to please,
> His fame would fire you, but his manners freeze;
> Like or dislike, he does not give a jot,
> He wants your vote, but your affections not.

Russell reflected the age in which he lived. When it was able to assess his whole life, *The Times* said in its obituary that foreigners might consider that Russell's career lacked brilliance and effect. It went on: 'Englishmen are not in sympathy with demands like these. In their eyes, pride wrapped in rigourous reserve and sobriety of expression, and demeanour approaching frigidity, are important elements in the dignified character of a Statesman.'[6]

Russell had been deeply involved in the 1832 Reform Bill, was interested in foreign affairs and served in both the Grey and Melbourne governments. When an election was held in 1847 and he became Prime Minister, the Whigs had an overall majority of only one and, therefore, could stay in office only with the support of the Peelites. As the Peelites were never going to support the Tories, however, it would take some political catastrophe to get the Whigs out of office.

In this climate, Greece at the beginning of 1847 had been a minor item on Palmerston's list of unfinished business. He'd given its development his best shot, but there were still plenty of major shortcomings, like the absence of a constitution, and minor irritations like George Finlay's compensation, or the Ionian Islands which would need ongoing attention. He was disposed to dislike almost everything about the Greek government and he was not in the least surprised when Edmund Lyons' dispatch from Athens announced yet another example of the Greek's inability to create a law-abiding nation. At the same time he had absolutely no idea that it was possible that, in dealing with this case of a Gibraltar Jew called David Pacifico, he could bring down the government – and the Foreign Secretary with it.

NOTES

1   Evelyn Ashley, *Palmerston* (Richard Bentley, 1879).
2   James Chambers, *Palmerston* (John Murray, 2004).
3   Ibid.
4   George T. Billy, *Palmerston's Foreign Policy 1848* (Peter Lang, 1993).
5   Kingsley Martin, *Lord Palmerston and Public Opinion, 1846–1852* (Allen & Unwin, 1924).
6   *The Times*, 29 May 1878.

10   Lyons on the attack

Sir Edmund Lyons was no fool and Palmerston had considered him good enough to sit shotgun on Otho from the beginning of the young king's reign in Athens more than ten years before. Moreover, Lyons was a keen student of Greek political intrigue, taught by that master of the art, Sir Richard Church. When Lyons heard of the riot at Don Pacifico's house, he knew exactly what he was dealing with and categorized it immediately as a robbery rather than an anti-Semitic demonstration.

After all, it didn't fit the pattern of anti-Semitic outbreaks. For one thing, although there were shouts of 'Death to the Jews' when the mob broke into the house, none of the Pacificos was really injured physically, and the head of the family, Don Pacifico himself, wasn't touched. The only serious concern was for young Clara Pacifico as, wrote Lyons: 'his eldest daughter was made hopelessly ill from the terrible fright'. Why the restraint on the part of the mob? Logically, because Baron Rothschild was in town to talk about the Greek loan and wouldn't arrive for the meetings in a better mood if the president of the local Jewish community or his family had been badly hurt. Yet this, after all, was the country where 5,000 Jews had been murdered a quarter of a century before, just on suspicion of killing the Greek patriarch.

Why, however, should an anti-Semitic mob be interested in keeping a visiting banker happy? That was an objective for the government, not for a bunch of thieving yobbos. Therefore, the rioters must have been organised by someone close to the government. It wouldn't have been an accidental gathering. To keep the Pacificos in one piece, there might even have been members of the mob with instructions to see that they came to no harm. As Lyons could recognize, there had been official observers: those sons of the Minister of War. This allegedly spontaneous robbery had been well planned.

The behaviour of the Greek government was also impossible to understand if this was an anti-Semitic riot. They had already banned the harmless burning of the effigy, to avoid upsetting Rothschild. Having done that, how could they permit the house of the president of the Jewish community to be looted instead? Was Rothschild going to be concerned if the mob had the bonfire, but indifferent if they went on the rampage against Pacifico? It's true that the Greek government might not have known that Pacifico was the conduit for the synagogue building fund for the Jewish congregation: that he was holding the money from James de Rothschild in London and the Rothschild's Vienna branch. Nevertheless, there is no reason to believe that the attempt to raise the necessary funds had been a secret; permission had been given for the synagogue's construction by the Athens authorities. Furthermore, the propensity of the Jews for giving and collecting charity had been a fixture of their behaviour for ever. At worst, the robbery was a reasonable risk for the perpetrators, even if someone rich and powerful was going to be very annoyed that the money had been stolen.

With Rothschild in town and knowing the government's precarious financial situation, Lyons would have expected the police to race to stop the riot, not twiddle their thumbs for three hours. What's more, if you wanted an anti-Semitic riot, why choose to storm the biggest house that was going to cause you the most trouble?

There was also the point that the British were well known to consider all the Jewish communities in the Middle East as being, to some extent, under their protection. The British had intervened before. Palmerston had, in fact, written to all his embassies after the Damascus Blood Libel in 1840, to tell them to keep a benevolent eye on any Jewish congregation in their area. Palmerston had written:

> Whenever a case is brought to your knowledge in which Jews resident within your district should have been subject to oppression or injustice, you will make a diligent enquiry... and will report fully thereupon to Her Majesty's Ambassador at Constantinople... Upon any suitable occasion you will make known to the local authorities that the British Government feels an interest in the welfare of the Jews in general, and is anxious that they should be protected from oppression.

The word would have got round and so, to that extent, Pacifico was off-limits. If, however, anti-Semitism wasn't the simple explanation, then robbery was the logical alternative. Robbery would explain the presence of those Tzavellos boys. Kitsos Tzavellos, the Minister of War, could hardly be there himself to see foul play, but his sons could go in his stead.

As Lyons confirmed, David's wife, Clara, had been seen wearing expensive jewellery at public social gatherings. That was abnormal, as it was asking for trouble for Jews to display their wealth in an alien atmosphere. Don Pacifico normally kept a very low profile, feigning near-poverty. As the British minister in Athens was to point out in the future: 'It was common in the East to meet amongst persons of M. Pacifico's persuasion all the externals of poverty with a large amount of hidden wealth.'[1] The Jews knew that if they appeared to have money, they were more likely to be attacked. So why was Mrs Pacifico flaunting the jewels? The obvious explanation was that she was modelling them at diplomatic parties, so that other ladies could admire them and ask their husbands for a birthday present.

For Tzavellos, buying jewellery was not his normal practice. Stealing it, yes. Buying it, no. There was a problem about stealing it, however. If you were going to set out to commit a robbery, you didn't know in advance where the desirable goodies were kept. They wouldn't just be sitting around on the bedroom dressing table. Tzavellos would have known he might have to take the house apart to find them, which could hardly be done thoroughly in the normal way unless he was prepared to arrange for the occupants to be tied up or quietly murdered in their beds, in order to buy his own people enough time to search the place. It would take only one servant to get out and sound the alarm for the whole thing to become a fiasco, and in any case you couldn't murder the Pacificos. It would ruin any chance of getting a loan from the Rothschilds and, as Don Pacifico had been in the diplomatic corps, the international publicity would make it very difficult to resist a proper enquiry.

Suppose, however, that there was what *appeared* to be an anti-Semitic riot? Backed by enough riffraff, you would have all the time you needed to ransack the building. The government could express regret for this disgraceful action, claiming that it was totally against the precepts of the Greek constitution. They could hold to the position that it was simply an unfortunate religious demonstration which had got out of hand. Even better, Easter was the perfect time for Rent-a-Mob, when the crucifixion was on everybody's minds.

For Tzavellos, as Minister of War, it would be easy to have a quiet word in the right ear and see that the army stayed well out of the way. If he cut in Kolettis, who was Minister of the Interior as well as Prime Minister, that would square the police. Tzavellos and Kolettis needed money for bribery and corruption, which are activities with heavy overheads. Tzavellos had to pay for a private army in the area of Greece he controlled. The slush fund would be built up nicely with the proceeds from the sale of Clara Pacifico's jewellery. After all, Don Pacifico valued it at £125,000 in today's money.

Before Lyons got fully involved, Pacifico had complained to the Greek authorities, and the Greek Attorney General had initiated an enquiry. It was three days after the initial complaint that Pacifico also asked for the help of the British.

The Greeks acted quickly. The Criminal Court of Athens considered the matter as early as 3 May and handed down a judgement. Five possible culprits – P. Nicola, P. Trasta, G. Sclarwaki, Turcovaso Dritza and M. Kantamadi – were ordered to be arrested. Five, out of several hundred rioters, was hardly a mass crackdown, but the question arose, in any case, of whether the accused would be able to pay for what had been stolen. The court did not have any suggestions on that score but, apart from the custody order, said it could do nothing. The fact that the two sons of the Minister of War had been recognized, and that a request had been made by Pacifico to search the family home, was ignored. None of the judiciary in their right minds would give a legal ruling that the house of Kitsos Tzavellos was to be searched – not if they wanted to stay in office and in good health. The president of the Areopagus court had already been dismissed by Otho that year; in politically sensitive cases, you either came up with the judgement the government wanted or you were soon unemployed.

So Lyons took up the cudgels. He told Palmerston it was looting, but realised he could hardly accuse two ministers of the Greek Crown of common burglary. So the wheels of diplomacy began rolling with a stern but properly restrained communication from Lyons to the Greek government. As he reported to Palmerston in May 1847, he had complained to Kolettis that Pacifico: 'had been exposed to one of the most barbarous outrages ever committed in modern times at a seat of government, in the presence of a numerous garrison [and] a large police force'.

In the extremely bloody history of the first half of the nineteenth century, Lyons' sense of proportion on barbarous outrages could have been questioned, but at least the Greeks should have recognized that he was taking the robbery seriously. One of their problems with the whole Don Pacifico affair was that they never could believe that the great British government was serious in protesting about the treatment of one expendable Jewish individual. It was always felt, until it was too late, that the British were just posturing.

The days passed and there was no reply to Lyons' complaint from the Greek government. Sir Edmund held on to Pacifico's letter for three weeks and then sent to the Foreign Office 'a letter I had received from Chevalier Pacifico'. The letter arrived on 1 June. As 1847 was a busy year for the Foreign Secretary, a reply wasn't sent until 19 July, when Palmerston told Lyons that he wanted a detailed statement from Pacifico of his losses. In the meantime Lyons had had to report on 9 July that he was still waiting for a reply from the Greeks to the letter he'd sent on 26 April.

Foreign Office files contain a mass of properly recorded information. Nowadays you find them all neatly typed, collated by date and containing totally accurate records of the past. What you can't know is what has been left out. The non-contentious material appears still to be in the files. What seems to be missing, among other papers in Foreign Office File 881 443, is what would have been Palmerston's obvious reaction to the news from Athens. Lyons is complaining about a riot which has destroyed the home of a British citizen: 'poor Mr Pacifico', as he refers to him on one occasion in the correspondence – a phrase, incidentally, which suggests that Pacifico was not regarded by Lyons as just an insignificant British victim. It would be amazing if Palmerston hadn't reacted by asking: 'What do we know about this Mr Pacifico?'

There is only one letter from Lyons in the file that throws light upon the relationship of the British government with Pacifico. It comes in the dispatch that Lyons sent to Palmerston on October 1st 1847. In it Lyons says:

> With regard to M. Pacifico's claim on the Government of Portugal of which the title deeds were destroyed in the general havoc, I think it right to inform your Lordship that M. Pacifico asked my good offices in the matter whilst the deeds were still in existence, and that I wrote to his old acquaintance, Sir William Parker, who then had his flag flying on the Tagus, but Sir William considered the moment unfavourable for urging the claim...I have every reason to believe that M. Pacifico's claim is just and proper.[2]

Lyons had indeed involved Parker in 1843, four years before that fateful Easter Sunday. Now, in ordinary circumstances, this would have been a case of a British citizen asking the British minister in Greece to get involved in a purely Portuguese matter. There was no possible benefit to Britain. What was more, Lyons would be interfering in the affairs of a country where one of his colleagues, the British ambassador, was supposed to handle Anglo–Portuguese relations. It was surely a highly unusual method of handling a complaint.

Why didn't Lyons write to the British minister in the embassy in Lisbon? He wrote instead to Parker, but then he describes Pacifico and Parker as old acquaintances. Lyons would have known from Pacifico that they had been in contact when Parker was on the Tagus station in years gone by, at the time Mad Charlie Napier took on the Miguelite fleet during the War of the Two Brothers. Parker also had that watching brief when the Duke of Terceira was moving his troops to the mainland, so he would have known the senior liberal players – and the commissary responsible for feeding the troops was definitely a key contact. Many of the details of Pacifico's claim on the Portuguese might well have been known to Parker as legitimate. Certainly Parker knew Lyons at the time, as a colleague in the days when Lyons was in the navy as well.

So Pacifico was a British subject, someone who had supported the British war effort in the Napoleonic Wars and held down a major role on the British-sponsored side in the War of the Two Brothers. It's a very different picture from the popular image of a Jewish con artist living off his wits. If Palmerston had had enquiries made in London – and Palmerston was not a man to leave a stone unturned – he would also have found another Pacifico: it was an unusual name. This was cousin Emanuel, the doctor who was one of the first directors of the Atlas Assurance Company – the firm whose policies were held in such high regard that they were able to advertise that William IV was among their clients: a considerable endorsement. Pacifico obviously came from a respectable family.

As a consequence, Palmerston could never have been taken in by the calumnies which would be heaped on Pacifico's head in the newspapers and the accusations that he was just a cheap crook. With his father, Jacob, a British diplomat, Emanuel at the Atlas and Solomon helping to finance the exchange building in Gibraltar, David would have had to be the black sheep of the family not to be judged as a man of good character. What was more, black sheep didn't usually get appointed as diplomatic consuls by the Portuguese. Even so, the viscount kept what he knew to himself; sometimes for a very long time and sometimes for ever. That was standard Palmerston practice.

The Foreign Secretary was told that Pacifico claimed British citizenship because his parents were both born in Gibraltar. As Pacifico wrote in August 1848: 'My family has been English upwards of a century'. Surely another question would have been asked: 'Is anything known about them in Gibraltar?' If Palmerston was considering sticking his neck out on behalf of Pacifico, he was going to check the man out wherever he could. The information that came back would have cast a totally different light on Pacifico's claim to British citizenship, because Palmerston would have been told about Pacifico's father being the minister in Rabat. This information isn't in Foreign Office File 881 443 either, but is recorded in the annals of Jewish families in Gibraltar.[3]

None of this came out: neither Jacob's service in Rabat nor Don Pacifico's activities in the wars. They were never mentioned in the papers or in the Houses of Parliament debates. Again, an explanation is necessary. It is well known that every Foreign Office plays its cards close to its chest. It tells the public the absolute minimum it needs to know. The suggestion that a Foreign Office should go to considerable trouble, on behalf of people who have served its interests in the past, is an internal consideration. The public want to be satisfied that the Foreign Office is always acting solely in the best interests of the nation, not of its former employees or friends. 'Better to keep it in the family', could well have been the decision. 'What they don't know, they can't criticise'.

It is generally appreciated that the contents of despatches from and to the embassies were edited for the records. The official explanation was that the British were more open in their internal relations with their colleagues than was the practice in many foreign countries. So it was held that it might embarrass those friendly nations if the information in the official government blue books was in the public domain in Britain but not on the Continent.

The way the story develops indicates that Palmerston knew very well that Pacifico was not just some British expat trader who had run into problems. Others, besides Lyons, would have told him. Pacifico cast his net wide; he even asked the Spanish Embassy in Athens to help, and claimed to be a Spanish citizen which, of course, he wasn't. He appealed to the French Jewish politician, Adolphe Crémieux, who had been instrumental in helping the victims of the Damascus Blood Libel, backed financially by the Rothschilds again. Crémieux actually wrote to Kolettis, but the Prime Minister was on his deathbed.

There were other people in London to comment as well. If James de Rothschild had wanted to be invited to one of Lady Palmerston's soirées, he would have been very welcome. Pacifico had lost the money Rothschild had sent to the Jewish community, and the banker would have told Palmerston so and asked for help to recover it. The

Rothschilds were already out of pocket from picking up the tab for the interest on the Greek loan in former years. In the course of business it might be necessary to be officially robbed. To be unofficially robbed as well would be too much.

Rothschild wouldn't have taken the loss lying down and neither would his relations in Vienna; the five family branches worked closely together. Furthermore, the Rothschilds were an immensely powerful financial house at the time. Surely Rothschild would have supported Pacifico's claims and asked Palmerston to compare Pacifico's account with that of the Greeks. Palmerston needed the Rothschilds and it was reciprocal. So whose word would you trust? Pacifico or Kolettis? The loyal Gibraltarian would get the vote. There is, in fact, nothing in the Rothschild's archives on the subject, but this was a question of charity funds going astray, rather than a business matter, so it probably wouldn't have been considered for the records. The Rothschild archives could also have been filleted.

Certainly the Rothschilds were often used by Palmerston as unofficial sounding boards on foreign policy. In November 1846 Palmerston had written to Normanby in Paris: 'Rothschild said to me last night that he heard from Paris that the government there would not mind our squadron going into the Tagus.' As the purpose would have been to protect Queen Maria, the Rothschilds were obviously working at the highest level.

Pacifico wrote to Palmerston that summer in London to add his own plea to the representations from Lyons:

> I am an English subject and of the Jewish religion; I have seen my wife, my children, insulted; my house rifled, my furniture, my goods pillaged, my money stolen...A strong hand, a firm will, are necessary to compel the Greek government to perform a duty of equity and of justice. That strong hand can only be yours, my Lord; that firm will my just rights lead me to hope will be your's likewise.

It is noticeable again that Pacifico mentions insults, not physical violence, although one of his daughters sustained a wound.

Kolettis died on 12 September 1847. It removed one thorn from Palmerston's hide because Kolettis had, of course, led the French party in Greece. Kolettis was said to have whispered on his deathbed: 'Remember me to M. Guizot and M. de Broglie – I have done all that they bid me'. In recognition of his support, the French put his bust on display in Versailles. It was Pacifico's chief suspect, Tzavellos, who took over as Prime Minister, although Palmerston's choice had, of course, been Mavrokordátos, the leader of the British party.

If it had been extremely unlikely that the Greek judiciary would prosecute members of the family of the Minister of War, it was totally out of the question for them to charge the children of the new Prime Minister. Lyons wrote to Palmerston to that effect early in 1848. He reported 'an opinion given by Greek lawyers to the effect that members of the Prime Minister's family were beyond the reach of the law'.[4]

The two sons of Tzavellos were now perfectly safe, and they knew it. On 13 September, the day after Kolettis' death, they led their friends to the vandalised Pacifico house and invaded it again. This time they were there to mock him for his now total inability to have them dealt with by the judiciary. There wasn't anything left worth stealing anyway. The police were called and arrived quickly this time to disperse the youngsters. Pacifico immediately complained to Lyons, who was furious and wrote to Glarikis for an explanation. The Greek Foreign Minister dismissed the intrusion as the action of playful children and not worth considering. He said:

> Towards the end of the month of September, about 30 children ran together in pursuit of an individual, and having taken the direction of the dwelling of M. Pacifico, approached thither, crying out against the object of their pursuit, and they made the Israelite believe that this mob was directed against him, and that they were going probably to invade his house. It is true that in passing under his windows those children uttered at the same time some exclamations, but this was all . . . it is from the mouth of the Sieir Tzarmitzi himself, whom M. Pacifico speaks of as a witness and protector of his domicile, that these facts were reported to them (the police).

Sieir Tzarmitzi – so Pacifico had got the family a minder, but it was still a nasty moment for them.

On 14 September when Lyons was still waiting for an official reply to the April letter, he again wrote to the Greeks asking for compensation. The British minister wanted an assurance that 'the main question of compensation for his losses on that occasion is in a fair way of settlement'.[5] It wasn't. Meanwhile Pacifico had provided details of his claim against Portugal and a list of his lost property. This was sent to London on 9 September. There had been a payment for the land Pacifico had sold to Otho for his palace gardens, but it was less than Pacifico had paid initially. The payment was probably calculated at the rate the Greek landowners had agreed to accept for their share.

The details of Pacifico's claim were set out by the chevalier at this early stage. He said he relied on his memory and, with Clara's help, there should have been little difficulty in producing a reasonably accurate statement. There would be two areas for his opponents to dispute. The first was the reason why he contended that the Portuguese government owed him the best part of £1.5 million in today's money. The second was the value he placed on the goods in his house which had been stolen.

Pacifico was still trying to get the money he was owed for his services to the Portuguese during the War of the Two Brothers between 1832 and 1834. He felt the destruction of his Portuguese papers would severely prejudice his chances of obtaining the £26,619 involved. Apart from the interest on the debt, over the years in which it had been outstanding, there were two main items. Nearly half the claim, around £11,000, was for that 'loss of 4 commanderies held at Alentejo for three years' which had been confiscated by the Miguelite authorities 'because I had done good to all the Liberal emigrants'. The second major item was for putting up the archbishop and 'the whole of the Liberal emigrants' (which was an exaggeration) in the two houses he owned in Gibraltar. That came to over £4,000. As the rent he had agreed with Pedro's representatives was £27 a month for each house, the refugees must have been living there for some years, but many liberals were refugees for more than a decade at the time.

Minor claims included his salary as Portuguese consul, where he estimated the arrears at over £900, and his pay as commissary and paymaster for the Duke of Terceira, which came to over £600. He asked for nearly £400 to pay him back for the pillaging of his corn warehouses and his house in Mertola in 1833 when the liberal army was fighting the Miguelites on the way to Lisbon. You can add some small items for services like 'Muskets given to Colonel Almeidas for the defence of Olhio, as proved by Baron de Faro's receipt'. It might be argued that the muskets weren't first-class military hardware, but they were better than pitchforks, which were all many of the Portuguese supporters of Pedro could muster in the countryside, and they had come from Gibraltar.[6] It was perfectly feasible that the profit margins were high in wartime – even outrageous – but that didn't mean that the contracts hadn't been approved. If you were trying to buy muskets and there was only one source of supply available, you would be unlikely to argue the toss over the price with the enemy at the gates. Commissaries trying to buy supplies were always in this invidious position.

Pacifico claimed he hadn't even been paid his expenses for travelling to Greece in the first place, although he said these had been approved in advance by the Marquis de Loulé. The Lisbon correspondent of *The Times* would agree in 1850:

> there can be no doubt that these items, with interest, make the £26,000 which Don Pacifico demands from Greece for the value of the papers...but unfortunately for him the claim had been repudiated by the Portuguese Government, which only held £200 to be due to him for consulate salary and expenses, and thus the matter has remained during the last six years. The Portuguese consider that Don Pacifico never had any claim, and that even if he had confesses himself paid in full by his nomination as Portuguese Consul at Morocco; that his claims up to 1834 not being accompanied by the certificates and sentences required by the decree of 1835, could never be maintained after 1837.

The Portuguese had stalled long enough, in fact, to invalidate Pacifico's claim. For Loulé it would have been simple enough to manage. The Morocco position was, financially, a valuable one and might well have cleared Pacifico's debt. When Loulé wasn't able to deliver the post, there was still ample time for Pacifico to provide the necessary legal certificates to attest to his losses. Would Loulé have told him that he needn't bother? That a valued colleague and devoted member of the party didn't need to go through such formalities? That the government knew exactly what he had nobly sacrificed and would, naturally, repay him in full? It was hardly possible to argue that the liberal refugees hadn't been put up in Pacifico's houses in Gibraltar or that Pacifico hadn't lost the *commanderies*. There would have been ample witnesses to confirm his statements – including members of the government. Terceira himself was a very senior member of it. If there was anything wrong with the papers, it would be the best way for the Portuguese to get out of paying part of the government's debts. Loulé could have successfully managed to talk Pacifico out of lodging the documents, that were officially needed, in time.

Cash had been stolen as well, of course. Pacifico's house had seemed the safest place to keep the money belonging to the Jewish community in Athens. This came to nearly £300. There was also £84 of his own cash stolen. The damage to the house was considered to be £200, the value of the furniture and the china to be £2,182 and of the food and wines in the house at the time, £98. The value of the food and wine seems excessive until you consider the contents of the cellars of the enemies of the Portuguese liberals. If the contents had been sold as cheaply as their other goods at the post-war auctions, Pacifico could have got some very fine vintages for very little. Only a wish to lay down a merchant's stock would account for the possession of two dinner services for twenty-four of English china, another set for twenty-four for dinner as well as tea and coffee services, and twenty-seven silver soup ladles. In fairness, if you were trying to create a fraudulent but credible claim for lost possessions, is it likely that you'd include an item for twenty-seven silver soup ladles! The unbalanced miscellany of objects points to a stock rather than household goods.

Pacifico also wanted compensation for the fact that he could no longer take in lodgers because of the state of the house. In the absence of any developed hotel industry, there would have been a number of occasions when visitors would seek lodgings in private homes and the more important you were, the better the accommodation you wanted. Lastly, there was, perfectly reasonably, a substantial figure of over £5,000 for interest on the debts; after all, some of them had been outstanding for the best part of twenty years.

Pacifico claimed: '(1) The interest on my claim upon Portugal from the 24th July until such time as I shall be paid, (2) An indemnification equivalent to the rent of my house, which I can no longer let, as I did before that calamity, because it is uninhabitable, (3) Indemnification for the expenses which I have incurred in consequence of my wife's illness and my daughter's wound, (4) Lastly, an indemnification for the injury which so lamentable an occurrence has occasioned to my reputation and my credit.'

As far as the claims for the damage caused at his house by the riot, Pacifico provided Lyons with a long list. Among the items were:

Three drawing room cushions	–	£75.
Damask tablecloths	–	£10 each.
Four dozen serviettes	–	£15.
One dozen dessert serviettes	–	£36.
Three copper frying pans	–	£2.10.0 [£2.50].
Two pudding moulds, over	–	£1 each.
A warming pan	–	£4.
etc.[7]		

To translate those amounts into today's money, you need to multiply by sixty-four and, on that basis, some of the figures look wildly exaggerated. How can three drawing room cushions be worth £1,600 each? Or a dessert serviette £192?

There are four points to take into account. The first is that the items might well have been brought to Greece by Pacifico to sell. He was a merchant and he had to make a living; he knew it wasn't going to be forthcoming from the income he would get as the Portuguese consul-general. A merchant puts a markup on his goods and what the consul's job did for him was to open the doors to all the best homes in Athens. He could sell expensive merchandise to those who could afford it – and the word would, inevitably, have got round that he kept his stock at his home. It would seem to Pacifico that it was safest there and the former regent's house would have had plenty of storage room. He had bought the scarce and fine goods to Athens to sell to the court, the expats and the rich Greeks. If for no other reason, that would make his home a target for Tzavellos.

The second point is that quality merchandise was very hard to come by in Greece. The country was a backwater and the local products were very rough and ready. There was a small market for the good stuff but it wasn't well served. If Pacifico could get it delivered from Gibraltar or England, it could be worth a great deal more in Greece than you could get for it in the country of origin. Pacifico, as a merchant, had a wide variety of contacts, and early on he could have had the goods brought in as part of the diplomatic bag. Correspondence survives of his dealings with people in Trieste before the riot, as well as in England, Portugal and Gibraltar.

Third, any of the items could well have been those which went on sale after the War of the Two Brothers, which would account for their quality.

Fourth, it is often the case that claims are subject to negotiation. The claimant feels he is entitled to a higher level of compensation than the insuring organization considers justified. Discussions take place, both sides give a little and a compromise figure is reached: it happens all the time. Pacifico was a merchant; this type of procedure was standard practice in the world he had worked in all his life. Of course, he was prepared to compromise, but he would want to start from a figure which gave him room to do so. In an ideal world the original claim would be accepted by both sides, but that certainly wasn't how the Greek government did business in 1847. It was all very well criticizing the size of Pacifico's claim, but over the years the Greeks had hardly acted with the financial integrity of the Bank of

England. The Greek governments were recognized as totally unscrupulous in avoiding their debts. Starting from a higher than justified figure could have been seen as a sensible precaution.

There was another element in Pacifico's claim which illustrated that point once again. It was the fact that Pacifico – and others – had still not been paid for the land they had sold to King Otho for his palace garden. This had been dragging on for years and Finlay was still regularly airing his grievance to Lyons and the Foreign Office on the subject without any concrete result.

The silver which had been looted was estimated at £98 and the family jewellery at £1,959. It would be asked why, if Pacifico was so rich, he had raised a loan from the Bank of Athens for £30 on the security of some silver. His answer would be that he lent money, like a banker, and, without an income from the Portuguese after he lost his diplomatic post, he would need to make his capital work harder to keep himself afloat. The silver he pledged was earning him nothing, but the money he raised on it could earn him a greater level of interest than the cost of borrowing.

The official lending interest rate of the Bank of Greece at the time was 15 per cent and the public who turned to moneylenders would probably have to pay the kind of annual percentage rate that modern department stores consider a reasonable return: up to 25 per cent or more. The politicians and critics in London could never grasp this point – or wouldn't want to. With the Portuguese items, it all came to £31,534 but, for the time being, Pacifico was destitute.

News of the varied British complaints against the Greek government soon alarmed many of the European states. One of those stirring the political pot was Prince Wallenstein of Bavaria, who was worried about increasing Russian influence in Greece. He wasn't impressed by Lyons and suggested to Milbanke, the British representative in Bavaria, that a new start by new people would be a good idea. The French minister, Piscatory, had already been sent to Madrid, so why not get rid of the old seafarer as well? Milbanke passed the message on.

Palmerston told him to explain to Wallenstein in no uncertain terms that he didn't care whether Russia had influence on Greece or whether the Greeks were pro-British or not. What Palmerston wanted was constitutional government, as agreed in 1830. Palmerston rebuked Milbanke:

> I do not see that the death of Mr Coletti who misgoverned Greece, or the promotion of M. Piscatory to the Post of

Ambassador at Madrid apparently as a reward for the course which he has pursued at Athens can afford any reason why Sir E. Lyons should be removed from his present post; and I have upon that latter topic only to request that you will never in future allow yourself to be made a Channel for any application of a similar nature in regard to any of your Colleagues abroad. Any foreign government which has any such communication to make to Her Majesty's Government should be left to employ its own diplomatic Agents for such a purpose.

The new Greek Foreign Minister was G. Glarikis and he did his best to persuade Lyons that Pacifico should put his case before the Greek courts and not involve the British government at all. He wrote to Lyons:

> Whatever happens, the inquest was not lacking and if it did not produce the right effect because of insufficient proof, it had at least identified the person against whom M. Pacifico intends to mount a civil action with the help of the King's prosecutor at the tribunal.
>
> I come now to reply to the part of your office on the 22nd of this month, that has to do with the affair at hand. and which had particularly drawn my attention. You say, in fact, M. Chevalier, that the British government will fix as soon as possible the sum that he proposes as compensation for the damage and suffering that M. Pacifico had to endure at the hand of the populace.
>
> Such a demand would have been more solid had, as I had the honour of saying before, M. Pacifico followed the regular route, if he had proven in the inquest that the aggressors of his house had been helped, instead of being repulsed by soldiers and that in this criminal act, they were accompanied by persons whose presence on the spot made believe to the populace that the acts that they had committed would be condoned by the Greek government. But before these accusations, so grave and damaging to the national pride, could be proven, M. Pacifico took it upon himself to be the judge and to demand an indemnisation that would please him. He had misled the legation that had taken him under her protection and the British government that he declared recently being her subject. These are, you agree I hope, accusations that the Greek government and any other government that appreciates its dignity and independence, should consider inadmissible.

M. Pacifico should not take the diplomatic ways, but should be reasonable and follow the rules applied to all strangers. And if, after all, his cries were not heard or was refused all compensation, then he could address the British legation, armed with proofs, he could prove the injustice that has been done to him, then the Greek government will not close its ears to his demands.

This procedure, he suggested was the principle that all European governments applied. Palmerston's position on this subject, however, had been clearly stated when the Venezuelan government had made the same suggestion in a dispute in 1833: 'As to the laws of Venezuela, the people of Venezuela must, of course, submit to them, but the British government have shown that England will not permit gross injustice to be done or gross oppression to be inflicted upon British subjects under the Pretence of Venezuelan law.'

David Pacifico replied at some length to Glarikis in October 1847:

I think that M. Glarikis is wrong in thinking that his opinion are more conformed to the European principles than mine are. I have followed the method indicated by M. Glarikis. It is the failure of my attempts that led me to seek justice from the ministry of His Majesty in Greece. It was the only way left for me. It is up to a government to research, punish and compensate the victim. A thousand examples justify this system, but I will mention only a few.

Pacifico specified a $20,000 payment of compensation forced on the commune of Ithaca by the British some years ago. Then there was the £20,000 the Portuguese had to pay for Miguel imprisoning General Milly Doyle. A Mr Ascoli, mugged in Lisbon more recently, got £5,000 through British intervention.

On the question of whether he was even British, Pacifico wrote that he:

came to Greece as a Portuguese representative, but this job did not make him lose his British nationality, like Mr. Mestrani, a Greek subject is Consul-General from Portugal to Athens, does not lose his Greek nationality. M. Pacifico, born in Gibraltar, is a British subject and the passport that he ceded to the British Consulate in Athens [when he arrived in Athens in 1839] proves that it is valid and correct...

that M. Glarakis presented that M. Pacifico could follow his advice and persist in a never-ending debate and delays, always refuted and ignored is really astonishing! . . . what an abuse of words to say that I was the principal actor in this case. I was victim, incapable of knowing who the guilty were . . . I did what I could, naming the sons of General Zevallas on the 12th June against whom nothing was done, whose houses hid objects that were stolen from me but were not searched.

In my position as an Israelite I could not act as a Greek citizen and go into their houses. Had I done that, I would have been massacred. The prejudice against my religion is shared by all the Greeks and because the crime was committed against a family of pariahs, persons outside the common law, and against whom injuries are allowed, the Greeks turned a blind eye.

Lastly M. Glarikis advances an argument against which he seems to think all of M. Pacifico's accusations should fail. 'without the weakness of the police, there would have been more arrests, quick punishment would have ensued'. And this is a minister of the Greek king who dares write such declarations. So it is not enough to be a victim of people's fanaticism, but also to be a victim of police weakness?! Because the authorities have failed to protect all citizens? Because they were afraid of a handful of bandits? It is surprising that they find it inconceivable that M. Pacifico should complain about injustice and should go to the British ministry, his natural defender! In truth, we don't know which is more extraordinary; such a denial of justice or the courage of sophism by which they had the nerve to pretend to justify?!!

The inquest resulted in discovering one of the criminals. Why did they not arrest him? Not enough proof! After 10 months, can I hope for any justice, after all the traces have vanished, and after the criminals had ample time to sell and dispose of all effects? Can I hope to amass sufficient proof to succeed in my action when the King's prosecutor lacks proof himself? Because it would be terrible to suppose that justice, recognising a criminal and having him under their nose, and armed with proofs, had refused to punish him! Even so, suppose he is convicted, it would only be of one object or more. Is he going to pay? I say 'no'. Either he is poor, or he is rich, having a lot of defenders and I would have added one more enemy to my already numerous ones! He would have prolonged his defence, his appeal, while I labour, impoverished – where can I find the money for a civil action that M. Glarikis is advising me to take.[8]

On the question of how he could be British if he had been
appointed as the Portuguese consul-general, Pacifico explained his
view of the law in response to the arguments of Constantine
Colocotrony, the new Greek Foreign Minister, in the autumn of
1848. He wrote to Lyons: 'I was by chance in the service of Spain
and Portugal but you know that under the English constitution a
British subject is granted permission to accept employment abroad
and, after he has left that employment, he is allowed to return to the
bosom of his mother country without losing any of the rights of a
British citizen.'

Palmerston, from the start, was primarily interested in whether
the claims would hold up under critical examination. He told Lyons:
'If the claims appear to be just and reasonable and if his statement is
supported by satisfactory proof, you will present a note to the Greek
minister for Foreign Affairs requesting His Excellency to direct that
the sum so claimed shall be paid to Monsieur Pacifico.'9

Lyons felt that the claims were fair. This wasn't because he
disliked Kolettis – although he did – but because he had studied the
claims in 1844 before asking Parker to intervene. He promised to
ask for further proof from Pacifico, but obviously the claim was
based on the destruction of the objects of value, and producing
convincing evidence that they had existed was going to be difficult.
The Portuguese government had their own copies of the Pacifico
claim papers and the house could be seen to have been looted. As for
the contents of the house, David Pacifico could remember them but
not produce them.

Palmerston, following his predecessor, Aberdeen, was also trying
to get the Greeks to move on Finlay's claim. It was now over ten
years since his land had been incorporated into the palace grounds
and he still hadn't been paid a drachma. Palmerston took pleasure in
reminding the Bavarian Otho of the behaviour of a German royal
icon, Frederick the Great of Prussia. When Frederick built his great
palace, Sans Souci, Palmerston recalled to Otho that a cottager
refused to sell his land to the king. The cottage still stands in the
middle of the grounds: a memorial to Frederick's democratic
principles – which, admittedly, weren't always so noticeable on other
occasions.

The Greeks had made an offer to Finlay of compensation in 1847
but he said it didn't reflect the value of the land. The Greeks who
had sold other parts of the grounds did take the money on offer, but
Finlay wouldn't – and asked for 15 per cent interest on the
outstanding bill as well. The Greeks offered arbitration, which

Finlay accepted, but then the Greeks didn't produce the right documentation and the arbitration lapsed. It is difficult to know whether the Greeks were stalling or just incompetent: very possibly both.

At the end of the year Lyons reported again to Palmerston in London. He said he had had no answer from Glarikis to the letter he had sent him on 2 October and that Pacifico 'is known to be in great distress in consequence'.[10] With no funds to carry on his business, with Glarikis obviously determined to thwart both him and Lyons at every turn, and with the constant fear that the British might get sick of the whole business and give it up, the prospects were distinctly bleak. Supposing there was some major event in Europe which distracted Palmerston and to which he had to give his maximum attention. What then? And a whole series of such events was just about to happen.

NOTES

1 Sir Patrick Wyse to Baron Gros, 1850.
2 Foreign Office File 881 413.
3 José Maria Abecasis, *Genealogia Hebraica, Portugal e Gibraltar* (Lisbon, 1991).
4 Foreign Office File 32, 20 September 1848.
5 Foreign Office File 881 413.
6 A copy of the deposition of witnesses in front of a judge in Faro in 1834 was provided to the foreign office in 1851 and supported Pacifico's claim.
7 Foreign Office File 881 413.
8 Ibid.
9 Ibid.
10 Ibid.

11 Europe on fire

Nobody in business has 'problems' any more; chief executive officers are now determined to regard them more positively as challenges. If you were the British Foreign Secretary in 1848 you certainly didn't have to look for challenges. If the unprecedented upheavals in foreign affairs all over Europe weren't deadly enough, the years 1848 and 1849 also saw a cholera pandemic which killed over a million people around the world. No less than 21,000 died in Britain as a result in 1848 alone. It has to be acknowledged that the possibility of catching a dread disease can be distracting for the most focused of minds, and Palmerston needed all his concentration at the time. Throughout the year the political problems were pouring in thick and fast from all over the Continent and from Ireland as well. Even his colleague, the Home Secretary, was facing a possible revolution.

For 1848 was the year of the liberal uprisings. The baby of constitutional government that Palmerston had espoused, defended, succoured and helped finance for twenty years suddenly grew up and became a violent teenager. Few European governments in power at the beginning of the year enjoyed 1848 very much. As revolutions broke out across the Continent, Palmerston could certainly have been excused for neglecting the problems of a single British subject in a relatively unimportant country. Nevertheless, hardly a month went by without his giving Don Pacifico's problems his attention.

It was the perceived excesses of autocratic governments that triggered the uprisings. In January there were revolts in Italy and, in February, the first major administration to collapse was that of France, when Louis-Philippe abdicated rather than face a civil war over the widespread demand for liberal reforms. If the king had taken a firmer stand against the mob, the administration would probably have survived, but he wavered and hesitated. Watching from across the Channel, Palmerston would have recognized the futility of Louis-Philippe's approach. When there were similar problems in Britain in the near future, they would be dealt with very differently.

The news of the successful uprising in France, carried swiftly on the telegraph across Europe, encouraged other revolutionary movements to try their luck and, as a consequence, governments started to collapse like ninepins. Trouble flared in Berlin and Milan almost immediately. In Austria, in March, the previously all-powerful Metternich had to flee Vienna, an ignoble end to thirty years as one of the key players in European politics.

As far as Palmerston was concerned, the good news was that many European statesmen, who had been broadly against Britain's belief in the format of constitutional monarchy, were now out of the picture. François Guizot, the unseated French Prime Minister, and the fleeing Metternich, had always been strong supporters of absolutist monarchs, like Don Miguel in Portugal. The other side of the coin was that a consistent foreign policy was difficult to follow in 1848. The foreign government you were dealing with today could so easily change to one with a totally different agenda tomorrow. There was a constantly shifting European political kaleidoscope that year and Foreign Office position policies had to be regularly adjusted. At the beginning of 1848, for example, Palmerston thought the likely doubles matches would be Britain and Germany vs France and Russia, but that wasn't the way it worked out.

The success of the liberal revolutions encouraged everybody else of a like mind to consider the same dream coming true in their own country. Even liberal England was not immune from this. There were two radical movements at home which initially gathered new strength. The London Working Men's Association had produced what it called the People's Charter which, primarily, wanted the removal of the duty on imported corn. It formed a movement called the Chartists, who added to their list of demands universal suffrage, payment for MPs, annual Parliaments and other substantial political changes. The other movement was the Irish nationalists under Daniel O'Connell, who wanted the British out of their country altogether. Of the two, the Chartists were, potentially, the greater danger, but if the pair of them joined together and acted in unison, they could easily constitute a grave threat to the nation's stability.

There were, in fact, two Irish movements, split across what have become traditional lines. There were O'Connell's nationalists who wanted to get things done peacefully, and then there was the Young Ireland movement who weren't so particular as long as they achieved their objectives. Usually, the two movements worked together in some sort of harmony. Certainly, the Irish had a very strong case for wanting Westminster out. By dealing with the effects of the disastrous potato famines far too late and with far too little humanity, Russell's government had been at least partially responsible for the death of a million people and the emigration of another million a few years earlier. In the 1820 census 30 per cent of the population of the UK lived in Ireland. Today, combining the population figures for the Republic of Ireland and Northern Ireland, it's about 10 per cent, and that decline started with the terrible results of the failure of the potato crops.

It was only to be expected that the Irish nationalists would set out to try to get the promise of foreign help if they took to the revolutionary barricades. They could also use some technical assistance on the actual construction of barricades and the French had plenty of experts. Palmerston hoped that this could be prevented as well, but the new administration in France had much the same outlook as the Irish. Over the centuries Catholic Ireland and Catholic France had Protestant England as a common enemy. The Irish leaders had reason to hope – as they had on occasion in the past – that France might come to their aid. In the spring they sent delegations to call on Alphonse Lamartine, the new French head of the provisional government. Lamartine accepted the gift of an Irish tricolour, eulogised O'Connell and made all the right noises.

Palmerston was unhappy about these occurrences and told his ambassador in France to spell it out plainly to Lamartine that Britain wanted there to be no further official statements of support, no speeches promising intervention and no enthusiastic welcome for any forthcoming Irish delegations. Otherwise, Palmerston threatened to withdraw the ambassador, which was often seen as a warning of an approaching declaration of war.

Lamartine was a moderate at heart. He was also a realist and he knew very well that the new government in France was potentially under threat from the absolutist powers of Europe, who might join together to restore Louis-Philippe. The excuse that this was to nip in the bud the threat of another Napoleonic War would easily suffice. France couldn't take them all on, and so Lamartine desperately needed Britain not to join in any such alliance. On the contrary, he wanted France to become more closely allied to Britain, who could be relied on not to support the absolutists – according to Palmerston – unless France pushed her into the other camp by encouraging the Chartists and the Irish. The quid pro quo was obvious. It was true that Victoria and Albert saw the overthrow of any monarch as a calamity, but the British government, if it came to a crisis, would stick to its own policy.

The new French government was very much on the side of the Irish and some of its members said so in the French Assembly. One member told a group of visiting Irish lobbyists that the British government didn't have the total support of the people. That was all Palmerston needed and he told Lamartine again to stop taking sides. When Lamartine addressed visiting Irish groups that spring, he had little option but to tell them, regretfully, that they could expect no more support from France, who would not interfere in the internal affairs of another country. Lamartine didn't add the codicil that this was an inviolable French policy – unless it was a small country! The will of the Irish nationalists to try to start their own revolution was seriously weakened, to the disgust of the Young Ireland movement.

As a quid pro quo, Palmerston told the absolutist governments in Europe that Britain did not see France as a threat to peace on a Napoleonic scale. He agreed that the new French Cabinet had said that the time had come to put aside some of the anti-French codicils contained in the Treaty of Vienna thirty years before, but Palmerston still wasn't joining any coalition against a new constitutional government.

As the autocratic governments came under further fire in February and March, the Chartists began to look an even greater threat to British stability. To resist an armed uprising, the obvious key necessity was to have sufficient men on home soil to tackle any emergency. That might be vital for the Home Secretary, but the inevitable result would be that the Foreign Office's freedom of action overseas would be curtailed. Palmerston needed troops all over the empire to keep it under control, and the country's armed forces would be severely stretched if, as happened, 30,000 soldiers had to be stationed in Ireland and another 30,000 on the British mainland. Palmerston had men brought home from South Africa and it was quite clear that any action in Greece, in 1848, couldn't involve the use of troops. Intervention in Athens went strictly onto the back burner.

The Chartist public gatherings had been violent on occasion in past years. There had been fatalities and looting. A tax protest had produced a crowd of 15,000 in London on 6 March 1848. As the news of successes on the Continent spread, the Chartists planned a monster demonstration in the capital in April and the delivery to Parliament of a petition demanding reform, said to have been signed by over six million people.

As a countermeasure, the government resolved to put on a show of irresistible force. Wellington was hauled out of retirement at the age of 78, to take command of 4,000 police in the capital, plus 6,000 troops and no less than 85,000 newly-recruited special constables. Similar forces were recruited in many other parts of the country and the middle classes flocked to the colours to oppose what was perceived to be, primarily, a proletarian movement. Indeed, the situation was considered so critical that Victoria and Albert were packed off to the Isle of Wight, where they could be more easily protected. Palmerston took the precaution of arming the Foreign Office staff with muskets and cutlasses to defend the building from the expected insurrection. If the Chartists were successful, however, the condition of the Foreign Office would not be the greatest of Palmerston's problems. It was highly likely that his estates in Ireland would be confiscated.

On the appointed day a vast crowd did gather in London on Kennington Common, but Feargus O'Connor, the Chartist leader, realised that he would only be leading his followers into a potential bloodbath if they moved against Parliament, protected by an army of close to 100,000 ready to take them on. Unlike the Gordon Riots in 1780, when the mob was able to control the City for six days, the authorities were ready this time. So O'Connor took the only sensible decision; he told the crowd to disperse and the vast majority of them followed his instructions.

For Palmerston and the government, the events of that April were frightening, and if they'd managed to come out of it as one of the few stable great powers left in Europe, they still couldn't let down their guard for a long time. Only Britain, Russia and Belgium had been unaffected by a revolution of one kind or another, a few months into the new year.

The Chartists had dispersed, gravely disappointed with O'Connor's leadership, but they might be back. Neither side thought it was the end of the story and an estimated 60,000 Chartist demonstrators marched round Trafalgar Square in May. Habeus corpus was suspended in Ireland in July. In spite of the debilitating effects of the famine on the protesting movements' supporters, only betrayal stopped a general Irish insurrection planned for August, and the movement became a running sore. In addition times were economically bad. Trade doesn't flourish in the midst of European-wide civil war. Consequently, Parliament couldn't afford to pass bills calling for vast increases in expenditure on the armed forces. Palmerston's diplomacy had to take into account the paucity of his financial as well as numerical reserves in an emergency.

As the autocratic governments fought back, the success of Britain in seeing off the Chartists was highly praised. There was massive support for the Whig government, but few were aware of how stretched Britain's resources had become. After all, this was the most powerful nation on earth. It had 26,000 merchant ships, compared to the second largest, France, with 14,000. It exported 47 million tons of coal where the runners-up, Germany, managed only 5.6 million, and two million metric tons of pig iron compared to France's 600,000. Moreover, Britain had 252 warships, which would rise to more than 300 in 1850. France had 140. As Palmerston told his eventual successor: 'You have no idea until you know more of your office what a power of prestige England possesses abroad.'[1] Palmerston knew this was no time to go to war with anybody, but he hoped that a skilful and determined use of Britain's influence and diplomacy might help significantly to increase the success rate of the liberal parties in Europe.

Prestige abroad was one thing. Prestige with the new Queen of England and her consort was quite another. By 1848 Victoria and Albert disliked both the character of their Foreign Secretary and his policies. As an unapologetic rake, he was a survivor of the Regency period, which Victoria had hated. She always intended to set a totally different and more respectable standard of behaviour for society. Palmerston, by his sheer presence, reminded her that many of the most powerful people in the country might not see things entirely her way.

Both Victoria and Albert were appalled to find that the policy of the Foreign Office was persistently directed – in France, Switzerland, Austria, Italy, Portugal and Sicily – in favour of the revolutionaries. The queen considered that Palmerston was becoming almost an independent power and she said so. The truth was that Palmerston mirrored the views of most of his fellow citizens in feeling contempt and dislike for autocratic European rulers. When he saw public uprisings against them, and the dictators being chased along the corridors of power they had abused, it gave him tremendous pleasure. As so many of the resulting royal political eunuchs were related to Victoria and Albert, Her Majesty's reactions were much more supportive of the absolutists. Victoria would ask indignantly whether the Foreign Secretary had forgotten that she was the Queen of England. The truth was that Palmerston didn't think that particularly important if it was going to get in the way of his objectives.

Albert was particularly aggrieved because he had not been brought up to constitutional ways. He became very angry, not least because he had no power to alter the government's approach. He saw the situation in Europe as being one where mob violence was taking the place of paternal royal leadership. There were so many revolutionary areas of contention where his family and friends were to be found; a Saxe-Coburg was married to the Queen of Portugal, Otho in Greece was a Bavarian prince and Albert had lots of relatives among German royal families. The British royals were unable to help and, as far as Albert was concerned, Palmerston was a coarse, reckless egotist with no principles.

This was a very unfair assessment of Palmerston but, as the Foreign Secretary seldom bothered to defend his actions and persisted in keeping the facts to himself as often as possible, he had to take a lot of the blame for Albert's opinion. Albert was always worried that Palmerston would go too far and plunge Europe into war. He ignored the fact that, as most of the European countries were extremely busy with their internal affairs, they were most unlikely to want to take on Britain at the same time. After all, they knew very well that their armies had no chance of even reaching her shores. Palmerston, for his part, had sublime confidence that everybody was panicking unnecessarily and that his policies constituted the only sensible course for Britain.

Palmerston found the queen's use of the monarch's right to advise her government on its policies a considerable irritant. As he saw it, he was dealing with a monarch who was a young woman, who didn't know all the facts and whose views would have been totally ignored if she hadn't been the queen. After all, in 1847 Victoria and Albert were 28 and Palmerston was 63. He took avoiding action on many occasions: 'Important Foreign Office dispatches were either submitted to the Queen so late that there was no time to correct them, or they were not submitted at all; or, having been submitted, and some passage in them being objected to and an alteration suggested, they were after all sent off in their original form.'[2]

Palmerston, of course, came up with any number of lame excuses. He told the queen that he couldn't understand how it had occurred; that he would remonstrate with his civil servants; that it would never happen again; that he was always anxious to hear the queen's opinion; that it had been a human error, and that there had been a misunderstanding. One of his better explanations was to remind her that 28,000 dispatches were handled by the Foreign Office every year.

The queen's aggravation was understandable. First, she thought that she was being treated with less than the respect she deserved as the monarch. Second, she was rightly concerned that potentially serious crises would come to light only after matters had come to a head; for example, in 1847, Palmerston had been on the point of breaking off diplomatic relations with France and hadn't told either the queen or the Cabinet. Victoria would vary her tactics and ring the changes of her forms of disapproval; she wrote Palmerston heated memos, she lectured him in person and she sometimes went into a sulk and wouldn't communicate with him at all. Nothing had much effect.

There was one occasion when Lord Clarendon, the Lord Lieutenant of Ireland, was invited to dinner at Buckingham Palace. He reported:

> The Queen exploded, and went with the utmost vehemence and bitterness into the whole of Palmerston's conduct, all the effects produced all over the world, and all her own feelings and sentiments about it...After she had done, Albert...asked him to call on him the next day. He went and had a conversation of two hours and a half, in the course of which he (Albert) went into every detail and poured forth without stint or reserve all the pent-up indignation and bitterness with which the Queen and himself had been boiling for a long time past.[3]

Clarendon, who would serve as Foreign Secretary five times in the future, did not feel it would be politic to give them his own opinion on the subject. He told his friends that he believed the queen was 'wrong in wishing that courtiers rather than Ministers should conduct the affairs of the country'. This was a reference to people like the Princess Lieven, who had come to London as the wife of the Russian ambassador as long ago as 1812 and was still deeply into court politics. Clarendon believed that the royals 'laboured under the peculiar mistake that the Foreign Office was their particular department and that they had the right to control, if not to direct, the foreign policy of England'. The queen asked Clarendon to pressure Russell, as Prime Minister, to fire Palmerston, but Clarendon refused to commit himself.

In fact, no pressure was really needed. Russell would have been delighted to see Palmerston go. The Prime Minister definitely had the worst of both worlds. Because of his Foreign Secretary he was attacked by Victoria and, at the same time, he was always likely to be ignored by Palmerston. The problem for Russell was what would happen if Palmerston wouldn't go. Could the Foreign Secretary bring the whole government down with the support he had from the Radical Whigs? Russell wasn't keen on finding out.

So Russell told Victoria that whilst he understood that Palmerston had lost the queen's confidence, this was surely on public rather than personal grounds. Victoria hit the roof again. 'The Queen interrupted Lord John by remarking that she mistrusted him on personal grounds', although she had to agree that Palmerston had been right in the view he had taken of foreign problems thus far. Albert, in a memo, said that he (Russell) was afraid that, if Palmerston went, it might break up the Cabinet and bring Palmerston back as Prime Minister. Russell said he 'thought Lord Palmerston too old to do much in the future, having passed his 65th year'. That was a poor forecast; Palmerston was elected Prime Minister at 71 and, with a brief interlude, stayed in the office until he was 81.

If Palmerston felt he was sailing too close to the wind, he would back down a jot. At one point Victoria sent Russell a very stiff memo setting out how she wanted Palmerston to behave towards her. Russell got Palmerston to call on Albert and apologise for his past behaviour. The prince noted that Palmerston 'was very much agitated, shook, and had tears in his eyes, so as quite to move me, who never under any circumstances had known him otherwise than with a bland smile on his face'. Palmerston apologised and Albert was suitably frigid with him. Following that performance, Albert asked him straight questions about foreign policy for an hour and, according to the prince consort, Palmerston didn't give him a single straight answer. Within a few weeks the Foreign Secretary was back to his normal dismissive attitude towards the palace.

Victoria and Albert's strongest royal connections were, of course, with Germany but the traditional friendship of the two nations was under threat. The Germans had started forming an economic union, the *Zollverein*, to cut tariffs between the 300 German states and improve economic co-operation. It was the model for the twentieth-century European Common Market. The *Zollverein* would not include all the German states until the 1860s but its growth was watched with alarm by Palmerston. As the tariffs fell by the wayside in Germany, they continued to be applied to British imports. Palmerston called the *Zollverein* 'a league founded in hostility to England' and he tried to get the north German states not to join it.

Politically, Britain and Germany were still allies. A liberal revolution broke out in Berlin on 15 March 1848. Frederick William IV of Prussia refused to support it, particularly as its leaders wanted to attack Russia in Poland to unite Germany in a common cause. The uprising fizzled out by May. The king had been afraid that the French would invade and support the rebels, so he asked Palmerston for an assurance that Britain would come to his aid if he was attacked by France. Palmerston couldn't give that assurance because he hadn't got the men, but in Prussia's case he was prepared to back the absolutist monarch rather than the liberal revolutionaries. As a result he later had to deal with Otto von Bismarck, which was not good news for any liberal.

Nicolas I of Russia was the one with plenty of soldiers, and the czar initially planned to send 300,000 of them to the Rhine to repel the expected French invasion. Palmerston watched from the wings, convinced that the French threat was a non-event. He reckoned the new French government wouldn't risk coming in on the revolutionary side. He told Frederick William that it was only if Prussia was attacked by Russia that they should move. Palmerston was always wary of Russia. One of his main political objectives was to keep the Russians out of the Bosporus where they could threaten the British route to India. Nevertheless, in the present circumstances, Russia had one of the few stable European governments and Palmerston found himself in an unusual alliance with the most autocratic state in Europe, in order to keep the peace.

Frederick William appealed to Queen Victoria, on the principle that monarchs ought to stick together. The young queen wished she could do more to advance the principle. Then the Prussians went to war against the Danes over a disputed area called Schleswig Holstein. The idea was to expand the size of the German state. Russia sided with Britain against Prussia because they considered Scandinavia part of their sphere of influence. Certainly, what happened in the Baltic was of prime importance to them. Palmerston didn't want Prussia to have better access to the North Sea; he considered that one great power in that area – Britain – was quite enough.

Now Palmerston found himself allied with absolutist Russia against more liberal Prussia. Palmerston agreed to act as arbitrator in the dispute and his support for Denmark helped that much smaller country against its massive neighbour. Queen Victoria was, of course, on Prussia's side and so Palmerston's position was another cause of dispute between them. The situation wasn't made any better by Palmerston not telling her in advance that he was going to be the mediator. This time Prussia backed down. It was a tangled web that everyone was spinning.

Yet with all this going on in Europe, Palmerston still found time to pay attention to what was happening in Greece. To Lyons, representing the British Crown in Athens, the uprisings in Europe were of small consequence. Of more importance was a tiny cause célèbre which is known today as the *Fantome* Incident. In the early part of the year a boat from HMS *Fantome* had landed on a relatively deserted part of the Greek coast near Patras. Two British naval personnel got out and were halted by a passing guard. One ran away and the other was arrested and taken to the local *nomarch*. He identified himself as a midshipman on the *Fantome* and was released and taken back to the boat. The only damage was a lost boat hook. Even so, the captain of the ship demanded an apology from the *nomarch* and reported the matter to Lyons in Athens. The minister made official representations and the Greek government refused to say they were sorry. This affair rumbled on too. Palmerston put it on the list of aggravations he had with the Greeks.

Indeed, the Greeks held Britain responsible for some of their own internal problems. In 1847 the Greeks discovered a conspiracy against Otho by a dissident called General Grivas. The government accused the British consul in Prevesa of giving the general safe refuge in the consulate. It was an attempt to suggest there were sins on both sides but, in January 1848, Palmerston had told Lyons to both refute the claim and inform the Greek Foreign Minister that 'Mr. Glarikis will do well for the future to abstain from unfounded accusations against Her Majesty's government'.[4]

For Don Pacifico 1848 was a terrible time. At the turn of the year it had been eight months since the riot and little progress had been made in obtaining any redress for him. The family were back in the house, but it must have been miserable to wander through the rooms of his home, once so comfortable and elegant, and now see them bare, scarred and ruined. It was said later that he appealed to his former diplomatic colleagues for financial help. His friends had certainly rallied round but he must have known that he was an embarrassment to many of his Jewish community. They would have preferred him to accept his fate, rather than get his foreign friends to attempt to put pressure on the government. Who knew what the Greeks might do if things turned nasty? Surely, many would feel, it would have been better to keep a low profile and hope that there would be no more – and no worse – outbreaks.

It wasn't Pacifico's way. At heart he was no cringing victim to be trodden on when it took some thug's fancy. His family had sailed their privateer out of Gibraltar to fight the French and Spanish in the Napoleonic Wars. He had been prepared to battle against the tyranny of Don Miguel, even at the risk of his life. Certainly, he could retreat to the Rock or even to England with his tail between his legs; he had family in both places and they would help him get back on his feet. What chance did he have in a foreign country against the massed ranks of the Establishment? Well, as far as he was concerned, they weren't going to get away with it. Come hell or high water he was going on.

In the previous December, Palmerston had told Lyons to prosecute the sons of Tzavellos. The case would be brought in Pacifico's name but he should be reassured that the bill would be paid by the British government. With considerable regret Lyons had reported back that there was no possible chance of success in a court action. Palmerston had also talked to his own law officers. He told Lyons to renew British demands for compensation and now to add £500 for the ordeal Pacifico had suffered. He was also to insist on another 10 per cent being added to the value of the Portuguese part of the claim as interest; what was more, he should claim it from 1845 when he believed Pacifico had taken up the case again.

Lyons duly wrote once more, pointing out that he had now tried to get a result from the Greeks in letters sent on 26 April, 3 October and 10 October 1847. He assured Palmerston he was doing his best. On 8 January 1848, the Greeks, in the person of Glarikis, had finally sent a note to Lyons. It contained the expected denials and excuses. The only recommendation was that Pacifico should rely on the Greek courts. Lyons sent the letter on to Palmerston, together with a rebuttal from Pacifico. On 24 March Palmerston wrote that he'd read both; he didn't agree for a moment with Glarikis, and he told Lyons to continue to pursue the Greek government.

Palmerston did give some thought to the extraordinary size of Pacifico's claim against the Portuguese. Was this, he asked Lyons, for the loss of some debentures: some bonds which had a cash value on presentation? No, said Lyons, nothing like that. Palmerston also wanted to know how the claim could be so itemised if the original papers had all been looted. It was explained that the rioters had indeed taken away everything, but thinking the papers were worthless, they had dropped them in the street. The sheet with the claim on it had been miraculously recovered. This seems very far-fetched, although it could have been true. The British appear to have taken the view that there undoubtedly had been a claim and if Pacifico had reconstructed it from his memory, the loss of the papers could be overlooked.

In reaching his conclusions, Palmerston looked on the Greek government with a very jaundiced eye indeed. As he wrote to the British ambassador in Paris at the time:

For many years past King Otho has been encouraged in his vicious system of government by all the Powers of Europe with which he has diplomatic relations, with the single exception of England... the government of France might indeed have been looked to for support for the constitutional liberty of the Greeks, but the French Government, under the late Monarchy, abetted in Greece the same system of corruption and illegality which in France has brought the Monarchy to the ground.[5]

With barefaced effrontery, Glarikis was quite prepared to treat the Pacifico case with disdain, but still to appeal to the British to help him when he had problems with the treatment of his own Greek citizens abroad. A Greek had been cruelly treated in Cairo, which remained under Turkey's control, and Glarikis asked whether the English minister in Constantinople could intervene on his behalf. Lyons said he would ask the ambassador:

who will, I am very sure, do all that is right in the interests of Justice and humanity without allowing himself to be influenced in the slightest degree by the reflection that whilst His Hellenic Majesty's Government expect him to support their demands for redress for ill-treatment received by a Greek subject in Egypt, they do not satisfy the demands of Her Majesty's Government for redress for ill treatment received by persons under the British protection in Greece.

When Palmerston heard, he told him to add that 'there is as little of dignity in the application for aid made by the Greek Government as there is justice in the denial of redress'.

The Tzavellos ministry collapsed in March 1848. Georgios Kountouriotis became Prime Minister and Drossos Mansolas took the Foreign Office portfolio. Very little changed. Whenever there was a new foreign minister in Greece, the new incumbent had the ready-made excuse that it took a long time to make himself au fait with the work of his predecessor. This, he would say, accounted for the long delays in responding to the letters of ministers from other countries. When it is remembered that in the first 175 years of the modern Greek state there were 219 different tenures of the office, held by 123 individuals in all, an ambassador was likely to deal with a new foreign secretary about every ten months. There were only slightly fewer prime ministers.

In April, Lyons told Mansolas that, at the very least, the Greeks should pay Pacifico £500 for the trauma. As he had reported to

Palmerston in March 1848, nearly a year after the robbery: 'Your Lordship will observe that M. Pacifico is reduced to the greatest distress and depends on the benevolence of his friends for his daily bread.' Mansolas paid no attention whatsoever and the hot summer dragged by without any further progress. One reason was the distraction at that time of a revolt in Hungary where the popular leader, Lajos Kossuth, declared independence from Austria. It was only with difficulty, and to Palmerston's disappointment, that the uprising was crushed.

There were also continuous problems with Italy, where Austria was trying to maintain its control in the face of other independence movements. Venice had revolted successfully against Austria in March. The Austrians wanted to reconquer it. The French warned them that, if they tried, France would come in on the side of the Venetians. They would use their newly formed and discouragingly-titled Army of the Alps for the purpose. With the French anxious to replace the Austrians in Italy, Palmerston was seriously concerned to avoid a major conflict there as well. There's no doubt that the summer of 1848 was a very busy time for the Foreign Secretary. Nevertheless, another major plank of Palmerston's foreign policy was to keep the French out of Italy. This was also considered necessary to protect the British route to India. Fortunately, the Austrians had to sort out their own revolutionary problems, so Venice remained a pawn in the struggle for Italian unity and France had no excuse to intervene.

Mansolas didn't last long in Athens and in July came M. Colocotroni, who adopted the same line as his predecessors. Lyons started to press him in September and October, and pointed out that Pacifico hadn't been paid even for the land he'd sold for the palace gardens. How the Greeks hoped to avoid this, Lyons couldn't imagine. While the Greeks may have been in arrears with Pacifico's land, Finlay wrote to Lyons in November to mark no less than the thirteenth anniversary of not being paid for his acreage. Palmerston remained unconvinced by the Greek arguments, as he told Lyons in September, and said that he had hoped the Greek government 'would not have pursued this evasive course in regard to these matters which was adopted by their predecessors'.

The Greeks switched prime ministers again in October, appointing Konstantinos Kanaris, who had managed to serve in the office for a month in 1844. By the end of the year Lyons' letters to the Greeks were becoming more insistent but that was about as much as could be said for 1848. As Lyons reported to London:

The refusal to pay M. Pacifico for the land purchased from him for the use of King Otho in the face of the proofs he gives of the sale, is altogether incomprehensible, nor is it easy to understand how the Greek Government can expect to escape indemnifying him for the losses and injuries he sustained in consequence of the attacks upon his house.[6]

As far as the land was concerned, Otho had blandly stated that he couldn't find the original contract for the purchase of the land. Pacifico offered him his own copy – it might have been lodged with the lawyer who drew it up, as it apparently wasn't stolen with the rest of his papers in the robbery – but Otho said he couldn't accept it as valid. It was such totally insupportable prevarication which led Lyons to get ever more testy.

Colocotroni died at the beginning of 1849 and in the February the Greek government finally agreed to settle its account with Pacifico for the land. They tried to apply one condition; they wanted Pacifico to sign a document saying he had received a smaller payment than had actually been the case. The Greek landowners had accepted a very low figure for their acreage and the Greek government was embarrassed that it was having to pay a foreigner more, even though Pacifico was getting back only what he'd paid for the land originally. Pacifico refused; he wasn't going to help the Greeks with their problems and risk being accused of some form of chicanery in the future.

The pressure Lyons was applying led his opposition to try to undermine his diplomatic credibility. After months during which there had been any number of complaints about Lyons from the Greeks, the French and the Russians, Palmerston thought it wise to get an opinion from his own side. As a consequence, he told Stratford Canning, the British minister at Constantinople, to go to Athens and give him a report.

Canning was a very senior and experienced diplomat – the brother of Palmerston's old guru – and while he immediately recognized that many of the complaints were politically motivated, he did advise Palmerston that more progress might be made if there was a change. It wasn't that Lyons was a poor minister; Lord Aberdeen, Palmerston's predecessor, had thought enough of him to see that he was made a Knight Commander of the Bath. If Lyons had faults they were a tendency to make mountains out of molehills and a proclivity to speak his mind, as he would have done in the navy, sometimes using language that would not normally have been considered appropriate for a diplomat. There was one occasion when he was invited as a guest to the opera in Athens and not given a seat in the royal box; he made a terrible fuss about this perceived insult.

Palmerston took Canning's advice and transferred Lyons to the safe and elegant surroundings of a quieter berth in Berne in Switzerland. In his place, in April 1849, he appointed Sir Patrick Wyse, who was a distinguished Irishman from Waterford. Where Palmerston was Protestant, Wyse was Catholic, but they were both Whigs. Wyse was born in 1791 and he had been sent to school in England before he went on to Trinity College, Dublin where he won gold medals in English, Latin and Greek. He always considered himself an English gentleman and one of his friends left an affectionate account of him:

> His person is small, and rather below the middle size; he has, however, an exceedingly gentleman-like bearing, which takes away any impression of diminutiveness. He holds himself erect, and seems a little animated by a consciousness that he belongs to an ancient family and is the owner of the manor of St John. He is exceedingly graceful in his manners, and at once conveys the conviction of his having lived in the best society.[7]

In 1815 Wyse went on the Grand Tour and stayed in Greece as the guest of Lucien Bonaparte, who was Napoleon's brother. Whilst there he met Laetitia Christine Bonaparte, who was the prince's third daughter. She was only 11 at the time and grew up to be a charming extrovert, artistic and full of life. Somewhat reluctantly she agreed to marry Wyse in 1820 and they had a son, Napoleon Alfred. Laetitia was supposed to have a substantial dowry but that was never forthcoming.

The young couple went back to Waterford, and William Charles soon arrived to swell the family, but the marriage was tempestuous and in 1828 Patrick and Laetitia separated. After that she caused great embarrassment by taking a series of lovers and Wyse found himself in time the very much estranged brother-in-law of the future Emperor of the French, Louis Napoleon. The new French ruler had been elected in December 1848 to head the government and would go on record as saying that 'the agent of Palmerston's treachery had been the wretched Irishman who abandoned his sister'.[8] Neither Palmerston nor Wyse would have pleaded guilty to Louis Napoleon's charges.

What Palmerston needed was a man for the long haul. The Greeks had already stalled for nearly two years in Pacifico's case and for around thirteen years over Finlay's land. In Wyse, Palmerston knew he had a man who wouldn't give up. He had fought for years for Catholic emancipation and had been one of the first to be elected to Parliament after the Catholics had finally been granted religious equality in 1829. He was elected for Tipperary in 1830 and was the Liberal Unionist Member for Waterford between 1835 and 1847. Much of his time in Parliament was devoted to trying to create a national school system for Ireland and in this he was also successful. His ambitions for the Central Education Society that he founded in 1836 were democratic control of the schools and school inspectors. He was well in advance of his time.

In 1849 there was further unrest in the Ionian Islands. In the autumn there was a revolt on Cephalonia, one of the islands. The British governor, Sir Henry Ward, took stern measures to put down the revolt, flogging and executing priests and peasants alike. He used the processes of court martials to try the cases and arrested many of the intellectual leaders of the party which wanted union with Greece. He had them transported to the disputed island of Cervi, where they were cast ashore and promptly given political asylum. Palmerston then ordered Ward to assert British sovereignty over Cervi, for which he had only a very weak case. It was a messy situation, getting messier all the time, as the British accused the Greek government of encouraging the insurgents. Political activists from the area were certainly received by Otho.

Glarikis was still involved in foreign affairs and still incorrigible. In September 1849 he asked Wyse for help on behalf of some Greek citizens who lived in Leghorn in Italy and who had been made to pay a tax to help the area fight a war. The war now being over, the Greeks wanted their money back. This time Palmerston had no hesitation in saying 'No'. He added:

> Her Majesty's Government... cannot refrain from expressing their surprise that the Greek Government should venture to ask the good offices of Her Majesty's Government to prevail on a third Power to satisfy the claims of subjects of the King of Greece while there are so many just claims of British and Ionian subjects still remaining unsatisfied by the Government of His Hellenic Majesty.

Meanwhile, Finlay had finally agreed to accept arbitration, as long as he felt the arbitrators would judge his claim fairly. When he got the proposed names of the arbitrators, however, he didn't think they would measure up to that modest requirement and so wouldn't accept them.

Wyse took over from Lyons at the age of 58 and started to pressure the Greeks again. He was cultured and charming, but very tough when he needed to be. It was a case, however, of the irresistible force meeting the immovable object. In December 1849 Wyse had to admit to Palmerston: 'all my efforts for the settlement of M. Pacifico's claim have proved ineffectual.' To keep the record straight, he reported back to the Foreign Office on 18 January 1850:

> I left untried no opportunities or means of persuasion which could bring the question to an amicable conclusion. M. Glarikis on five separate occasions promised me that it should be entered on and on each proved unwilling or unable to redeem his pledge. Worn out at last by continued and ineffectual solicitations I informed him, and he agreed to the arrangement, that I should consider his silence as tantamount to a refusal of the demand.

The Greek government had finally got off the fence. There was no possibility that it was going to agree to what the British wanted. Pacifico's claim was no further forward at the end of 1849 than it had been thirty-three months before. For the Greeks it was the calm before the storm.

NOTES

1 George J. Billy, *Palmerston's foreign policy, 1848* (Peter Lang, 1993).
2 Lytton Strachey, *Queen Victoria* (Chatto & Windus, 1921).
3 Edward Pearce (ed.). *The Diaries of Charles Greville* (Pimlico, 2005).
4 *The Times*, 17 January 1848.
5 Foreign Office File 27, 3 October 1848.
6 Foreign Office File 32, 2 October 1848.
7 Richard Lalor Shiel.
8 James Chambers, *Palmerston* (John Murray, 2004).

12   Blockade

Andreas Londos saw in the New Year of 1850 with mixed feelings. On the one hand he was the new Greek Foreign Minister in the Cabinet of the fourth prime minister in two years, Antonios Kriezis. This had to be very good news. On the other, it was a bitterly cold winter and the country's farmers were struggling desperately to survive. This was bound to put more pressure on the new government.

It was also proving difficult to get the British minister off his back. Sir Patrick's insistent calls for the settlement of the long-standing British claims were increasingly aggravating. Londos knew that the standard response was to promise to take action and do nothing at all but this was an increasingly risky procedure. The possibility had to exist that the British wouldn't put up with prevarication for ever, even coming from him. He might be considered to be more pro-British than many of his predecessors, but some of the disputes had been dragging on for years. It was lucky that the main claimant was a Jew. The likelihood of a major nation putting the interests of a Jew ahead of its own relationships with other major powers was surely very small.

So the New Year might bring its problems but at least he could face them surrounded by the trappings of power. The days in the capital passed pleasantly enough, until 13 January, and the day dawned without the slightest premonition of disaster.

On that morning, however, down on the coast, five miles from the city, in the beautiful Salamis Bay, a sail appeared on the horizon. It looked pretty large to the local fishermen, and surely that was another – and another – and another. Slowly and majestically there sailed into the harbour, what would be called today, three British battleships, three heavy cruisers, one light cruiser and six destroyers. They were armed with a total of at least 750 guns. Londos was immediately told and naturally his first thought was to wonder if Palmerston in London might have lost patience at last.

Leading the battle squadron, under the command of Pacifico's

former colleague, Vice Admiral Sir William Parker, was the state-of-
the-art HMS *Queen*, launched in Portsmouth as recently as 1839
and carrying 110 guns. British warships were divided into six
categories at the time. First-rate were the largest and Parker had
three of these: HMS *Queen*, HMS *Caledonia*, a 40-year-old veteran
of many famous battles – one under Cochrane – and HMS *Howe*,
another 35-year-old warrior, and, like the *Caledonia*, armed with a
massive 120 cannon. The second-rate ships, the next most powerful
on view, were HMS *Ganges*, built in Bombay in 1821, HMS
Powerful, built in Chatham in 1826, and HMS *Vengeance*, built at
Pembroke Dock in 1824. All three had individual complements of
eighty-four guns. The light cruiser was the eighty-gun *Bellapheron*,
the same ship which had first brought Otho to Greece back in 1833,
if no longer captained by Sir Edmund Lyons. Even if they had almost
all been launched a good twenty years before, these seven warships
could take on any fleet in the world. Backing them up were six
steamers of war – today's destroyers – smaller but definitely very
useful: the *Odin*, *Firebrand*, *Dragon*, *Resound*, *Bulldog* and *Spitfire*.

Of course, Londos tried to reassure himself, this could be just a
friendly visit by one of the powers that guaranteed Greek
independence. It didn't have to presage any sort of hostile action. So
an invitation was immediately sent to Parker to call on the king the
evening he arrived, together with Sir Patrick and Parker's naval
officers. It was a pleasant occasion with the British admiral and
officers resplendent in their full dress uniforms and the king at his
most charming. It was cordially agreed that the admiral and his
captains would return for dinner with the king on 17 January. The
only cloud on the horizon was that Wyse had taken the opportunity
to ask for an informal meeting with Londos the following day. The
new Foreign Secretary was now rightly concerned; if this was all
leading up to a military confrontation, Londos knew full well that
the Greeks would be able to muster only one ageing battleship, the
Otho, on their side. It would not be a fair contest. In fact, it wasn't
a feasible contest at all.

Admiral Parker, as everybody knew, was on his way back to his
base in Malta from the Dardanelles. He had served as the First Sea
Lord in London in 1846, but he was then needed to protect the
Turkish Empire from a possible assault by the Russians. Many of the
Hungarian and other refugees, from the unsuccessful 1848 and 1849
uprisings against the established governments, had taken refuge with
the Turks, and the Russians wanted them extradited. The revolutionaries had asked the Turks for asylum, on the perfectly accurate

grounds that their lives would be in considerable danger if they were sent back. The Turks agreed and said they could stay. A cadre of resident revolutionaries, who understood the weaknesses of Western governments, might come in useful. Furthermore, the Turks didn't like the aggressive Russian tone that St Petersburg used when calling for extradition.

Palmerston took the same view, but this was because he still supported every liberal movement he could. If someone wanted to overthrow an autocratic government, Palmerston was invariably available. Parker was sent off to patrol Turkish waters in case the Russians tried to use force against Constantinople. The fleet actually arrived too late to be of any consequence in the row, because the Russians and the Turks had managed to cobble together an agreement before it hove into sight, but the Turks would be grateful for the gesture of solidarity anyway.

From Palmerston's point of view, he now had a massive force available in the Mediterranean, so why not use it to get the irritating Greek questions sorted out once and for all? As Wyse had reported, he had five times received promises of a settlement by Glarikis, but the Greeks had reneged on each occasion. Enough was enough. Palmerston wrote to Parker on 30 November 1849 and told him to take the fleet to Athens and take his orders from Wyse. He wrote to Wyse on 3 December:

> My dear Wyse, I have desired the Admiralty to instruct Sir William Parker to take Athens on his way back from the Dardanelles, and to support you in bringing at last to a satisfactory ending the settlement of our various claims upon the Greek Government. You will, of course, in conjunction with him, persevere in the *suavity in modo* as long as is consistent with our dignity and honour, and I measure that time by days – perhaps by some very small number of hours. If, however, the Greek Government does not strike, Parker must do so. In that case you should embark on board his fleet before he begins to take any hostile steps, in order that you and your mission may be secure against insult. He should, of course, begin by reprisals...the best thing...would be to seize hold of his [Otho's] little fleet...the next thing would be a blockade of any or all of his ports; and if that does not do, then you and Parker must take such other steps as may be requisite, whatever those steps may be...of course, Pacifico's claim must be fully satisfied. You should intimate to the Greek Government...that

we cannot go on requiring the people of this country to pay fifty thousand a year [the interest on the Greek loan] to enable King Otho to corrupt his Parliament, bribe his electors, build palaces, and lay up a stock purse for evil time, which his bad policy may bring upon him.

As always, Palmerston did not mince his words when communicating with his embassies. He provided clear instructions and strong leadership, but the impression remains that he could never resist making a witty remark if one came into his head while writing his despatches to his own people.

As arranged the previous evening, Sir Patrick went to see Londos on 13 January and gave him the news he had been fearing. He told him, confidentially, that Greece had twenty-four hours to pay the claims. If not, Wyse would be back the next day to tell him so officially. If that didn't produce the necessary results, the British minister couldn't answer for the consequences. Parker, who accompanied him, confirmed to Londos that he had his instructions to support the demands by the most effective methods available – which included his 7,000 marines and 750 guns.

What was threatened was, to all intents and purposes, a blockade, and such a strategy had been used for many years to enforce demands on small nations by the great powers. In Palmerston's time, he had sent the West Indies fleet to blockade New Granada in 1837. The British consul had been imprisoned for six years as the result of a street brawl, and this was considered the best way of getting him out. In 1838 the French had blockaded Mexican ports, again because French subjects had not received the protection they were deemed to have needed from the local courts. In the same year the French blockaded Buenos Aires and the Argentine coast. In 1842 and 1844 it was the turn of Nicaragua, and in 1845 the British and the French had blockaded Argentina again.

A blockade of Athens was potentially very dangerous for the Greeks, because most of their food supplies for the capital arrived by sea. The hills surrounding the city made any other method of mass communication almost impossible. The rationale for the blockade was quite clearly defined: 'Most of the cases Palmerston took up with foreign governments were those in which British traders resident abroad had their property seized ... or whose commercial privileges, as guaranteed by treaty, had been interfered with.'[1] As far as non-combatants were concerned, the accepted principle during a blockade was that neutral shipping should not be molested if it could be avoided. In the last resort, however, neutral ships would have to be confiscated as well.

Palmerston fully approved of the manner in which Wyse and Parker had presented their ultimatum. As he wrote to Normanby in Paris on 1 February:

> Parker would not have been justified in assuming beforehand that the demands, which Wyse was to repeat, would be refused. Parker, therefore, on his arrival, saluted as usual, and with his officers paid his respects to the King before Wyse repeated his demands. This was in good taste and well judged, because it took off from his arrival the public appearance of a menace, and left the Greek Government at liberty to yield without the appearance of constraint. I should have blamed Parker if he had come in with a swaggering air of threatening preparation, with his tampons out [the wooden stopper for the muzzle of a gun] and his men at their quarters.

Parker and Wyse were the epitomisation of the iron fist inside the velvet glove and they both knew the Greeks would throw up smokescreens in all directions. First, the senior Greek ministers and the king met together and decided to try to involve the Russians and the French, as the co-signatories of the London Agreement, which they invoked. They took the line that the British action was 'an attack on the independence of Greece, a disturbance of her tranquillity [and] an encroachment on her resources' and that 'through their amicable mediation, the matter might be adjusted'. France was close enough to get further involved in Greece, but the truth was that a major part of its army was far too busy in Italy at that moment to spare the time to attack Britain, even if that was considered desirable.

The French certainly pretended to be upset that they hadn't been given any prior warning of the British intentions. Indeed, Edouard Thouvanel, the French minister in Athens, tried to get the nearest French admiral to come to the Piraeus to confront the British fleet. The admiral declined the pleasure, saying that he would wait for instructions from Paris before doing any such thing. The political situation in the French capital was still extremely fluid and Thouvanel was a relatively junior minister. This was no time to be creating international incidents unless you were told to do so in writing from the top. It would also not have escaped the admiral's notice that he would have been well outgunned by the British squadron. Canning in Constantinople had, in fact, sent an instruction that the British Sebastapol fleet was to be prepared for sea as the French flotilla was stopping in Smyrna instead of heading for its own ports.

Thouvanel was writing without authority, which was rash for a diplomat whose own position was tenuous. He had been doubly lucky to get the diplomatic post in Athens. First because his chief, M. Piscatory, had been transferred and second, because he was going to be replaced after the 1848 revolution in Paris but the new government changed its mind. Thouvenel was only 32 years old in 1850 but he intended to make his mark, and he gave the Greek government all the support he could, and put as many obstacles in the way of Wyse as he could manage.

The attempt by the Greek government to involve the Russians would go badly wrong. First of all, Kriezis sent a man who had been known to represent the czar in Athens. With that background he was hardly likely to put Greek interests ahead of the Russian. When Kriezis found that he was acting specifically on behalf of Russia, he had him recalled, but he wouldn't come. Furthermore he sent one of Otho's former tutors to Constantinople, to repair the breach between the Orthodox churches and bring the Synod of Athens back into the Russian Orthodox fold. It was then agreed that the Greek government would no longer have any control over the church in Greece, and Russia made that stick in the future. Instead the control reverted back to the Russian Orthodox archbishop in Constantinople. As, however, the archbishop never knew when he might need Russia's protection, the effective control was in St Petersburg.

This was not what the Roman Catholic Otho had had in mind at all. From the Greek Church's point of view, the only advantage of the Constantinople agreement was that at least it meant that they would no longer be regarded as schismatic; the supply of sacred oil from Constantinople for consecrating bishops could be resumed.

The Russians did agree to try to help the Greeks with the blockade. As Wyse reported without too much concern: 'They have apparently complied with the request of the Greek government and placed their men of war at its disposal.' The only problem for the Greeks was that the Russian ships were a very long way away and had shown no signs of wanting to tackle Parker in the last few months when he was threatening to help the Turks and straying into the Dardanelles.

In the meantime Londos was told to refuse to settle the claims. Perhaps Wyse was bluffing. Sir Patrick wasn't. On 15 January he told the Greeks that Parker's ships would start blockading the port of Athens if there was no settlement. At half past three on the afternoon of 17 January, the day of Parker's dinner with the king, the Greek government rejected the ultimatum. At three o'clock, half an hour before the ultimatum expired, their one battleship, the *Otho*, had sailed out of harbour in an attempt to act independently. The steamer, HMS *Bulldog*, was quickly despatched to bring her back. Meanwhile the dinner went ahead in what must have been a somewhat strained atmosphere. On 19 January Wyse collected the archives from the embassy and led all the British legation staff, which included Lyons' adult son, onto HMS *Queen*.

Don Pacifico and his family were lodged on the *Caledonia* and he must have been delighted to meet Admiral Parker again after such a long time. It had been over twenty years since he had been transported by Napier to invade the Algarve with Terceira. Parker had been there too and it must have been comforting to have been able finally to relax after nearly three years, knowing that he was now again in safe hands. On 21 January Wyse gave the rest of the British residents in Greece forty-eight hours to board British vessels if they were worried about the Greek reaction to the blockade. Most declined and were left undisturbed, as few thought they were in any actual danger and this proved to be the case.

Parker was cordial to his Gibraltarian visitors but he kept his distance. Pacifico was a hot potato and he wasn't sure he could trust him. Parker wrote to friends that he *thought* he remembered Pacifico, when the truth was he had been considering his Portuguese claim at Lyons' unusual request only six years before. He must also have remembered Pacifico from the Portuguese civil war. To further jog his memory, on those evenings when he entertained Pacifico to dinner in the wardroom, he had listened to the chevalier's talk of his Portuguese claims. Parker still wasn't happy but he was there to do a job, and behaved correctly to all the parties. As far as the Greeks were concerned, 'we have unceasingly endeavoured to spare them unnecessary annoyance'.[2]

The reaction in Europe was very similar to that of *The Times* when they learned of the action:

> What he now required was to bring a British fleet of seven line-of-battle ships and six steamers of gigantic power, with their 7,000 fighting men, their cannon, and all the mighty apparatus of naval war, to give a little reality to those obsolete and unacknowledged bits of lost paper... in a generous hour that

same bill was endorsed by Lord Palmerston in the name of England.[3]

The *Otho* was impounded and the *Odin* and the *Dragon* were ordered to the Piraeus where a Russian corvette and the French steamer, *Vedette*, were anchored. It was just a precaution in case they considered interfering while the fleet started to collect Greek merchant shipping as well. Even after the protracted negotiations over nearly three years, the Greeks still professed themselves astonished at what was happening. Parker proceeded to raise the pressure a notch; British marines were drilled to go ashore and head for the royal palace. The guns were made ready to bombard the Piraeus.

There were minor setbacks. Palmerston had instructed Wyse to impound as much shipping as was necessary to satisfy the outstanding British claims. This was not easy to do:

> The detention of the few vessels, for the most part in a wretched condition, and far below the amount of the compensation claimed, constituting the King's fleet, has touched the pride of the Government, but has not induced it to yield. The *Otho*, a schooner and a few gunboats have been detained; a corvette has been discovered at Patras, but so unseaworthy as not to be worth the removal, and our steamers are in pursuit of others.[4]

Wyse had proposed to blockade the Piraeus and the neighbouring ports of Patras and Syra. Attacks on private property and Greek commerce would follow if necessary. Eventually around fifty ships were seized. In Salamis Bay there were two columns of powerful British naval vessels and between them the confiscated Greek ships with prize crews on board. The British consul at Patras said that the five at Corfu alone were worth £47,000, so the value available was disputed. Naturally, many ship owners took avoiding action. In a blockade, it was not only unacceptable to commandeer vessels that were registered in neutral countries, but in addition, goods which had been brought from neutral countries in non-combatant boats certainly couldn't be confiscated. Consequently, as many items as possible were soon registered as non-Greek. As Parker wrote to the Secretary of the Admiralty: 'Since the first rumour of the embargo being contemplated every subterfuge has been resorted to, by tampering with the papers of Greek vessels, to exempt them and their cargoes from detention on the ground of their having been chartered by foreigners...and to stamp the cargoes as the property of Russians, Austrians and Turks.'[5]

The French and Russian ministers in Athens, Persiany and Thouvanel next tried the tack of persuading Wyse that the Greeks couldn't possibly afford to pay the compensation. Wyse commented to the Foreign Office on 7 February: 'financial stringency did not prevent the simultaneous appointment of expensive missions to Paris and St Petersburg, intended, presumably, to urge the continuance of French and Russian support'. Thouvanel told Wyse that the Greeks' money was needed to service the loan debt. As the French had never pressed the Greeks to live up to their obligations to pay the money in the past, this reasoning annoyed Palmerston very much indeed.

Persiany took the same line on behalf of the Russians, who had previously been even less willing to support Lyons in pressing the Greeks to come through with the interest. The Russians were indignant with the British as a result of Persiany's despatches, and Palmerston told the British Ambassador in St Petersburg to explain to the Russian Foreign Minister that his resulting protests to London were 'evidently written under an impression founded on an imperfect knowledge and erroneous supposition as to the circumstances to which it relates'.[6]

The Greeks also appealed to the Portuguese government to help them to undermine Pacifico's claim, and it was delighted to oblige. According to Finlay, when writing his massive *History of Greece*: 'All the foreign ministers at Athens did everything that lay in their power to foment the quarrel.'[7] The Portuguese Finance Minister, Count Tojal, wrote to the Athens papers to put the Portuguese side of the argument. Loulé, who had talked Pacifico into the Greek post in the first place, was still around and, on his record as a turncoat, would have believed that attack was the best form of defence. It had been very convenient for the Portuguese that Pacifico's papers had been destroyed, and there remains the unanswered question of why the looters should have bothered to carry the documents away; one would have thought that their arms would have been full of household goods rather than papers. It is perhaps far-fetched to wonder whether the Portuguese had been a party to the original riot, but is has to be a possibility. Pacifico decided that he must respond to the Portuguese statement and issued a retort from his cabin, apartment seven, on the *Caledonia*.

> I have refrained from answering the numerous falsehoods that have appeared from time to time in the public papers from a feeling that they were too contemptible to be noticed; but having seen today in the Observateur d'Athenes' extracts from

two letters written by Count Tojal to the Portuguese Vice Consul at Athens I think it right to show the world how little the said extracts are to be relied on though they proceed from so high a quarter. First, with regard to my nationality, I was born in Gibraltar; my father was also born there, and my grandfather was born in London to disprove that I became a naturalised Portuguese in 1822. I possess two documents, one a dissolution of partnership between my brother and myself made at Lagos in the very year 1822, attested by a Portuguese notary public and by the British Vice Consul, thereby both of whom I am stated to be a British subject. The other document is a letter of introduction dated September 11th 1828 from the Governor of Gibraltar [General Womm] to the British Vice-Consul at Tangiers, in which he mentions my nationality.[8]

The fact was that Pacifico's paternal grandfather was born in Italy but his maternal grandfather could well have been born in London. If the 1822 dissolution states that Pacifico was British, it would have been made before he became a naturalised Portuguese in that year. There was no General Womm in Gibraltar in 1828 but General Sir George Don had been lieutenant governor at the time and Pacifico's memory may have been slightly at fault on nomenclature, after nearly twenty years and without the necessary documentary references. The Tangier introduction would be evidence of Pacifico's interest in North African trade before Loulé offered him the diplomatic post in Morocco. Obviously, if Pacifico could produce these documents, the ones which were stolen during the riot specifically referred to the Portuguese claim. How Pacifico rescued the others was never explained.

The big question so many people found difficult to answer at the time and, indeed, in the years which have passed since, was why Palmerston bothered to fight Pacifico's corner so strongly: 'The fact that a British fleet was ordered to support the lawsuit of a Jew against a Christian government created a great sensation in Europe. Not only Russia, France and Prussia boiled over with rage, but also a strong coalition in England [embracing Gladstone, Disraeli, Cobden and the Prince Consort] endeavoured to overthrow Palmerston.'[9]

Of course, when the blockade started, the co-signatories of Greek independence – the Russians and the French – had thrown up their hands in shock, horror. They imparted the clear impression that the action of the British came as a complete surprise to them. This was purest humbug.

As long ago as August 1847, Palmerston had written to the British ambassador in St Petersburg:

> No orders have as yet been sent to Parker to compel the Greek Government to comply with our various demands; but you should not conceal from Nesselrode [the Russian Foreign Minister] and the Emperor that such orders must soon be sent, if Colette [Kolattis] does not render them unnecessary by voluntary compliance...we are too palpably in the right to make it possible for France to oppose us by force of arms; and we are stronger than she is in the Mediterranean, and, therefore, there is the best possible security for her good behaviour.

So the Russians knew what was in Palmerston's mind. What about the French, who evinced outrage as well? Palmerston had written to Normanby in Paris on 1 February 1850:

> I think you can put to Lahitte [the French Foreign Minister] what a contrast there is between the conduct of English agents towards France and that of French agents towards England. The French representative in Morocco...made demands on the Morocco Government...which the Moorish Government was most unwilling to accede to. Our Consul-General, Mr Hay, first spontaneously, and then by instructions from me, bestirred himself with as much zeal and activity as if the case had been one in which his own Government had been concerned, and by an infinity of trouble persuaded the Morocco Government to comply with the French demands, and thus saved France from the necessity of employing force to obtain redress. In Greece we have demands for redress which have been pending for years, and the neglect and refusal of which we have borne with exemplary patience, and when at last we find it necessary either to abandon or enforce them, we send our fleet to support the demands of our diplomatic agents, we find the French minister, faithful to the course which French diplomacy has for years past pursued in Greece, encouraging the Greek government to refuse.[10]

Palmerston was seriously vexed that the French did not reciprocate by supporting British demands in Greece. After all, he pointed out, he hadn't interfered when he witnessed: 'her exploits at Tahiti and the Sandwich Islands, where she, on false pretences, bullied the Queen of the first into a surrender of her independence and plundered the King of the other because he would not alter his tariffs on brandy and compel his Customhouse officers to learn French.'

For his part, de la Hitte told the British ambassador in Paris that it was overkill to send 'so fine a fleet...to enforce such trivial and unimportant demands at a moment's notice from a feeble state.'[11] Palmerston commented that even though Anglo–French relations were exemplified by 'perfect good understanding and cordial co-operation', that didn't mean that de la Hitte should 'become a party to demands in which France had no concern and which regard solely the interests of British subjects'.

Normanby in Paris tended to be critical of Wyse, but Palmerston was having none of it. He annotated one adverse report with: 'This can be put away.' If, however, Palmerston had expected the Greeks to cave in almost immediately, with or without French and Russian support, he was disappointed. On 5 February, when the blockade had been in place for nearly three weeks, Wyse wrote to the Foreign Secretary to explain the delay:

> The intrigues of the court: the almost incredible ignorance of the Ministry of the nature and extent of our demands; the encouragement given by the Russian Chargé d'Affaires and Party and by the French Minister (by proffering their services and promising the support of their respective governments) to this resistance of the Greek Government to our claims, continue to be the chief causes of this delay. The Greek government still uses every effort to mislead the public both here and elsewhere as to the real nature of the case. They are vehemently, I might add virulently, seconded by the Russian organs of the Greek Press. The British government is still represented as having made a sudden and peremptory demand, within 24 hours for compensation, to an enormous and unproved amount, to a Jew of doubtful nationality; all notice of previous remonstrances and continued indifferences on the part of the Greek Government continues to be suppressed, and the conclusion is drawn that these demands are mere pretexts set up to conceal a design to subvert (by fomenting discontent and embarrassing the public revenues) the present order of things, to dethrone the King and convert the Kingdom into a British dependency etc.

Palmerston had been over-optimistic when he wrote in jaunty terms to Normanby about the capture of the *Otho* on 14 February, before he had received Wyse's 5 February note: 'In the meanwhile the Greeks were beginning to understand the rights of the case, and when they saw us detaining the *Otho*, they said we were taking away the wrong one.' What the Greeks might have said, behind the king's back, certainly didn't come out in public. In Athens' cathedral a massive 'Te Deum' was performed on Otho's birthday and vast, apparently loyal crowds came to support their monarch.

The date was significant because the French ambassador in London, Édouard Druyn de Lhuys, was writing to his own government at the same time:

> I laid before Lord Palmerston a very animated picture of the bad impression which the news from Athens had produced upon the President, the Council, the diplomatic body, the whole Assembly and upon public opinion. I dwelt upon all that was offensive for us in these sudden and violent resolutions taken without our knowledge against an allied nation...Lord Palmerston, diminishing the importance of what had passed at Athens, replied that this affair appeared to him so simple and of so little consequence that he had not thought it necessary to speak to the French government about it.

Druyn de Lhuys was deputed by his government in Paris to try to get Palmerston to suspend the blockade. The two met on several occasions, often for hours, but progress was very slow. The ambassador offered French assistance to try to arbitrate in the dispute but Palmerston rejected this out of hand. An arbitrator has power to get the two antagonists to compromise and Palmerston was not in the mood for compromise. He also remembered 1831 when a Frenchman got a stiff sentence from Miguel for a political crime. The French wanted the sentence quashed,, and the judge and the chief of police to be dismissed. Palmerston had offered to mediate at the request of the Portuguese government and the French turned him down and threatened to bombard Lisbon. Lhuys offered the good offices of France if the blockade was raised and the merchantmen, which had been seized, released. Palmerston said that was out of the question and Lhuys had to go back to the drawing board and drop the demands.

The blockade certainly did not go down well among the courts of Europe, and Palmerston was well aware of that fact. Writing to his brother on 15 February, he said: 'King Otho is the infant gâté de l'absolutisme [the spoilt child of absolutism], and therefore all the arbitrary Courts are in convulsions at what we have been doing... what has happened may serve as a hint to other governments who turn a deaf ear to our remarks, and think to wear us out by refusals or evasions.'

Palmerston was also certain that the real reason for the opposition from France and Russia was that 'they are furious at seeing [Otho], whom they have been encouraging on for many years past to insult and defy England, should at last have received a punishment from which they are unable to protect him'.[12] What also gave him a great deal of satisfaction was that 'it was gall and wormwood to the French and Russians that the negotiations should be going on in Athens, with the guns of the British fleet on the spot ready to support the Minister'.[13] Palmerston was not concerned about the united approach of the French and Russian opposition to his actions. While they might agree on the Pacifico issue, he knew they were far too antagonistic towards each other on a wide range of other topics for any joint military action to be a feasibility.

The Pacifico affair first came up in Parliament on 4 February when the leader of the Tory opposition talked of 'acts of injustice and violence... against a friendly power, or rather... a weak friendly power'. In a short debate, Lord Lansdowne, the leader of the House of Lords, put the government's case and Lord Aberdeen, a former Foreign Secretary, supported the opposition party, although he agreed that he couldn't say much in favour of the Greek government. That same day it came up in the Commons and Palmerston referred to the case of 'A Gibraltar subject, not a Portuguese Jew, as stated by my honourable and learned friends' whose home 'was violently broken into at midday by a mob, of which part were soldiers, in the service of the King of Greece, some gendarmes, the son of the Minister of War leading and encouraging them.' Sir Robert Inglis, who was one of the leaders of the opposition to the emancipation of English Jews, suggested that neither Pacifico nor Finlay were really British. Palmerston told him curtly: 'The parties are both British subjects.'

There was a further exchange on the subject on 14 March when Palmerston was asked when the blockade might end. His reply was quite true, as far as it went, and he made the one point that mattered to him:

> There never has been what was strictly called a blockade of any of the ports of Greece. A blockade meant the prevention of the entry or egress of any vessel either belonging to a particular country or to neutrals. No such blockade had ever been resorted to on this occasion. Greek vessels were prohibited from

leaving the ports; but that measure was discontinued by an order of Sir W. Parker on the 1st of the present month, in consequence of a communication which he received from Her Majesty's government recounting the acceptance of the good offices of France.

Palmerston was quibbling and what he didn't say was that Parker had no instructions to release the ships he had impounded. He carefully placed it on record, however, that the French were providing good offices but not mediation. The affair came up briefly twice more before the end of March but it rumbled on more loudly in the papers than in Parliament.

Back in Athens, Wyse was not winning:

> The Greek government shows no sign of yielding to our demands; and the French Minister and the Russian Chargé d'Affaires not only continue to countenance their resistance but attempt ... to convert a question simply affecting British and Greek interests, into a controversy between Great Britain and the two other Great Powers; they have also apparently complied with the request of the Greek Government, and placed their men-of-war at its disposal.[14]

Moreover, there was a lot of pressure from European governments on behalf of their merchants, whose cargoes had been impounded in Greek ships. The Greeks carried a great deal of cargo and the potential risks to the foreign merchants, of giving them the business for the indefinite future, was now a greater threat to the Greek economy even than the confiscations. Palmerston knew this very well and also knew how powerless the Europeans were to do anything about it. As he wrote to Wyse:

> As to the claims of foreigners, Prussians or others, on account of the detention of their cargoes in Greek vessels, our answer would be, that a man who chooses to put his property on board a vessel belonging to another country must take his chance as to any difficulties in which that country may get with other Powers, and all the remedy he can justly have is to get his cargo back again on proof that it really belongs to him. Last year, during the Danish hostilities against Germany, many of our merchants had cargoes on board German ships. Those ships were captured by the Danes, and the only remedy our merchants had was to prove ownership before the Prize Court in Copenhagen and thus to get their goods delivered up to them.[15]

Prince Albert was still getting flak from his relatives on the Continent, and he continued to try to get Russell to dismiss Palmerston, but the Prime Minister made it clear to him in March that this really wasn't at all likely. Albert drafted a memo:

> Before leaving town yesterday we saw Lord John Russell who came to state what had passed with reference to Lord Palmerston. He premised that Lord Palmerston had at all times been a most agreeable and accommodating colleague, that he had acted with Lord John ever since 1831 and had not only never made any difficulty, but acted most boldly and in the most spirited manner on all political questions; besides he was very popular with the Radical part of the House of Commons as well as with the Protectionists so that both would be ready to receive him as their leader; he (Lord John) was therefore most anxious to do nothing that would hurt Lord Palmerston's feelings nor to bring about a disruption of the Whig Party, which at this moment of party confusion was the only one which still held together. On the other hand, the fact that the Queen distrusted Lord Palmerston was a serious impediment to the carrying on of the government. Lord John was therefore anxious to adopt a plan by which Lord Palmerston's services could be retained with his own good will and the foreign affairs entrusted to other hands.

Discussion between Palmerston and the French ambassador in London continued throughout February. The ambassador made implied threats, although Palmerston knew they were not serious. Lhuys felt that the dispute threatened Europe: 'the tranquillity of which might be compromised by the incident'. Palmerston finally agreed that he would accept the good offices of France, so long as it was clear that any representative they sent was there to make the Greek government realise that they had no option but to agree to the British terms: 'on the question of the principle of the claims against Greece, there was nothing to discuss. It had to be accepted.'[16]

The difference between an arbitrator and the use of good offices was crucial, but the anti-Palmerston forces would keep trying to insist in the future that the French were arbitrating when they were never offered that role. In fairness, the envoy they chose was told by de la Hitte, before he left for Athens, to tell the Greek government only of proposals of which he personally approved.

Palmerston agreed that Parker would be told not to capture any more shipping while the negotiations continued, but he was not about to release any ship which had been confiscated already. Palmerston also made it crystal clear that he had no intention of trusting the Greeks to keep their word. He did, however, tell Wyse that he would listen to any arguments, even if they involved a reduction in Pacifico's claim. The only stipulation was that if there was any question unresolved, then Pacifico should get the benefit of the doubt. He also insisted that there should be a time limit of three weeks for the envoy to succeed or fail. If the Greeks hadn't agreed to the terms by then, the pressure would resume. Eventually, he relented and allowed the period to be considerably extended.

The French choice of diplomat was Baron Jean-Baptiste Louis Gros. He was a professional and had served his country in the Americas as the chargé d'affaires in Mexico and Colombia. He had recent experience of blockades because he had been involved when the French squadron blockaded Buenos Aires in 1847. Gros was a man of many parts and his passion was photography. The first successful form of this had been invented in France by Louis-Jacques-Mandé Daguerre in the 1830s, and Gros became an expert at producing beautiful daguerreotypes. He was an accomplished diplomat but, from Palmerston's point of view, he would always represent the French interest and that meant supporting the Greeks in this dispute. Gros travelled to Athens to see what he could do in March, but it was never going to be an easy mission. He met with Wyse on the SS *Vedette* on 26 March. At that point no less than fifty-six ships were in custody.

Palmerston had written to Wyse on 22 February with further instructions. He particularly singled out Pacifico's claim: 'if his documents are right, as I believe them to be, his claim is as clear as the rest. We must have money ... and not promises to pay ... the word of the Greek Government is as good as its bond, and the bondholders can tell us what that is worth.'

According to *The Times*, which was hardly pro-Palmerston, Gros had been told by de la Hitte 'to recommend the Greek government to refuse no satisfaction which equity could demand or justify, and even to deal somewhat liberally with the estimation of what it had to give'.[17] Palmerston had, however, made it perfectly clear to Lhuys that all he wanted Gros to do was persuade the Greeks to pay up.

The mere appointment of Gros exacerbated the increasingly poor relations between Wyse and Thouvanel in Athens. Thouvanel immediately wanted the arrival of the envoy to be portrayed as a great victory for French diplomacy. As Palmerston complained to Lhuys, Thouvanel had 'run through Athens saying that "all was finished, that England was at the feet of France"'. Lhuys denied it, but Wyse's view at the coalface was that the French had poked their noses into a purely British dispute with the Greeks when they were neither wanted nor needed. Wyse was right to be concerned. Baron Gros did not carry out his brief simply to use his good offices. As Palmerston reflected in a letter to Wyse afterwards: 'His game was first to beat you down as low as he could, and then to come back to say that he could not bring the Greek Government up to that point and that you must, therefore, come down lower still or else he would go away.'[18]

Finlay wrote later that Gros 'acted the part of a court of review, but he sought for evidence only from the agents of King Otho and the Greek government, without making any attempt to procure proof of the facts from the agents of the claimants'.[19] This was unfair because Gros saw both Pacifico and Finlay, although he didn't change his mind about the way in which their claims should be handled. It is true that Gros followed de la Hitte's instructions not to recommend anything to the Greeks of which he, himself, disapproved, which meant he behaved like a mediator.

In Paris there was a strong anti-Palmerston faction. It was led by Madam Lieven, still a close friend at court of Victoria and Albert when she was in England. She was an inveterate schemer who wanted to exercise power, and whose ambitions in London Palmerston had helped to stifle. When she finished up in Paris, she was very keen to bring Palmerston down in revenge. With the Russians anxious to split France from England in European matters, the Franco–Russian conspirators had a lot of common ground.

Amidst all the international furore, a small voice was totally ignored. It belonged to Thomas Chisholm Anstey MP who took a particular interest in constitutional law. He raised the point in the House of Commons that 'whatever the rights and wrongs, the institution of a blockade without the authority of the Queen in Council was illegal. It should certainly not have been instituted by a private letter from a secretary of state, as in this case.'[20] This flouting of the rules has modern parallels as well, and it was just one more black mark for Queen Victoria to put on the record of the Foreign Secretary. Palmerston had formally told her of the Greek and Russian reaction to the blockade at the outset but, as she noted: 'the levity of the man is really inconceivable'.[21]

The conversation between the Greeks and Gros dragged on, with Wyse adamant that he wasn't going to give an inch. Gros insisted that Pacifico had appeared to have only moderate means before the riot and even to be in financial difficulties. Wyse retorted: 'I observed...that they [Jews] found it necessary to conceal rather than display in the midst of an envious and hostile population. The testimony of Greeks in reference to Jews was always suspicious and at the present moment most particularly so.'[22] Gros' hidden agenda was to fail in Athens and get the matter referred back to Paris where the British fleet would not be available to threaten the Greeks. He stalled all he could; he had gone through the motions of seeing Pacifico, but concluded to Wyse only that the old man had 'greatly moved the Baron's compassion but did not furnish any additional proof'.[23] To try to help resolve the situation, Pacifico now agreed in early April to reduce his claim by 30 per cent.

Back in London, on 7 April, Lhuys wrote to de la Hitte, now the new French premier, to say that he had finally agreed a settlement with Palmerston. The amount that the Greeks would have to pay in compensation was settled; there would be an apology for the *Fantome* Incident and a commission would be set up to enquire into Pacifico's Portuguese claims. On 15 April Lhuys had confirmed his view to Palmerston that Britain, Greece and France would never agree to a settlement in Athens, so they should come to an agreement in London instead. It would be approved by Britain and recommended to the Greeks by France. This Palmerston accepted.

Palmerston couldn't tell Wyse all this until the French in Paris had accepted the deal. De la Hitte decided to do so, and sent a despatch to Gros to that effect. After the draft was agreed in London on 16 April, there were a number of developments on 24 April, in Athens. First, the SS *Vauban* arrived from France carrying details of the Palmerston–Lhuys deal. Gros passed the message on to Wyse verbally but the ambassador said he didn't believe it. He'd had three-and-a-half hours of hard negotiating with Gros on 12 April and made no progress. Little mutual trust remained between the two diplomats. Indeed, Gros had threatened to withdraw from the whole affair, which didn't faze Wyse in the slightest. His instructions were from Palmerston and nothing had been written to him by the Foreign Secretary telling him to change course. He suspected that Gros was continuing to stall to avoid the blockade starting again.

Gros had admitted to him the day before the *Vauban* arrived that he had been unable to get the Greeks to agree to a settlement. Wyse had said he understood, and the blockade would start again on 25 April. When the message arrived on the *Vauban*, Gros went off to Otho to show him the news of the settlement, so that the king could tell the Greeks that he had defended their position to the last, had no part in the discussions in London, and had been forced to accept the result of the negotiations.

So without Palmerston's confirmation, which was still in the post, Wyse told Parker to reinstate the blockade. When that news reached Paris, there was fury. The agreement which had been made with the British was said to have been flouted by Wyse. At this point, however, the Greeks had had enough and decided to give up and pay the bills. On 28 April it was agreed to give Pacifico 120,000 drachma, which was about £5,460 and the extra £500 for his ordeal. The Greeks also agreed to pay 12 per cent interest on the £500 from 12 March 1848 to 4 April 1850, which was another £60. The total of over £6,000 is more than £350,000 in today's money. As a quid pro quo, Wyse agreed to release all the commandeered ships. It was only on 2 May, five days later, that Palmerston's confirmation of the London settlement reached Wyse.

When the Greeks eventually capitulated, the reasons given were many. That the Russians had recommended they do so as a way of showing up the bullying tactics of the British. That they gave up in order to save life or to stop foreign shipping being affected. *The Times* hit the real nail on the head in its issue of 24 April: 'The corn trade in the South of Russia and the Danubian principalities is the great resource of the ship owners in Greece. But in a very short time the season will have passed for chartering vessels for the Black Sea and this branch of trade will then be lost for the year.'

The Greek ship owners leaned on the Greek government. They made £2 million a year profit from carrying cargo, and the longer the blockade continued, the more their reputation for safe passage was harmed. More and more neutrals were naturally not using Greek shipping. There was also the factor that the Greek's 'agricultural resources have very nearly been entirely destroyed by the unusual cold of this year'.

The Times was furious and vented its spleen by insisting that 'He [Palmerston] has enriched the Jew at the cost of the dignity and influence of his country...The gross exaggeration of the claims stamped the case with rottenness and malignity.' Palmerston was not concerned with the views of *The Times* now that the battle was won. What he did recognize was the need to save the French face after the Greeks settled without Gros' participation.

The French had been worried from the start that the affair would be brought to a conclusion without their having any share in it. De la Hitte, therefore, ignored the fact that Gros had told Wyse he could do no more. He said that the British had started the blockade again without allowing Gros to complete his negotiations. In the French National Assembly he denounced the British as guilty of duplicity. *The Globe* in London immediately proclaimed that 'claptrap', and a fitting tribute to the anti-British tradition of the previous French government. Palmerston indignantly denied any suggestion of duplicity to Lhuys.

Palmerston still realized that the French government had to be given some fig leaf of respectability to display to the deputies in the Assembly. On 16 May Lhuys went to Paris for further consultations, 'to be a medium of communication'. This action was also distorted by opponents of the government to make it appear that the French had withdrawn their ambassador, that possible prelude to war. It was perfectly obvious that this wasn't true, because Lhuys had not written to the queen officially to say that he was being recalled. Without this diplomatic nicety he couldn't be described as being in that position. Equally, Palmerston didn't consider for a moment withdrawing Normanby from Paris in retaliation. Russia and Bavaria did contemplate withdrawing their ambassadors but eventually thought better of it, as Palmerston was always sure they would. The papers could point to the unseemly absence of Lhuys from Queen Victoria's birthday party and were nearly as shocked that the French minister in Berlin didn't go to the official British ball there. That was about the extent of their demonstration of official disapproval.

Palmerston offered olive branches of protestations of the British desire to maintain good relations with the French. De la Hitte was having none of it, as Palmerston recorded: 'The French were beyond measure annoyed that the dispute should at last have been settled by our own means and not by their good offices.'[24]

It was, therefore, decided that the agreement would be signed in the presence of French plenipotentiaries, who would be seen as its guarantors. Furthermore, the terms of the settlement would be those agreed in London and not in Athens. There wasn't a great deal of difference but it enabled the French to agree to be mollified, even if Palmerston considered it was all play-acting for internal consumption. As he told Normanby on 17 May: 'It is clear that the French Government think a quarrel with us would be useful to them at home.' They felt: 'the quarrel is a mighty pretty quarrel as it stands, and it would be a pity to spoil it by explanation'. The real powerhouse in France, however, was now Louis Napoleon, who would become Napoleon III, and he agreed a compromise. If the British would return the deposit the Greeks had to pay to guarantee their compliance, then he would accept the agreement.

Now Palmerston had a problem. To return the deposit would make it seem that the French had browbeaten the British. A further compromise was needed. It was agreed that the deposit would be returned, but at a meeting with the Greeks in the presence of the French as plenipotentiaries and guarantors, when the Greeks would publicly agree to pay the compensation for all the claims, which finally amounted to £11,000. By such delicate diplomacy, the long-drawn-out conflict was brought to a conclusion. Otho signed the papers, 'recognizing denial of justice and ratifying the right of coercion against his government'.

The naval squadron could now be withdrawn and Parker wasn't sorry to be leaving. He was already one warship short as 'The *Ganges* is sickly and tainted with erysipelas and ulcers.'[25] Parker had sent it to Malta for the recuperation of the sufferers. Pacifico had sent him £180 to help compensate any Greek ship owners whose vessels had been damaged during the blockade. Parker sent the money back, suggesting it be delivered to the ship owners by some-one else. As he wrote to Pacifico: 'I cannot but highly appreciate the generous and honourable motive which dictates your liberal offer and induces me to suggest that some upright and disinterested indivi-dual unconnected with Her Majesty's squadron or functionaries, would with greater propriety execute your wishes.' Parker later told the Admiralty that the Greek government showed no signs of compensating the owners and got permission to give them £120 himself.

It further underlined a point that Wyse had made when writing to Palmerston earlier in the year: 'Whatever may be thought of the merit of our demands, all agree that extreme negligence and disrespect on the part of the Greek government have brought the country into its present serious difficulties.'[26]

Parker did offer to pay his respects to Otho before the squadron left Salamis Bay but, not surprisingly, the king declined to receive him. Parker remained unsure that Pacifico's case was watertight, but he had carried out his instructions and, as the last British sail disappeared over the horizon, Salamis Bay returned to the normal hustle and bustle of a busy port.

NOTES

1   Evelyn Ashley, *Lord Palmerston* (Richard Bentley, 1879).
2   August Phillimore, *The Life of Admiral of the Fleet, Sir William Parker* (Harrison, 1880).

3   *The Times*, 1 March 1850.
4   Foreign Office File 32, No. 3, 18 January 1850.
5   Admiralty 1/5603, 8 February 1850.
6   Foreign Office File 97, 2 April 1850.
7   George Finlay, *History of Greece*, vol. 7 (Clarendon Press, 1877).
8   1850 Government papers (24). LVI.
9   *Universal Jewish Encyclopaedia*.
10 Palmerston to Normanby, 1 February 1850.
11 Foreign Office File 27, 31 January 1850.
12 Palmerston to the British Ambassador at St Petersburg, 27 March 1850.
13 Ashley, *Lord Palmerston*.
14 Foreign Office File 32, 8 February 1850.
15 Palmerston to Wyse, 7 May 1850.
16 Albert Hyamson, *Proceedings of the Jewish Historical Society of England* (1953).
17 *The Times*, 17 June 1850.
18 Foreign Office File XX, 7 May 1850.
19 Finlay, *History of Greece, vol. 7*.
20 Hyamson, *Proceedings of the Jewish Historical Society of England*.
21 Francoise de Bernardy, *Victoria & Albert* (Harcourt Brace, 1953).
22 Foreign Office File 32, 2 April 1850.
23 *The Times*, May 29th 1850.
24 Ashley, *Lord Palmerston*.
25 Admiralty 1/5603, 12 May and 21 June 1850.
26 Wyse on HMS *Queen* to Palmerston, 29 January 1850.

13 The Newspaper war

Before cinema, radio, television and the wonders of modern information technology, newspapers were the best way of finding out what was going on in the world. When the Licensing Laws were discontinued in England in 1694, newspapers were freed to publish their views within democratic reason. John Wilkes famously used his publication, the *North Briton*, to advance his controversial anti-government views in the mid-eighteenth century. In their publication infancy there was no such thing as objective journalism – the unbiased reporting of a situation. In the eighteenth century the papers were either Whig or Tory and most governments were prepared to come up with substantial bribes to the publisher to influence him to favour their opinions. Indeed, even favourable theatre reviews had to be paid for by the theatre owners.

It was the debate over the philosophical ideas of revolutionary France which stimulated the growth in the number of radical papers, and in the first quarter of the nineteenth century there emerged a variety of publications of different views, such as the *Weekly Dispatch*, William Cobbett's *Political Register*, the *Globe*, the *Examiner*, the *Scotsman* and the *Manchester Guardian*. Despite prosecutions for offences as diverse as sedition and blasphemy, newspapers the government didn't want on the streets continued to be published. Cobbett even managed to issue his *Political Register* from prison.

The core of the industry was in London because that was where national and international news was most likely to arrive first. In London, in the first part of the nineteenth century, by far the largest number of readers ordered *The Times* but it was only slowly that the paper was able to afford to be independent in its views.

On the Continent, the absolutist governments, like Russia, used their newspapers as their official organs, a role that *Pravda* would perform for future Stalinist authorities. With the absolutist examples in front of them, the ruling classes on the Continent believed in the 1840s that *The Times* was used by the British government, overtly or covertly, as the perceived voice of the Establishment The newspaper's stature increased to the point where it was considered by many to be 'one of the powers of Europe'. The publications were far freer to state their case in Britain by this time; successive governments were prepared to take the rough reporting with the smooth. William Cobbett's *Twopenny Trash* and T. J. Wooler's *Black Dwarf* were only two of the radical papers that didn't follow any government's line.

The Times was the first to employ foreign correspondents. In many other ways as well it was streets ahead of the competition and became known as 'The Thunderer' because one of its journalists wrote 'we thundered out the other day an article on social and political reform'. By 1850 its circulation had risen, from 5,000 in 1815, to 50,000, at a price of 2½p, and it dwarfed its competition.

The Times' support came to be considered very valuable by the serving politicians. Peel said in the House of Commons at the time of the Reform Bill in 1832 that it was 'the principal and most powerful advocate of reform' in Britain. It had supported the move for the reform of parliamentary seats and it had been against slavery, although in the 1840s it had also been against the repeal of the Corn Laws. This last position pleased the Tory Party, but *The Times* was still prepared to support the legislation of a Whig government if it thought it appropriate. It could also be used by foreign powers to advance their own views. In 1840, Guizot, the then French ambassador, asked Charles Greville, the clerk to the Privy Council, to call on him. Greville's famous diary records: 'Guizot, however, did not take the trouble to send for me merely to tell me all this ... but to revive the energy of *The Times* ... and to get me to set that great engine again to work, especially to make them *show up* Palmerston by exhibiting the mistakes which he had already made. I told him I would not fail to see Barnes' (Barnes was the current editor).

It was in 1840 that Barnes handed over the editor's desk to one of the greatest newspapermen *The Times* ever had.[1] John Thadeus Delane was 23 when he became editor. He had been working for the paper for just ten months after taking his degree. *The Times* commented at the time of his death: 'He never was a writer; he never attempted to write anything except what he wrote better than most writers could do – reports and letters.'[2] The son of an Irish barrister, Delane went to King's College, London and Magdalen College, Oxford. He was a Londoner by birth and myopically expected public opinion to be created by the Establishment members in the capital. He tended to ignore the growing power and influence of the provincial manufacturing centres, which led to his stance on public affairs sometimes being unrepresentative of feelings in the country as a whole. He was known as a 'Crossbench man', one who belonged to no single body of opinion, but perhaps his strongest belief was that 'the business of the press is disclosure'.

One of his guides was his father-in-law, a former MP called Horace Twiss, who wrote editorials for him and covered parliamentary debates. Another was soon to be Lord Aberdeen, who struck up a firm friendship with the young man. The former Foreign Secretary put nothing in writing to him but 'hardly a day passed without John Thadeus Delane meeting Lord Aberdeen'. He was, therefore, well informed of what was going on at the highest level in politics.

He lived close to his office at 16 Serjeants-inn off Fleet Street, into which he moved in the spring of 1847, when he was also in the process of being called to the Bar. *The Times* later reported that the house had good panelled seventeenth-century woodwork and a fine wooden staircase. Delane apparently breakfasted at lunchtime, spent the afternoon in his study, rode out on horseback to meet his friends and spent the long nights at the paper. At home: 'Here in a noble dining-room, with the aid of an excellent French cook, and the no less excellent wine from his probably ancient and certainly roomy stone cellars, he gave little dinner parties for six or eight men at a round table.'[3] Alternatively, he dined out, and was welcomed everywhere. He was a power in the land and became one of Palmerston's main domestic opponents during the first half of 1850.

The Times first learned of Don Pacifico when the news of the blockade of the Greek coast arrived in London on 4 February 1850.[4] It took about two weeks for the information to travel such a long distance, although the invention of the telegraph massively improved the speed at which news circulated in western Europe. The first story to be transmitted by telegraph was the news of the birth of Queen Victoria's second son at Windsor in 1844. With this new ability to be au fait with current events so much faster, the popularity of reading newspapers became such that it spawned a whole series of shops devoted to selling them, and W. H. Smith's first bookstall duly opened at Euston in 1848.

The Times viewed the blockade with 'astonishment and regret' and 'surprise approaching to incredulity'.[5] After all, Consols, the government's gilt-edged stock, had dropped by half a point on the news of Parker's intervention! It was *The Times* that pointed out that the arguments of Palmerston were now backed up by a 'more powerful fleet than that with which Nelson fought the battle of the Nile'.[6] J. B. O'Meagher, its correspondent in Paris, was leaked details of the correspondence between the British and Greek governments, and a blue book from the British government followed at the end of February.[7] *The Times* studied the documents and made up its mind very quickly, reporting on 27 February that 'the evident exaggeration of these demands throws the utmost doubt on the whole transaction'.[8]

The opinion of the good and the great at the time was summed up in the Greville diaries. Greville, as the grandson of a duke, knew everybody worth knowing. He wrote in his journal on 10 February:

> It was a bad and discreditable affair and has done more harm to Palmerston than any of his greater enormities...as far as P is concerned, he will, as usual, escape unscathed, quite ready to plunge into any fresh scrape tomorrow, uncorrected and unchecked; he bears a charmed life in politicks, he is so popular and so dextrous that he is never at a loss, nor afraid, nor discomposed.[9]

Greville, who could spot trouble from a mile away, told his diary on 14 February:

> The Greek question is the worst scrape into which Palmerston has ever got himself and his colleagues. The disgust at it is here universal with those who think at all about foreign policy; it is past all doubt that it has produced the strongest feelings with those who think at all about foreign matters...the Ministers themselves are conscious what a disgraceful figure they cut and are ashamed of it...the Greek affair was not a measure well considered, discussed and agreed on by the Cabinet, but done in true Palmerstonian style, offhand, partly and casually communicated to his colleagues, but so managed by his own act, to which they indeed became parties, completely implicated, but in which they were not really consulted...Now that the whole magnitude of the scrape is revealed to them they are full of resentment and mortification.

The Times continued in like vein to pour scorn on Pacifico's claims, constantly bolstering its criticism by identifying his Jewish faith as reprehensible in many ways: 'In other words, ask all you dare and get all you can. That may be a mode of dealing familiar to Greeks and Jews but it is the reverse of those plain and fixed demands with which we are happily more familiar.'

Palmerston was never going to take this sort of prejudiced reporting lying down. While *The Times* was by far the most eminent newspaper in the country, there was still competition, and another respected organ was the *Morning Chronicle*. This had been published even earlier than *The Times* in 1772, but its circulation had not been driven upwards to anything like the same extent. It had a circulation of only 5,000 in 1850 although its readers were influential. Its main attraction over *The Times* was that it cost only 1½p compared to *The Times* 2½p.

With such a small circulation, the *Morning Chronicle* had a tendency to write its articles with the fierceness occasionally associated with a small dog. This was partly because Palmerston himself often wrote the leaders. As Greville recorded in his diary in October 1840: 'this morning the *Morning Chronicle* puts forth an article having every appearance of being written by Palmerston himself (as I have no doubt it was), most violent, declamatory and insulting to France'.

Then there was the *Morning Post* which started in 1772. By the 1840s its main claim to fame was the celebrity status of the people who wrote for it. During its lifetime Coleridge, Southey, Wordsworth and Charles Lamb were among its journalists. When it learned of the early stages of the naval blockade, the *Morning Post* fired a salvo in support of the government, denouncing 'the crawling sycophancy and pitiful disingenuousness of *The Times*'.[10]

Its main complaint about its rival was of a 'degraded spirit, whose base malignity has deprived it of all sense of generosity and truth'.[11] Furthermore, its pro-Greek tone was considered to be encouraging the intransigence of the Greek government, who were 'relying on such false hopes as *The Times*'. Whether the *Morning Post's* pro-Palmerston policy was influenced by the award of a baronetcy to its publisher in 1841 is, of course, difficult to assess, but it was unlikely to do much harm.

Looking at *The Times*' editorial policy, to call it malign and degraded may have been unfair, but it wasn't the whole story anyway. Unknown to Delane, his correspondent in Athens, Patrick O'Brien, was taking bribes from the Greek government to write copy which was carefully selected, heavily slanted and sometimes palpably false – such as saying about Pacifico's home in Greece: 'Everyone in Athens will bear witness to the truth of what I say. The house in which Don Pacifico resided was a mean habitation.'[12] This was in spite of the fact that it was a home good enough for the regent of the country just a few years before. In fact, Lyons had described it in his early letter of complaint to Kolettis as a 'large and conspicuous house'. O'Brien worked on the basis that it was going to be hard to check on his copy from Athens, and if he threw enough mud, some of it would surely stick. He was described later as vain, biased and venal and he toed the Greek government line until he was found out and dismissed by Delane in October 1850, just a few months later.

Delane, however, had been prepared to believe the dispatches from his correspondent in Greece, even though they would have strained the credulity of the man on the Clapham omnibus. Who could rationally believe, for example, that 'Not a single word has been said against England in the Greek press', as O'Brien wrote in the middle of the blockade.[13] The readers were asked to accept that the Greeks heaped the total blame on Palmerston. That was certainly the paper's line: 'Lord Palmerston has falsely taught King Otho to regard this country as his personal enemy, and has consequently driven his Ministers to seek support wherever they can find it.'[14]

The Foreign Office tried to point out the errors in O'Brien's reports but this only increased the wrath of *The Times*: 'To the peremptory and insolent contradiction which the organ of the Foreign Office has been ordered to give to the last important communication of our correspondent in Athens, we oppose our entire confidence in the accuracy of his statements.'[15] If O'Brien was being bribed, even without that incentive, many *Times'* writers had their own prejudices. For example, Reeves, who wrote many of the Leaders, was strongly pro-French. Delane himself was determined to denigrate Pacifico and attack the government, without considering the possibility that Palmerston had better cause for his actions than might be immediately apparent.

The *Morning Post* opposed the views of *The Times* rather than approving Palmerston's actions. The paper had stopped supporting the government automatically when it was bought by the followers of Sir Robert Peel in 1848. It had condemned Palmerston's Spanish policy as 'nonsense'. That didn't stop the Foreign Secretary from using the *Post* – and any other paper he could influence – to support his policies. Where others might consider 'dealing with newspapers was dirty business',[16] Palmerston was 'constantly directing that information should be supplied to the Press'.[17] The Foreign Secretary spent more than £50 a year on newspapers, although 'it was said to be Palmerston's habit to throw his copy of *The Times* into the fire.'[18] That would be only after he had read it carefully.

In October 1849, the comfortable relationship between the *Morning Chronicle* and Palmerston was resumed when Peter Borthwick was appointed editor. Borthwick knew politics from the inside; he'd been the MP for Evesham from 1835 until 1847. Within three months Palmerston was telling Clarendon that he found the paper 'much improved' and 'not indisposed to view with candour the conduct and course of the government'.[19] Palmerston became very friendly with the editor and went back to often writing the political leaders for the paper himself. When he didn't actually write them, he was certainly the government leak which provided the paper with its inside information.

The Times was a more difficult nut for the Foreign Secretary to crack. It was a press battle to be savoured: Palmerston, the experienced journalist politician, against *The Times*, a journal with more politicians in its camp than any of its contemporaries. If newspapers were the principal source of information for the general public, they were also, as a consequence, the largest moulders of public opinion. *The Times* now had a potential daily readership of between 100,000 and 150,000. It also had close connections with two men who served as foreign secretaries: the Earl of Clarendon and Delane's constant informant, Lord Aberdeen. They were backed up by leading politicians and senior civil servants like Sir Denis le Marchant, the undersecretary at the Home Office, who also leaked information to them. If Palmerston seemed inclined to hand out Foreign Office information strictly on a 'need to know' basis, it was partly because he suspected that what he told even his colleagues today could be in *The Times* tomorrow. He feared this, even if Aberdeen and Clarendon were careful to make sure that their names couldn't be linked with the reporting.

The Times and Palmerston hadn't always been this far apart in their views on Greece. When Kolettis died, *The Times* dismissed him as 'the Prime Minister of Athens'.[20] The *Morning Post* chimed in with the accusation that he had always been 'the willing slave of French intrigue'.[21] The question was what to do about Britain's enemies abroad. When Delane took over as editor of *The Times* in 1841, the paper's jingoistic attitude changed. Delane was all in favour of non-interference in the affairs of foreign countries: 'it is not for us to decide whether Sicily be independent, whether Spain be governed by Moderados or their opponents, or what are the territorial divisions of Italy'.[22] That might have been Delane's viewpoint but Palmerston had a much wider vision of the interests of his country.

The Foreign Secretary knew that his competition, the absolutist regimes, were not going to take a disinterested view of the politics of countries with whom they had close relations. If Britain adopted an isolationist policy, it would leave the field open to countries whose own interests might well run counter to those of the United Kingdom. There were many nations where Britain did have a very definite interest in their continuing adherence to democratic government. It would make them far more likely to be allies in the future. Portugal under Miguel had been a typical example of the opposite eventuality, because the Miguelites were strongly supported by the absolutist Metternich in Austria. In many cases Britain, as a world power, could not just stand aside unless, of course, all the other interested nations were equally prepared to be on the sidelines – and not always then.

It was a rock solid part of Palmerston's philosophy that he was going to stand up for British citizens abroad whenever he could, and this was enthusiastically endorsed by the *Morning Chronicle*. It felt that there could be no other argument, 'unless, indeed, one of them be held by *The Times* and the other by the rest of mankind'.[23]

Those whose actions ran counter to the views of the newspapers were, of course, considered the enemy. When Lyons received the Order of the Bath in 1844, *The Times* commented: 'We are all delighted, as no man deserves better of his country, and his services of late have been most arduous. I hear also that King Otho takes it as a great compliment that England should thus reward her Minister at his Court.'[24] As Thomas à Kempis said 500 years before: *sic transit gloria mundi* – how quickly the glory of the world passes away. By February 1850 *The Times* was referring to 'some random dispatches of Sir Edmund Lyons whose spirit still seems to haunt the scene of his former absurdities'.[25]

Having decided that a policy of non-intervention was the right approach, *The Times* set out to achieve its own objective. It thundered that it was seriously concerned about the effect the blockade would have on Britain's international relations. It was also quite prepared to distort the facts if that would make its case more influential. It exaggerated the dismay of France and Russia at Britain's high-handed action and appealed to the country's philhellenism to try to get popular opinion to put pressure on the government.

The *Morning Post* did its own thundering and said that this course of action put *The Times* 'in a light more chequered, inconsistent and discreditable than has yet appeared'.[26]

Abroad, of course, the opinion of *The Times* continued to be considered the opinion of the British nation as a whole, as well as its government. It was indeed a newspaper with remarkable clout. Within Britain it was widely believed that it was sufficiently unbiased and independent to be able to write the news without a government spin being put on the facts. What was often overlooked was that, in place of the government spin, you might get a newspaper spin. There can be no doubt that most newspapers seek, if often unsuccessfully, to influence affairs through their comments. The difference with *The Times* was that it often could.

The problem for the paper, as far as the Pacifico affair was concerned, was that it didn't want its reporting to become confused by any contradictory facts which didn't fit its prognosis. It had come to a decision, based on its prejudices and those of its journalists. It wouldn't entertain the possibility that Pacifico might have a sound case and its sources didn't include anybody who would know, because the Portuguese claim was based on events which had occurred twenty years before in wartime. Its Lisbon correspondent usually got the facts right, as far as they were in the public domain, but that was insufficient to do Pacifico justice.

For most of the first four months of the year, Don Pacifico was aboard a British warship in the bay of Salamis. He was unable to influence what was going on in London and if the newspapers wrote libellous accounts of his actions, he was in no position to stop them. That might come later but, for the time being, he was unable to defend himself. In any event, his problems were in the hands of the British government and he would have taken no action without their permission.

The Times had a field day shredding his reputation:

His hearth rug is damaged by a coal – put down Portugal for thirty pounds...nay, there stood a chest by that chimney corner whose untold treasures were little known to the rout of boys who scattered its contents to the winds of Greece. Every shred of that paper was a claim of millions of reis. Mr. Disraeli (in his novels) has let us into some of the secrets of the Mosaic Arabs; a fellow with a greasy coat and a rough beard, who carries a bag and cries 'Old Clo', will retire to his inner luxuries in apartments of more than Oriental splendour...At any rate it would not have been superfluous to have investigated and ascertained a point so essential to our interference in this trans-action and the mere fact that M. Pacifico arrived in Greece with a British passport is very slender evidence in the matter.[27]

It was a mixture of anti-Semitic rant and unproved criticism, although *The Times* strongly denied that it was judging Don Pacifico through anti-Semitic eyes. It just referred to the two main petitioners against the Greeks as 'a Scotch speculator' and 'a Jew adventurer'.[28] The only calm comment in the paper came from an Ionian whose letter to the editor was printed on 13 February 1850. The unknown correspondent, writing from his London club, said that he knew the facts and that Pacifico's claim was 'more than the goodwill, stock in trade and premises of any other merchant'. The significant point is that he confirms that we are not dealing with the looting of a home as much as that of a warehouse and business premises. He also threw light on Finlay's claim. He said that Finlay was in Athens at the time of Greek independence with the very large capital of £500. He used it to buy an immense amount of land for 5p, 12½p and 25p an acre. He bought land all over Athens and this would certainly explain how he financed himself over the years.

Palmerston must take some of the blame for the doubts in everybody's minds. He didn't tell the Palace, the Cabinet, the House of Commons or the newspapers in advance of the blockade. It was an attitude absolutely guaranteed to put up the backs of everybody who considered that they were also powers in the land. Such behaviour says something about Palmerston's character. He obviously had a constant need to feel important. It went beyond cocking a snook at his colleagues or peers; there was often little justification, in terms of the national interest, for his high-handed manner. He obviously needed the kick it gave him, the heady feeling of power.

At the same time, Palmerston couldn't have been anxious for Pacifico's past to be too closely examined. If the newspapers started going into Pacifico's work as the Duke of Terceira's commissary, more details of British involvement in the War of the Two Brothers might emerge, to embarrass members of the present Portuguese government. It would certainly embarrass Terceira, who was now a powerful politician in Portugal and should have supported his old comrade-in-arms with his claim. The Portuguese might also have to spell out exactly what the complaints were against Pacifico as vice-consul in Greece and they might not enjoy that either. There were a lot of good reasons for not opening up a can of worms.

The line *The Times* took was not just for home consumption. Delane knew very well that *The Times* would be quoted widely throughout Europe and would be taken at its own valuation – as the voice of the British people. When *The Times* quoted newspapers like the Prussian *Kölner Zeitung* or the leading Greek *Courier d'Athénes*, it encouraged their editors to believe that they had wide support in Britain. The Greek government kept its own people in the dark about the true course of the dispute, and their newspapers enthusiastically supported a venal government. *The Times* characterised the Greek press as supporting the government, with the exception of two 'which are the creatures of Lord Palmerston'.[29]

As far as it could gather from the British government blue book covering the affair: 'we were not prepared for such a display of elaborate trifling and ill natured chicanery as we find in this bulky volume ... if we could suppose Lord Palmerston had ever seriously thought that this affair required his interference on its own merits, we should pronounce without hesitation he had been very grossly imposed upon'.[30]

In fact, *The Times* did not reflect the general opinion of the public. Justified or not in the stand it took – and arguments about intervention in the affairs of other states still rage today – the British, as a whole, felt good about the blockade of Greece. It was an illustration of their country in charge of world affairs and their pride and joy, the British navy, ruling the waves. The *Morning Post* also caught the public feeling when it stated: 'the incidents relative to Greece have come as a relief to the otherwise monotonous character of our recent continental intelligence'.[31] Palmerston was able to judge the mood of the country by his own postbag, so he knew that this demonstration of British power was going down well in the countryside. He dismissed the accusation of bullying small countries: 'What, we are to tax our people for the purpose of giving them a strong government, and then we are not to maintain the rights of our people because their government is strong. The weaker a government is, the more inexcusable becomes its insolence or injustice.'

The Times backed up its views by trumpeting the dangers of a European war breaking out as a result of the blockade, the idea being that either Russia or France would come hotfoot to the aid of the Greeks. This was pure pie in the sky and Palmerston knew it. What was Russia supposed to do? It was 1,500 miles from London to Moscow and the Russian navy was nothing like as good as the British. It would take weeks for a Russian fleet to arrive, if a Russian admiral could be found who fancied he had the slightest chance of success against Parker's armada. The Russians could bluster, but that was all.

When Nesselrode, the Russian Foreign Minister, wrote to Brunnow, his ambassador in London, that he feared the blockade would threaten the peace of Europe, the despatch was quickly leaked to *The Times*, who used it to hammer the government's position. When Nesselrode wrote a much calmer letter on 20 February, Brunnow leaked that as well, but on this occasion *The Times* chose to ignore it. Only when the *Morning Post* printed it on 12 March did *The Times* deign to follow suit.

The French would also settle for bluster. With the recent upheaval caused by Louis Napoleon's election as president of France in 1848, peace and quiet was what the French wanted rather than any serious conflict across the Channel. There might be angry demonstrations but there was little point in anything more drastic.

Palmerston was, nevertheless, treading a delicate line in Greece. The position could well be taken that, as Russia, France and Britain all guaranteed Greek independence, all three should be consulted over grievances. Palmerston was fully prepared to adopt this course of action if the interests of all three countries were involved – on the payment of the interest on the Greek loan, for example – but held that Pacifico et al were strictly British concerns and nothing to do with the other two partners.

Senior colleagues like Lord Aberdeen, the previous Foreign Secretary, didn't see it that way. Their view was that France should have been consulted and 'while Lord Aberdeen is silent in the House of Lords, his voice is heard through the paper mask of Printing House Square'[32], where *The Times* was published. *The Times* would support any French intervention and was very understanding about French indignation at Palmerston's behaviour. It kept on telling its readers that the best hope for peace was the mediation of Baron Gros, totally ignoring the fact that Palmerston had specifically told the French that he was not accepting Gros as a mediator.

The Times and the *Morning Chronicle* didn't have the field of political comment to themselves. Palmerston used other papers as an alternative to appealing to Peter Borthwick. When a particularly virulent article against France appeared in the *Globe*, Russell, the Prime Minister, thought he detected Palmerston's hand in the writing. Palmerston protested: 'I do not write the *Globe*, nor indeed do I always read it.'[33] The truth was that, on occasion, he did write for the *Globe*, and for the *Courier* and the *Morning Chronicle*, but he did so incognito.

The offending article had denounced a major speech in the French National Assembly and called it a fitting tribute to the previous administration's anti-British traditions. The *Globe* later reinforced its attack by saying of the French 'that their repressive tendencies at home were only equalled by their hatred of liberty abroad'.[34] This was very much Palmerston's position. On the other hand, another paper, the *Morning Herald* supported Edward Stanley, primarily because the Tory leader was not above writing articles for them as well. *Punch*, one of the most popular magazines, was another publication which was staunchly pacifist at the outset.

As the blockade proceeded, the tone of the newspapers became ever more strident. According to *The Times*, 'Lord Palmerston, his supporters and his organs, assume throughout that every man who objects to his policy is either a rival, a mercenary, a conspirator or a traitor.'[35]

This kind of hysterical copy certainly sells newspapers. All of a sudden the pro-Palmerston papers found a 'knot of conspirators', 'the Russian intrigue', 'the agents of Russia', 'the Muscovite faction', 'the employés of Austria' and 'the allies of absolutism' under every anti-government bed. *The Times* said that its critics inclined 'to the theory that a congress of Russian, Austrian and French plenipotentiaries is permanently sitting in Printing-House-Square and interchanging notes hourly with some English politicians at the west end'.[36]

The Russian ambassador wrote to complain of the language of both the *Globe* and the *Morning Post*, which had criticised the Russian emperor. Palmerston was very relaxed about it. As he wrote to the Prime Minister:

> Any articles in the newspapers to which he alludes were drawn upon the Russian government... by the boastful threats made by the Times newspaper as to what Russia would do to put a stop to our proceedings in Greece. The war of words is, no doubt, much to be deprecated, but the responsibility for any evils which it may produce must rest with those by whom it was begun.[37]

Every newspaper now re-emphasised to its readers that it represented public opinion. Posters were used to press these views as well. One called the Tories, Graham and Disraeli, the agents of Russia. The truth was that those of the good and the great who actually knew Otho considered him a joke, and the country, as a whole, couldn't have cared less about the rights and wrongs of the matter. The MPs in Parliament dissolved in laughter when Palmerston told them during the blockade that 'as a proof that no courtesy was omitted on our part, on the anniversary of the birthday of either the King or the Queen, I forget which, our fleet saluted with all the honours suitable to the occasion'.[38]

The exception to all this was the *Jewish Chronicle*, which was, apparently, mortified by the whole subject. At a time when the Jews were trying to get agreement that they could sit in Parliament without taking the oath 'as a Christian', the events in Greece were a serious embarrassment. Instead of the Jews being portrayed as respectable members of society, the spotlight was on Don Pacifico, and he was being derided as a cheap mountebank. The *Jewish Chronicle* never mentioned the blockade once in its columns. It confined itself to one reference to the affair when it was nearly over. In the issue for 26 April it commented: 'During the long pending question of the Pritchard Affair,[39] none of the journals who opposed his exaggerated claims ever concerned themselves about his religious profession; but since the Pacifico affair led to misunderstanding between England and Greece, the opposition journals attack Mr Pacifico, chiefly on the grounds of his being a Jew.' After that the *Jewish Chronicle* put its journalistic head into the sand and didn't say another word about Pacifico until it gave him a brief obituary when he died.

As the blockade started to bite, *The Times* remained loyal to the Greek cause. As late as 23 April 1850, the leader column assured Athens that 'sympathies will be increased for the sovereign of the country, and for the ill used people of Greece'. *The Times* retained its faith in Greek justice. It agreed that British citizens should be protected by the laws of a foreign country, 'but not to substitute for the authority of those laws arbitrary assessment of damages and a one-sided mass of uncontrolled evidence'.

On 24 April came another attempt by *The Times* to try to seize the high moral ground from the government. It told its readers: 'for the gratification of frivolous or immoderate pretensions the permanent objects of our policy are sacrificed and wasted'.[40] Even when the Greeks had agreed a settlement, *The Times* continued to attack the Foreign Secretary: 'England may be disgraced, Europe exasperated, Greece oppressed – what matters if the whim of the Foreign Secretary be gratified.'[41]

When Pacifico was eventually told of the attacks on him in the press, he decided – as usual – to fight back. The worst distortions – and there was a very wide choice – had been printed by the *Morning Herald*, whose Lisbon correspondent had written in March 1850: 'The Jew Pacifico, before his fraudulent bankruptcy at Constantinople, and before his consulship in Greece, held an inn in Portugal.' Pacifico was in court by 18 November 1850, barely three months after his arrival in London, for *Queen ex parte David Pacifico v Baldwin and another.*

On the same day that the case started, *The Times'* leader writer dipped his pen in purest vitriol and gave vent to his paper's rage at Pacifico having at last received justice and compensation for the looting of his house. Before any evidence was heard in court, *The Times* had made up its mind what the verdict ought to be: 'a respected contemporary is added to the list of his [Pacifico's] distinguished but unfortunate victims. The *Morning Herald* has taken the place of King Otho in the speculations of the indefatigable and ubiquitous Hebrew.' The *Morning Herald* 'in one of its anti-Pacifico days [was] seduced into publishing a letter from its correspondent in Athens which we would not have ventured to insert... Who will hear of the reappearance of this wonderful personage in a British court of justice, without a feeling near akin to horror?... It has indeed been darkly hinted that Don Pacifico is that remarkable personage who is condemned to traverse all time and space in quest of that peace which he can never obtain.'

Having compared Pacifico to the anti-Semitic legend of the Wandering Jew, the paper goes on: 'The British fleet was employed to extort it [payment] from King Otho, and some other tremendous agency will soon be brought to bear against our unfortunate contemporary. Hapless wretch! How will it escape from the coils of this monster... He will investigate all the newspapers of last year, and institute fifty prosecutions besides other enterprises... a hundred years hence the Pacifico claims will have taken the place of our national debt.' *The Times* was also anti-Catholic: 'With a Cardinal Archbishop and the Wandering Jew at large in our streets, we might as well be in an Indian jungle, at the usual dinner time of the residents... The *Morning Herald* is not always as civil as might be to the Hebrew profession, but sorry should we be to see it in the power of its foes, for they will certainly show it no mercy.'[42]

In the somewhat calmer atmosphere of the Court of Queen's Bench, Sir Alexander Cockburn, the Solicitor General, pointed out, on behalf of Pacifico, that his client had never been in Constantinople, had never been declared bankrupt and had never owed anybody a shilling (5p). By the time the case returned to court in May 1851, the defendants apologised unreservedly. They made the usual lame excuse that the article had come in late from their correspondent in Greece and had been printed without being checked. They admitted there was no foundation to any of the accusations. Pacifico agreed to the matter being settled by the payment of his costs and he never sued a newspaper again.

All in all, it was a pretty generous attitude to adopt, but then Pacifico was not the man the papers tried to portray him to be. On this single occasion when he had the chance to make his case in an English court, the defendant's counsel had to 'withdraw all which affected Don Pacifico's personal character, and to say that he was satisfied that the imputations were without foundation'.[43] Yet this vindication has not led later writers to wonder whether the other accusations against him might have been equally baseless.

Even when the result was known, *The Times* wouldn't admit it had been wrong. Instead it made snide comments about minor journalistic shortcomings being over-severely punished by the courts, even though Pacifico had settled for costs and no damages.

The majority of the newspapers would continue to be anti-Palmerston. In 1855 Greville wrote: 'Palmerston will soon find the whole press against him, except his own papers, the *Morning Post* and the *Morning Chronicle*, neither of which has any circulation of influence.' It has always been the desire of newspapers to control public opinion, but Palmerston's standing in the country didn't suffer noticeable damage from the invective of the newspapers who disliked his policies.

NOTES

1   This chapter owes a great deal to a thesis, *Press Comment on the Don Pacifico Affair 1847–1850* by Timothy Taylor, 1988.
2   *The Times*, 25 November 1879.
3   Ibid., 29 May 1941.
4   Ibid., 4 February 1850.
5   Ibid.
6   Ibid., 9 February 1850.
7   A blue book is a bound volume including all the pertinent parliamentary reports and other official parliamentary publications.
8   *The Times*, 27 February 1850.
9   Edward Pearce (ed.), *The Diaries of Charles Greville* (Pimlico, 2005).
10   *Morning Post*, 28 February 1850.
11   Ibid.
12   *The Times*, 4 April 1850.
13   Ibid., 19 March 1850.
14   Ibid., 8 April 1850.
15   Ibid.

16 T. Morley, 'The Arcana of that Great Machine', *History Magazine*, (1988).

17 C. Webster, *The Art and Practice of Diplomacy* (1961).

18 S. Koss, *The Rise and Fall of the Political Press in Britain* (1981).

19 W. Hindle, *The Morning Post 1772–1937*.

20 *The Times*, 1 October 1847.

21 *Morning Post*, 2 October 1847.

22 *The Times*, 22 June 1850

23 *Morning Post*, 15 February 1850.

24 *The Times*, 4 July 1844.

25 Ibid., 15 February 1850.

26 *Morning Post*, 14 March 1850.

27 *The Times*, 1 March 1850.

28 Ibid., 22 February 1850.

29 Ibid.

30 Ibid., 27 February 1850.

31 *Morning Post*, 23 February 1850.

32 *Morning Post*, 5 March 1850.

33 G. P. Gooch, *The Later Correspondence of Lord John Russell, 1840–1878, vol. 2* (1975).

34 *Globe*, 20 May 1850.

35 *The Times*, 29 June 1850.

36 Ibid.

37 Palmerston to Russell, 16 May 1850.

38 *The Times*, 29 June 1850.

39 A few years before a man called Pritchard had been expelled from Tahiti by the French. A commission was set up to decide whether he deserved compensation.

40 *The Times*, 24 April 1850.

41 Ibid., 15 May 1850.

42 Ibid., 19 November 1850.

43 Ibid., 10 May 1851.

14   The House of Lords debate

The Greeks may have given in, but the agreement to pay compensation had infuriated Queen Victoria and Prince Albert, the Tories and many of Palmerston's own colleagues in the Whig Party. Even Russell told Palmerston that 'the interests of the country required a change should take place in the Foreign Department', a remark some distance away from a rousing endorsement of his old friend's policy. Palmerston didn't take it to heart. He wrote to Normanby again, happy at the final discomfiture of Otho: 'All the accounts which come from Greece state that the Greeks complain, not of what we have done, but of what we have not done; they say the English brought Otho, the English ought to take him away.' On 23 May 1851 the deposit, which the Greeks had been forced by Wyse to give as a token of good faith, was returned to them. *The Times* remained absolutely furious and from 27 to 30 May the paper ran a daily leader on the subject, going through the timetable of events and pointing up every shortcoming it could find in the government's behaviour.

In its view on 27 May, the blockade 'has done as much as a dozen revolutions in endangering the peace of Europe'. It took the view that no claim should have been pursued, with 'one state exacting at the hands of another redress for injuries alleged to have been suffered in the persons of its subjects'. How the paper could have twisted the facts in its own mind to still consider the effects of the Easter riot to be 'alleged' is very difficult to understand, unless it was an extreme example of sour grapes. Had there ever been any doubt that a totally innocent man's house had been looted by a mob?

Of course, the biased reporting of the corrupted O'Brien, *The Times*' correspondent in Athens, twisted the facts to denigrate Pacifico: 'Previous to the attack on his house, so far from possessing property to any amount, [he] was in a state of pecuniary difficulty, [so] that subscriptions had been raised or proposed for him, and that he had been compelled to pledge plate to a considerable extent, which had not been redeemed.'[1]

The subscriptions had, of course, been raised for the new synagogue and the plate had been pledged for the business loan. What really bugged Delane and *The Times* was why it was Pacifico, a Jew, who gained the ear of the government. This was something they never did understand. After all, to the newspaper, Pacifico was an outcast. It played the mildly anti-Semitic card time and again. On 28 May it was 'the notorious Pacifico – Monsieur, Senor, Mr, Chevalier, Rabbi or Brother, as he may please to style himself'. With the specific reference to 'Brother', *The Times* was presumably wondering whether the explanation might lie in a masonic plot. It knew – and it considered it to undermine his credibility – that Pacifico was 'a Jew by creed and principle'. By implication, Jewish principles were, obviously, suspect. After all, he was 'hawking about for sale unintelligible claims'.

The Times still believed there could be no foundation whatsoever in Pacifico's case against the Portuguese. Hadn't the Portuguese explained that 'the claims had been dismissed as utterly groundless and ridiculous'? Pacifico was denounced as 'the unconscionable Hebrew' – although why a victim should have a conscience was not explained. The action was taken, *The Times* concluded, 'on the Jew's behalf'. By 30 May *The Times* had him categorised as 'this hybrid Jew' and 'insatiable mendicant'.

The government's opponents wouldn't admit defeat and if Palmerston's policy was to be publicly rejected, they felt that the House of Lords was the place to start. So a motion was put down on behalf of the Tory Party, to discuss the government's handling of the Greeks. In the nineteenth century the Tories always had a comfortable majority in the House of Lords. When there was a Tory government in power, the Lords hardly bothered to turn up. Admittedly, they didn't have to: 'Until 1868, when the ancient system of proxy voting was provisionally suspended and never reintroduced, peers did not even need to go to Westminster to influence the outcome of a debate. A friend could cast a vote on their behalf.'[2] The Commons was, of course, elected, but a considerable proportion of MPs came from the younger ranks of the aristocracy. The opinions of their fathers and uncles carried a great deal of weight.

As MPs weren't paid, a private income was essential, and more likely to be available if they were members of the aristocracy themselves. It was a very cosy set-up for the Tories. Realistically, with the exception of money bills, if the Tory majority didn't like a piece of government legislation, they could block it.

When the Whigs were elected, Greville commented that this 'placed the House of Lords in the new position of an assailant of the Queen's Government, frequently thwarting their most important measures'.[3] In debating the foreign policy of the government, however, the Lords were not in the same position as if they were trying to block or amend a piece of government legislation; Palmerston had not asked for their approval before he sent in the fleet. All the Tory peers could do was attempt to produce a majority in the House, who would disavow the government's policy and, thereby, embarrass it.

The debate was held on 17 June 1850 at five o'clock in the afternoon. Nearly 300 peers had assembled, a very large turnout, which illustrated the passions which had been aroused. There was, according to Greville, 'great curiosity and interest . . . the House was crowded in every part; I never saw so many Peers present, nor so many Strangers.'[4]

Nevertheless, the debate was conducted in the usual civilized manner on the motion:

> That while the House fully recognizes the right and duty of the Government to secure to Her Majesty's subjects residing in foreign states the full protection of the law of those states, it regrets to find, by the correspondence recently laid upon the table by Her Majesty's command, that various complaints against the Greek Government, doubtful in point of justice or exaggerated in amount, have been enforced by coercive measures directed against the commerce and people of Greece, and calculated to endanger the continuance of our friendly relations with other powers.

It certainly wasn't easy to forecast the result of the confrontation. The Tory Party knew they couldn't form a government if they brought the Whigs down. The split in the party over the reform of the Corn Laws a few years ago had resulted in them being little more than a rump of an opposition. Those Tories in favour of the repeal of the Corn Laws had left the party and gathered under Sir Robert Peel as a third force, which usually supported the Whigs. Russell's government was, for the moment, the only game in town.

Furthermore, the two Houses of Parliament did not enjoy debating matters of foreign policy at the best of times. As *The Times* pointed out: 'When we consider the extreme difficulty of inducing the legislative assemblies of this country to record their opinions on any question of foreign politics . . . we are doubly sensible of the moral importance of this vote.'[5]

When faced with a high percentage of opposition from the Continent, it was also the customary patriotic position for the parliamentary parties to sink their differences and present a united front to Britain's enemies. In 1850 the Tories had decided that such an approach was not applicable on this occasion. If their major objective was to gain votes, it was a risky line to take. The great majority of the British were always happy to see their country exercising its undoubted power.

The debate was opened by the leader of the Tory Party, Edward George Geoffrey Smith Stanley, first in line to become the next Earl of Derby. Stanley was the crème de la crème in the House of Lords, but his position was felt by many to be due to the fact that he was born into the right family; he was not considered a strong leader. Even his son said of him: 'My father is a very clever man, but he has no judgement, and would not do for a Minister of this country'.[6]

Even so, as Benjamin Disraeli, the Tory leader in the Commons, pointed out on one occasion, Stanley, in his early parliamentary career, had helped to abolish slavery, educate Ireland and reform the membership of the House of Commons. It was a distinguished record and he went back a long way with Palmerston and Russell. They had all three served in Lord Grey's administration during the historic battle over the Reform Bill in 1832.

Stanley had split with the Whigs in 1834 and gone over to the Tories. He was a brilliant speaker and was known as the Rupert of Debate, as he had been compared to the dashing Prince Rupert, the Royalist cavalry commander in the Civil War. The couplet ran: 'The brilliant chief, irregularly great/Frank, haughty, bold – the Rupert of Debate.'

Stanley was certainly in his prime as an orator as, with the chamber packed, he rose to attack the government on that long summer evening. As far as Stanley was concerned, the government's policy in Greece had nearly led to a war in Europe:

> by its extraordinary violence, by its unnecessary intemperance, by its improper abstinence from the necessary communications with other powers, and by its intrinsic injustice, has been calculated to endanger and has endangered the continuance of our friendly relations with foreign powers. That it has endangered that continuance no one of your Lordships is prepared to deny; if we escape scot free from our present embarrassments, as there is probable ground for believing that we shall, it will be more owing to good luck than to our good policy.

Before Stanley dissected the Pacifico case, he dealt with that segment of the British claims which was described as the *Fantome* Incident. Stanley took it seriously: 'I commence with that claim which is the most serious, as it is the only one which touches the national honour...One of her Majesty's steamers, the *Spitfire*, in pursuance of that kind and generous policy towards the Mediterranean states, called in at Patras and received on board a notorious rebel against the government of Greece, who found immediate protection under the British flag.' Later the Greeks had arrested a midshipman from HMS *Fantome* when he quite innocently landed at night.

It was a mix-up waiting to happen. As was pointed out later: 'The Greeks, bear you in mind, not speaking one word of English, nor the Englishmen one word of Greek...As soon as an interpreter was found, and it was ascertained who the Englishman was, he was at once liberated, and respectfully conveyed back to his ship.'[7] Total British losses were just the one boat hook. The *Fantome* had to leave Patras for other duties and so Lieutenant Macdonald, the captain of the *Spitfire*, which remained behind, sent a message to the Greek authorities which Stanley read out in full:

> The governor of the town had taken upon himself not only to display a hostile feeling towards the British Government, but also to permit a most unjustifiable outrage to be committed on an officer and boat's crew of Her Majesty's sloop, Fantome. I consider it my duty as the senior officer present at Patras, to prevent all communications between Her Majesty's sloop, Spitfire, under my command, and the town of Patras, except for the purpose of receiving the necessary supplies for the ship, through the medium of a boat belonging to the shore. I have further to request that you will be good enough distinctly to state to the governor, that I have represented to my own government the state of affairs, the more especially when I bear in mind the abominable falsehoods circulated by his authority and through a letter to yourself, accusing the officers and men of landing strangers under cover of the night. It is quite impossible under these circumstances that I can hold any communication for the future with an authority that sets all international law at defiance...My positive orders having been issued that in all future communication between the ship's boats and the shore, the Spitfire's boats are to be fully armed and equipped and fully prepared to resent any insult that may be offered to them.[8]

Stanley derided the *Fantome*'s captain's threat to arm any boat visiting the shore in future as a ludicrous safeguard against losing another boat hook. 'Was there ever such a mountain made out of a molehill?', he asked the House. He couldn't believe that this could be 'translated as a serious matter of international quarrel!'

Stanley would have been quite right if that had been the whole of the story. His Lordship, however, did not provide the House with all the facts, and possibly he didn't know them all, but, of course, Palmerston did. The train of events had actually started a month or so earlier than described, on 13 December 1847. There was widespread unrest in Greece as the malcontent, General Grivas, tried to start a general insurrection against Otho. In Patras the position was complicated by a row between two Greek officers – but no gentlemen – General Tzavellos and a Captain Méréditi of the Seventh Frontier Guards, a band of semi-brigands.

The captain said the general's son had stolen his watch. The general had the captain detained and put under house arrest. The captain, having made sure that his men would remain loyal to him, then invited the governor of Patras to the house for discussions. When he arrived, he was put in chains and Méréditi took his men off to rob the National Bank. They took about £6,000 (they gave the bank manager a receipt!) and then started looting. The *Fantome* happened to be in harbour at the time and when the captain heard about the pillaging, he sent a party of marines ashore with a cannon to protect the British consul.

The townsfolk realised that they couldn't overcome the captain's forces by themselves. So they appealed to the resident foreign diplomats to deal with Méréditi. The consuls agreed to try, met with Méréditi and reached an agreement that he would leave the town if he was paid a substantial bribe. They then pleaded with the captain of the *Fantome* to take the rebels on board and away from the vicinity. He, in his turn, agreed to do this, but when the insurgents embarked from the shore on the British naval boats, the townsfolk broke the agreement by firing on them. Five men were killed and fifteen wounded. As the British were doing the rowing, the captain of the *Fantome* naturally protested vigorously, but the Greek government later denied that any of this had happened and refused to apologise. The French newspaper, *Courrier Français* carried the official line that the British had rescued Méréditi, rather than that they had been asked to take him away.

So who do you believe? *The Times*' correspondent in Malta reported the events soon after they occurred and said he got the whole story from a private source. It is very detailed, it predates the *Courrier*'s account and it hangs together. Why should the *Fantome* captain have interfered if he hadn't been asked to? The correspondent in Malta had no axe to grind, the report is not from the biased Patrick O'Brien in Athens and the *Courrier* was certainly not going to put a pro-British gloss on the facts. There is also no reason for the Malta article to be inaccurate because the Patras events would not have seemed to have any startling importance at the time they were first reported.

So Lieutenant Macdonald of the *Spitfire* and the British in Patras were still smarting from the grossly unfair account of the December troubles in Patras and the double-dealing of the Greeks, not to mention the injuries to their colleagues. The *Fantome* Incident, weeks later, was just another example, as they saw it, of not being able to trust the local authorities. Macdonald sent a stiff note saying so. Lyons backed him up. Stanley didn't give the House of Lords half the facts.

Stanley then turned his attention to Pacifico. As far as his Lordship was concerned, the Pacifico case 'presents such an astounding combination of audacity and mendacity, of all that is ridiculous and disgusting, that I am ashamed to bring it under Your Lordships' notice'. This in spite of the fact that he had the decency to admit that 'it seems, indeed, from the papers that the police were deterred from taking such steps [to stop the riot] in consequence of persons who had high connections in the state being concerned in these outrages'. He didn't mention Lyons' comment, which must also have been in the papers, that the truth was that it was a well planned robbery.

Stanley had decided that the basic problem in Athens was that Lyons had never tried to be friendly to the Greek government. He saw his actions as springing from a determination to undermine any Greek parliamentary party that favoured the French – Kolettis' side. He felt that Lyons considered Glarikis and Colocotrony equally biased. Andreas Londos may have been labelled pro-British, but Stanley wasn't making any exceptions. He felt that Palmerston and Lyons had set out to bully the Greeks and, after Lyons, Wyse had been instructed to follow the same policy.

Stanley told the House that he also had little time for the other British subjects on whose behalf Palmerston had acted. Only Finlay 'has any right to be considered as a person of character and respectability'. It was the wrong choice; Finlay had bought the land which Otho needed for his palace grounds for £10 (the modern equivalent being £650). He claimed he should be paid £1,500 for it (nearly £100,000 in today's money). He also wanted 15 per cent annual interest (which, admittedly, was often the going rate in Greece) which between 1836 and 1848 added another 180 per cent. This brought the debt to £3,750, or nearly a quarter of a million pounds in today's money. In Britain in 2004 a judge declared the way a similar debt had escalated to be unreasonable, and cancelled it. In Victorian Britain, Finlay wasn't criticised in the House of Lords.

To prove his point against Pacifico, Stanley raked the ashes and resurrected the case in which David and Solomon were involved in 1817, more than thirty years before. He told the House that at that time, Pacifico had handed over a forged bond in exchange for $600 in Portugal. It was, in fact, $2,000. He said that only Pacifico's agreement in court to refund the money had prevented criminal charges being brought against him. Nobody considered that perhaps Pacifico had been as much taken in by the forged document as the recipient. Finding out that he had been cheated of his own money, he had paid the sea captain back in full. That had been accepted as satisfactory by the court at the time.

It was perfectly feasible, but Stanley had no first-hand knowledge of the case. He had merely been told of the event by 'reliable sources' in Lisbon. Stanley, speaking with parliamentary privilege, was sure the sources were to be believed and Pacifico, in his absence and without being given the opportunity to defend himself, was guilty of forgery.

There was only one logical source for Stanley's information: someone who had actually been there all those years ago and was in a position to know the facts. That man was Jeremiah Meagher, the British vice-consul in Lisbon. Meagher had started at the embassy as secretary to the vice-consul in 1810 and served in that capacity until 1821. He was then made vice-consul himself and didn't retire from that position until 1867. On three occasions during that time he acted as consul-general.

The proof that it was Meagher lies in the fact that Admiral Parker asked him for information on Pacifico during the blockade. Parker and Meagher had been friends for twenty years and it was from Meagher that Parker learned of the 1817 case. He considered him totally trustworthy. No one, he said, was 'less disposed to speak ill of another'.[9]

Parker had got Meagher's letter on 10 May in Corfu, where the squadron hove to after leaving Salamis Bay. He was surprised at its comments on Pacifico: 'I did not imagine that he was such a consummate rogue as Meagher can prove him to be.'[10] He learned that Pacifico 'was once detected in uttering a forged bill of £500'. He wrote that he had been told that Aaron Pacifico had paid out $2000 to hush it up. Notice that Parker referred to Aaron Pacifico by name. Not as 'Pacifico's brother' or 'the brothers compensated' but specifically Aaron. It suggests that Parker knew the family better than he was prepared to admit when they were so much in the public eye.

Parker was, apparently, not told that this was the same figure that the bill had been meant to cover. Undoubtedly the forged bill was an embarrassment for the brothers, but counterfeit notes often finish up in the hands of people who had no connection with their manufacture. It would be equally logical, in order to protect their good name as ship's agents, for the Pacificos to compensate the ship's captain handsomely for the unpleasant experience he had undergone as a result. After all, the man had finished up in court in both London and Portugal. Nevertheless, Pacifico didn't do so. He just paid what he owed.

Parker came to his conclusion without hearing Pacifico's side. He didn't ask himself why, if Pacifico was such a rogue, it had been necessary for the vice-consul to go back to 1817 to find evidence against him of any alleged wrongdoing. Meagher was never a high-flyer and he might well have considered the appointment of merchants as consuls to be unfair to professionals like himself. A lot of civil servants look down on political appointments and Pacifico had been brought into the Portuguese diplomatic service at a high level without any previous experience. The professional diplomats also tended to look down on the merchant appointees to consular posts.

Consider also that, if it was an attempt to defraud the ship's owner, it was a singularly stupid one. The forged bill was almost bound to be recognized as such when it was presented. When that happened, the offender, Pacifico, was easy to find. He hadn't left town and he was still acting as a ship's agent. Surely, if Pacifico meant to pass on a forged document, he would have chosen a victim who was less well known to him and whom he could hope to avoid meeting in the future. Unfortunately, Meagher's letter to Parker has not survived. Meagher volunteered his information when he was asked to by the admiral, but it seems very unlikely that Palmerston hadn't sought the same input as well. Again, there is no evidence in the Foreign Office files, but if Palmerston asked Lyons if the claim was reasonable, he would logically also have had a word with the embassy in the country subject to the claim.

Stanley described Pacifico at the time as 'an accommodating gentleman of the Hebrew persuasion'. He apparently considered his religion pertinent, just as *The Times*' concern about Pacifico's principles was supposed to originate from the same Talmudic source. Stanley ridiculed what Pacifico was claiming his lost property was worth. He quoted some of the items:

> 1 large couch in solid mahogany, British work, with double bottom, one of which in Indian cane for summer: £72. 1 bottom for the winter for the above, a cushion in tapestry embroidered in real gold (Royal Work): £25; 2 pillows and cushions for the back of the whole length of the couch in silk and wood covering, embroidered in real gold, as the bottom of the above couch: £75 . . . A double bed in solid mahogany, with 4 pillars richly carved, 2¾ yards long by 2½ yards wide, with the back and the end carved in carved mahogany and carved frame, and a set of brass castors, worth £150. Utensils of the finest porcelain.

There was a lot of laughter in the House. The likelihood of items of this quality being picked up cheaply, at auctions of the goods of Miguel's aristocratic supporters, after the War of the Two Brothers, never came up. Stanley either didn't know of these events or didn't think that mentioning them would strengthen his case.

Stanley stated quite baldly that Pacifico 'was born of Portuguese parents'. There was no truth in this at all, but it cast doubt again on the government's statement that it was helping a British citizen. Stanley deplored the fact that Pacifico had borrowed thirty pounds at a low rate of interest from a bank in Athens, and pledged the silver as a guarantee of repayment. He sneered at the objective being to lend the money to others at a high rate of interest. Victorian banks, however, lent money as well. When Portugal tried to get a loan in 1830 it was charged 31 per cent commission by the British lenders. This was put down to the City of London performing its proper function. It was perfectly respectable. Stanley encouraged double standards.

The British claims on the Greeks also included the compensation for their treatment of the abused Ionians. One Ionian, Stallio Sumachi, had been arrested in Patras in 1846 for burglary and robbery. He wrote to the British consul to complain that he had been tortured and eventually Lyons complained to Kolettis about 'this unhappy victim of official brutality'. The Greeks denied that Sumachi had been ill-treated, but tried the policemen concerned anyway. To no one's surprise they were found not guilty. Palmerston wrote to Lyons in language to which Stanley took exception, because he felt that it was totally undiplomatic:

> Her Majesty's government had hoped that such practices as these [the torture], which are unauthorised by the law and constitution of Greece, and are reprobated by the general consent of all civilized nations, had ceased to disgrace the executive government of Greece. But Her Majesty's Government cannot permit such things to be done with impunity towards British or Ionian subjects; you are, therefore, instructed to demand from the Greek Government that the police officers who have been concerned in this outrage shall be immediately dismissed, and that adequate pecuniary compensation be made to Stallio Sumachi for the sufferings he has undergone ... you will also state to the Greek Government that Her Majesty's Government hope and expect that you will be enabled to report by the next packet after you receive this dispatch that these just and moderate demands have been complied with.

The tone was certainly decisive, but the British had been told by the doctor who had examined Sumachi that he had been personally threatened by the Greek authorities if he didn't report that there had been no evidence of torture. There was, however, no doubt that the police officers, once acquitted, could not be tried again for the same offence. Palmerston was insisting that the Greek courts were not reliable and that the decision of the court should be ignored. To agree to this, the Greeks would have to disavow their own judiciary, which wasn't very likely, even if disavowal might have been a correct response to their behaviour.

Stanley also felt that Andreas Londos had been hard done by, because he had been in office for only three weeks when the blockade ultimatum came from Wyse and Parker. He ignored the fact that Londos was the fourth minister to deal with the Pacifico claim – Kolettis, Glarikis and Colocotrony having been in charge before. To Stanley, the intent of the Greek government to avoid its obligations, if humanly possible, was subsumed by its nobility when faced with Parker's threatened blockade. He quoted with approval the rebuke Londos sent Wyse: 'Greece is weak, Sir, and she did not expect that such blows would be aimed at her by a government which she reckoned with equal pride and confidence, among her benefactors.' Such utter humbug finds few greater contemporary parallels.

Greville was in the House and observed that 'Stanley spoke for two hours and three-quarters. He has made more brilliant speeches, but it was very good, moderate and prudent in tone, lucid, lively, and sustained.' It fell to the Third Marquis of Lansdowne, Henry Petty-Fitzmaurice, to reply. Lansdowne was also a political heavyweight. He had served as both Chancellor of the Exchequer and Home Secretary in a distinguished career, and was now Lord President of the Council. He had the advantage over Stanley in that he knew more about some of the key facts than had been disclosed thus far.

Lansdowne suggested that Stanley's speech was 'indebted much more to the eloquence of the speaker than its intrinsic worth'. He suggested that it was hardly likely that Pacifico was such a scoundrel, if 'the claims which had been made upon Greece had received the sanction of the Cabinet'. He pointed out that many countries took similar action to that of the British government when its citizens were badly treated, and that, even as he spoke, United States warships were on their way to Lisbon to support claims for redress on behalf of Americans against the Portuguese government.

The Marquis went on to refute the suggestion that the Greeks had originally been asked for a full settlement of Pacifico's claim. He said that the government just wanted 'compensation for what the Pacifico claim was worth'. Lansdowne did not want to insult the Portuguese in the House, but he did point out that 'it is stated that they [the Portuguese] undertook to give M. Pacifico the consulship as a substitute for the sum he was entitled to recover'. Never mind if the Portuguese now said that the claim was worthless. They hadn't thought that when they offered him the consulship.

Then Lansdowne dropped a bombshell which everybody afterwards pretended hadn't gone off. It was allowed to make no difference to the position of the critics of both the government and Pacifico, and future writers on the subject would ignore it. Lansdowne bluntly spelt out that 'Every one of these claims that involved any doubt with regard to a question of law was referred, with all the documents belonging to each case, to the Queen's law advisers, and in no instance has a claim been made in which, after full and deliberate consideration of the papers, they did not say the party had a right to obtain compensation.'

So Palmerston hadn't just been backing his own judgement. He had taken advice from the law officers as was, in fact, his invariable practice. He knew that the Portuguese were never to be trusted to repay their debts because they never had any money. The law officers said the claims were worth pursuing.

Lansdowne then made a telling point about Pacifico's position as the claimant. He pointed out that Lord Stowell, an eighteenth-century Admiralty judge, had made 'many splendid decisions on points of law though the people to whom his judgements referred were many of the slave dealers, pirates and adulterers'.

Lord Eddisbury also made a strong defence of Pacifico. As he pointed out: 'The case of Pacifico had been ridiculed as one too contemptible to be treated seriously, and yet nobody could deny that his was a case of hardship and oppression.' He snapped back with contempt at those who made light of the looting: 'How would the Noble Lord like, if his own house had been ransacked, to have his daughter's effects shown before the public in order to raise a laugh?'

Eddisbury went on to tackle the question of whether Pacifico was a forger and a confidence trickster. He reminded the House that a man's character had not seemed to be important to the peers in the past. What had been their reaction to John Wilkes, the great eighteenth-century defender of the rights of Parliament? There had been little doubt that Wilkes was both an inveterate gambler and immoral to boot. Nevertheless, Parliament supported his philosophy with enthusiasm. The noble lord was adamant; a man deserved justice whatever he might have done thirty years ago. Eddisbury went on to point out: 'In a commercial country like this – with interests spread over every part of the globe, with our fellow subjects in every port and our ships on every sea – it is of the utmost importance that nowhere should injustice be permitted towards those who rightly claim the protection of the British government.'

On the other side, Lord Brougham, who had fought hard for the 1832 Reform Act, took the criticisms of Pacifico at face value. He castigated 'Mr Pacifico, of whom he had never heard it predicated that he was most able, except in taking care of his own interest, or most learned, except in the art of making accounts, or most respectable in any point of view whatever'. What Lord Brougham had heard was not the whole story either.

Second only to Stanley, the most powerful gun in the armoury of the Tory opposition to the government's foreign policy was always likely to be the Earl of Aberdeen. He had been the Foreign Secretary in the Cabinets of both Wellington and Peel and no one knew more about the internal workings of the Foreign Office, apart from Palmerston. Aberdeen approached the subject as a lifetime lover of everything Greek. He had toured the country from 1801 to 1804 and excavated the amphitheatre on the Pnyx in Athens. Aberdeen founded the Athenian Society, wrote on Troy for the *Edinburgh*

Review and wore his philhellenic rose-coloured glasses with pride. Aberdeen was neither confrontational nor forceful. He was, however, a model for the caricature of the dour Scot. He was not the favourite companion of the more dashing politicians such as Palmerston and Disraeli. In 1853 Disraeli wrote of him:

> His manner, arrogant and yet timid – his words, insolent and yet obscure, offend even his political supporters. His hesitating speech, his contracted sympathies, his sneer, icy as Siberia, his sarcasms, drear and barren as the Steppes, are all characteristics of the bureau and the chancery, and not of popular and aristocratic assemblies animated by the spirit of honour and the pride of gentlemen.[11]

You might criticise his manner, but George Hamilton Gordon, Fourth Earl of Aberdeen, was a man of wide experience. It was when he was Foreign Secretary that Finlay had first appealed for help to get paid for his land. The earl knew the intricacies of the dispute over the Ionian Islands and he knew international law. He quoted two eighteenth-century authorities, Emerich de Vittel and Lord Mansfield. Vittel had laid down the accepted doctrine: 'The prince, therefore, ought not to interfere in the causes of his subjects in foreign countries, excepting in cases where justice is refused, or palpable and evident injustice done, or rules and forms openly violated, or, finally, an odious distinction made to the prejudice of his subjects, or of foreigners in general'.

Aberdeen refused to believe that his beloved Greeks could have done anything of the kind. He couldn't see that, in Pacifico's case, the Greek courts, as early as May 1847, had said they couldn't do anything to the perpetrators. He talked of giving Londos twenty-four hours to come to terms, as if this was the first the Greeks had known of Britain's protests. Aberdeen was right, however, when he said that all the governments in Europe suspected that there was more to it, and that Lyons was trying to bring down the pro-French Greek government and possibly even Otho himself.

Aberdeen went on to take some of the wind out of the sails of Admiral Parker. His squadron, he told the House, had set out from London and alarmed the foreign governments when it dropped anchor in Lisbon and Naples. It had then gone on to the Ionian Islands, providing whips to flog the rebels who were active at the time. As for suggesting that Parker had brought the Russians to their senses over their dispute with the Turks, Aberdeen reminded the peers that the disagreement had been settled before the fleet arrived in the Dardanelles. Indeed, Parker had had to apologise to the emperor for entering the Straits.

When Parker heard of the accusation that he had provided 'cats' to whip offenders, he denied it. He did, however, agree that he had given the authorities log lines which could be used for that purpose.[12] A log line was a rope used with a float to estimate the speed of a ship.

There were lesser contributions from many other peers. Lord Hardwicke tried to confirm that Parker had gone into the Dardanelles only because of bad weather. Lord Beaumont didn't like Pacifico, 'but the House ought to consider him as an injured individual, to whom redress had been refused when applied for to the proper legal authorities at Athens'. Lord John Manners emphasised that the government's policy depended on the strength of the opposition. He pointed out that a British subject had been taken off a ship in America and imprisoned, but Palmerston had done nothing about that.

The debate rolled on into the small hours, with the result always in the balance. When the last peer had had his say, the House divided at a quarter past three in the morning. The government lost by 169 votes to 132, an opposition majority of thirty-seven. Greville was very taken aback: 'I never was more amazed than at hearing the division never having dreamt of such a majority.' The peers finally went home and next day the government had to start to consider what it should do now. Greville wondered as well: 'reste à savoir what government (and P especially) will do. If he was disposed to take a great line, he would go at once to the Queen and resign.'[13]

At this point *The Times* wanted to quit while the going was good. It said that the vote 'has now brought the vexed question of Lord Palmerston's late proceedings in Greece to its appropriate close'.[14] The *Morning Post*, by contrast, considered that 'the result involves a paradox at present inexplicable; the argument was all one way – the numbers another'. Palmerston didn't lose any sleep over the reverse. He wrote to Normanby in Paris the next morning:

> We were beaten last night in the Lords by a larger majority than we had up to the last moment expected, but when we took office we knew that our opponents had a larger pack in the Lords than we had, and that whenever the two packs were to be fully dealt out, theirs would show a larger number than ours. When the Protectionists (the opposition to the repeal of the Corn Laws) have thought that a defeat on any particular

question in the Lords would make us resign...they have carefully abstained from mustering their whole strength. Last night they felt confident that we should not go out on an adverse vote of the House of Lords and they brought up all their men, even the hospital invalids.

The question was still, what next?

NOTES

1   *The Times*, 8 January 1848.
2   John Wells, *The House of Lords* (Hodder & Stoughton, 1997).
3   Ibid.
4   Edward Pearce (ed.), *The Diaries of Charles Greville* (Pimlico, 2005).
5   *The Times*, 18 June 1850.
6   Palmerston to his brother, 15 February 1850.
7   Richard Cobden, MP in the House of Commons, 28 June 1850.
8   *The Times*, 19 June 1850.
9   August Phillimore, *The Life of Admiral of the Fleet, Sir William Parker* (Harrison, 1880).
10 Ibid.
11 M. E. Chamberlain, *Lord Aberdeen* (London, 1983).
12 Phillimore, *The Life of Admiral of the Fleet, Sir William Parker*.
13 Pearce (ed.), *The Diaries of Charles Greville*.
14 *The Times*, 29 May 1850.

15   Civis Romanus Sum

The House of Lords voted against the government on Monday 17 June and the opposition wasted no time in taking advantage of the reverse. On the Thursday, Benjamin Disraeli, leading the Tory rump in the Commons, asked if the government intended to resign. Lord John Russell, the Prime Minister, was in no doubt about that. He might have wanted to get rid of Palmerston as a confounded nuisance, but he wasn't going to be pushed by any other party into taking the necessary steps. Even if the Queen felt the same way about Palmerston, which she certainly did, Russell would defend his government's record: 'The Prime Minister offered to resign but refused to make Palmerston the scapegoat for sins committed with the approval of the whole government.'[1] On the Wednesday there had been a Cabinet meeting to decide what to do about the vote in the Lords and the result was that they decided to do nothing.

Palmerston was completely unrepentant. He made himself abundantly clear that 'it was not the intention of the government to depart from the course of their foreign policy, that they had no intention whatever to bow to the decision of the other House, and that they certainly had not the slightest disposition to resign the reins of government'.[2] Presumably, but not necessarily, he had cleared his statement with Number Ten. In the House of Commons, on the Thursday, Russell had repeated the government's position. This was that British subjects abroad could expect 'immunity from any despotic, unjust or oppressive laws' of the countries in which they found themselves. When it was suggested that a list of such countries might be printed somewhere, there was no response from the government.

The vote in the Lords couldn't simply be ignored. It soon became obvious that approval of the government's policy would have to be sought in the Commons. Only a week after the peers had voted, the lower House convened to debate the pro-government motion 'that the principles on which the foreign policy of Her Majesty's government have been regulated have been such as were calculated to maintain the honour and dignity of this country'. The ground had been carefully chosen for the battle. The Commons were not asked to judge the Foreign Office's behaviour in the Don Pacifico affair alone, although everybody knew that was the main cause of contention. The subject was voluminously wrapped up in the whole of the government's record. This did not prevent most of the speakers from concentrating their fire on the recent situation in Greece. Of course, the blockade had not just been to get compensation for Don Pacifico. There was also the money due to Finlay for his land, the apology the government sought for the *Fantome* Incident, and the treatment of the Ionian islanders who had been arrested and badly treated by the police. These would be exhaustively discussed, but the key element was always Pacifico.

The Speaker took the chair at four o'clock that next Monday afternoon. The House was as packed as the Roman colosseum on the days when they threw Christians to the lions, with Palmerston the expected victim on this occasion. Every inch was occupied by spectators, settling down to hear what would be one of the great set-piece debates of the nineteenth century. This was a vote of confidence, and on the result of the debate depended not just the Foreign Secretary's future but the continuation of the government itself. The uneasy co-operation of the Whigs and the Peelites had been fractured over the Don Pacifico affair, and dependable pro-government voters like anti-Corn Law fighter, Richard Cobden, were certain to speak against the administration, backed up by other parliamentary heavyweights like Gladstone and Disraeli.

The Foreign Office debate was opened by John Roebuck, QC, who was a fine independent advocate and the founder of the Reform Club in London in his spare time. Roebuck, a barrister, was well qualified to dissect the evidence. He had no hesitation in homing in on the core problem in Pacifico's case: was the amount of the damages claimed unreasonable? Roebuck had done his own research: 'Going to an upholsterers, I said "[is there] anything extravagant or extraordinary in the prices?" The upholsterer said several peers had placed orders of a far more extensive kind . . . if you go to a particular drawing-room you will see things of quadruple that value'.

Roebuck contended that it was quite possible that the damaged possessions were worth what was claimed, even without mentioning the bargains available in the auctions after the War of the Two Brothers, of which he was probably unaware. Roebuck recognized and stated Pacifico's true position: 'He was, in reality, a tradesman who had the hope of selling those articles of furniture to advantage and of selling them to the very man who denied him redress.' The MP was scathing about the depths plumbed by those who sought to trivialise the situation. There had been jokes, he said, about the claim Pacifico had made for the cost of the marital bed: 'The joke was pointless in form as it was vulgar in sentiment.'

Roebuck then turned to another criticism of Pacifico's claim for damages, which was that he had not appeared to be a rich man, but Roebuck pointed out that 'hiding wealth is one of the means of safety where there is no law'. And Roebuck didn't think the Greek law was on a par with the British High Courts, even on a good day. He ridiculed the Greek investigators: 'though the occurrence took place in broad daylight on Easter Sunday, and the people who came there were known by name, the whole of Athens indeed knowing who they were, they could not find a creature'. So was Pacifico right in going to the British Embassy for help? Roebuck laid down the law: 'If you believe . . . that what you deem justice cannot be done, by all the rules of international law you have a right to make an appeal to the government of your own country'.

Roebuck reminded members, if that were necessary, of the implications for British trade of not looking after complainants: 'If you once relax the rules by which the people of this country are guarded when abroad, there is no safety for English commerce.' Could this not be done consistently without using force? Roebuck was clear on that point as well: 'If anybody hopes to preserve peace by making all the world believe that nothing will induce us to go to war, he is greatly mistaken.' The Member for Sheffield was also dismissive of the anger of the French at the way the Foreign Office had acted. As far as France was concerned, its behaviour was no role model for the British: 'Freedom does not exist in France. No man can discuss a political question of the day. One after another the newspapers are put down. Yet they talk about the honour of France.' The House could happily resound to a chorus of 'Hear, hear': knocking the French always went down well in the Commons.

It was the evening of the second day before Palmerston rose to speak to a House which was deeply split on the motion before it. More than anything else, the government's survival depended on what Palmerston could say to defend his record. Happily for Russell and his colleagues, the gravity of the situation didn't put off a politician who had been involved in affairs of state for more than thirty years. At 66, Palmerston had no difficulty in speaking fluently for four-and-a-half hours without a note.

The Foreign Secretary started by mildly remonstrating with Disraeli for calling for the government's resignation as a result of the vote in the Lords. Surely, he said, such a demand should have come only if the Commons had voted likewise. He then went on to make the case for gunboat diplomacy:

> The resolution of the House of Lords...lays down for the future a principle of national policy which I consider totally incompatible with the interests, with the rights, with the honour, and with the dignity of the country, and at variance with the practice, not only of this, but of all other civilized countries in the world. The country is told that British subjects in foreign lands are entitled – for that is the meaning of the resolution – to nothing but the protection of the laws and the tribunals of the land in which they happen to reside. The country is told that British subjects abroad must not look to their own country for protection...The House of Lords has not said that this proposition is limited to constitutional countries. The House of Lords has not said that the proposition is inapplicable, not only to arbitrary and despotic countries, but even to constitutional countries where the courts of justice are not free...The country is simply informed by the resolution, as it was adopted, that, as far as foreign nations are concerned, the future role of the government of England is to be, that, in all cases, and under all circumstances, British subjects are to have that protection only, which the law and the tribunals of the land in which they happen to be, may give them.
>
> Now I deny that proposition. It has been said 'we do not apply this rule to countries whose Governments are arbitrary or despotic, because there the tribunals are under the control of the Government, and justice cannot be had; and, moreover, it is not meant to be applied to nominally constitutional Governments, where the tribunals are corrupt.' But who is to be the judge in such a case, whether the tribunals are corrupt or not? The British Government, or the Government of the State from which you demand justice?...I, say then, that our doctrine is, that, in the first instance, redress should be sought from the law courts of the country; but that in cases where redress cannot be had – and those cases are many – to confine a British subject to that remedy, only, would be to deprive him of the protection which he is entitled to receive.

Then the question arises, how does this rule apply to the demands we have made upon Greece?...By treaty in 1832...the three powers determined that Greece should henceforth be a monarchy. But while England assented to that arrangement, and considered that it was better that Greece should assume a monarchical form of government, yet we attached to that assent an indispensable condition that Greece should be a constitutional monarchy. The British Government could not consent to place the people of Greece, in their independent political existence, under as arbitrary a government as that from which they had revolted...When Prince Otho of Bavaria...was chosen, the three powers, on announcing the choice they had made, at the same time declared that King Otho would, in concert with his people, give to Greece constitutional institutions.

It was, however, understood, that during the minority of King Otho, the establishment of the constitution should be suspended...King Otho came of age, but no constitution was given...I do not mention this with any intention of casting the least reproach upon Russia, or Prussia or Austria. Those three governments, at that time, were despotic. Their advice was given, and their influence was exerted to prevent the King of Greece from granting a constitution to his people...Therefore, from the time when the King came of age, and for several years afterwards, the English Government stood in this position in Greece with regard to its Government – that we alone were anxious for the fulfilment of the engagement of the King, while all the other powers who were represented at Athens, were averse to its being made good...

One of the evils of the absence of constitutional institutions was that the whole system of government grew to be full of every kind of abuse. Justice could not be expected where the judges of the tribunals were at the mercy of the advisers of the crown. The finances could not be in any order where there was no public responsibility on the part of those who were to collect or to spend the revenue. Every sort of abuse was practised.

In all times, in Greece, as is well known, there has prevailed, from the daring habits of the people, a system of compulsory appropriation – forcible appropriation by one man of that which belonged to another; which, of course, is very disagreeable to those who are the victims of the system, and exceedingly injurious to the social condition, improvement, and prosperity of the country. In short, what foreigners call brigandage, which prevailed under Turkish rule, has not, I am sorry to say, diminished under the Greek sovereignty. Moreover, the police of the Greece Government have practised abuses of the grossest description...

Well, this being the state of things in Greece, there have always been in every town in Greece, a great number of persons whom we are bound to protect – Maltese, Ionians, and a certain number of British subjects. It became the practice of this Greek police to make no distinction between the Maltese and Ionians and their own fellow-subjects. We shall be told, perhaps, as we have already been told, that if the people of the country are liable to have heavy stones placed upon their breasts, and police officers to dance upon them; if they are liable to have their heads tied to their knees, and to be left for hours in that state; or to be swung like a pendulum, and to be bastinadoed as they swing, foreigners have no right to be better treated than the natives, and have no business to complain if the same things are practised upon them. We may be told this, but that is not my opinion, nor do I believe it is the opinion of any reasonable man ... [there is] the necessity of putting a stop to the extension of these abuses to British and Ionian subjects by demanding compensation ... the granting of which would be an acknowledgement that such things should not be done towards us in future.

In discussing these cases ... it is often more convenient to treat matters with ridicule, than with grave argument; and we have had serious things treated jocosely; and grave men kept in a roar of laughter, for an hour together, at the poverty of one sufferer, or at the miserable habitation of another; at the nationality of one injured man or the religion of another; as if because a man is poor he might be bastinadoed and tortured with impunity; as if a man who was born in Scotland might be robbed without redress; or, because a man is of the Jewish persuasion, he is fair game for any outrage...

...it has been, and still is, the practice of the [Greek] government, instead of punishing brigands, to amnesty and pardon them; and indeed it is even supposed that the officers of police sometimes go shares in the plunder. That, however, is a matter of opinion; but it is a fact that the robbers are almost always pardoned; and such is the encouragement thereby given to the system of plunder, that the robbers go about armed in bands, and sometimes actually attack and occupy towns.

Then we come to the claim of M. Pacifico – a claim which has been the subject of much unworthy comment. Stories have been told, involving imputations on the character of M. Pacifico; I know nothing of the truth or falsehood of these stories. All I know is, that M. Pacifico, after the time to which these stories relate, was appointed Portuguese consul, first to Morocco and afterwards at Athens. It is not likely that the Portuguese Government would select for appointments of that kind, a person whose character they did not believe to be above reproach. But I say, with those who have before had occasion to advert on the subject, that I don't care what M. Pacifico's character is. I do not, and cannot, admit that because a man may have acted amiss on some other occasion, and in some other matter, he is to be wronged with impunity by others.

The rights of a man depend on the merits of the particular case; and it is an abuse of argument to say that you are not to give redress to a man because in some former transaction he may have done something which is questionable. Punish him if you will, punish him if he is guilty, but do not pursue him as a pariah through life.

What happened in this case? In the middle of the town of Athens, in a house which I must be allowed to say is not a wretched hovel, as some people have described it, but it does not matter what it is, for whether a man's home be a palace or a cabin, the owner has a right to be there safe from injury – well, in a house which...was...the residence of the Count of Armansperg, the Chief of the Regency...M. Pacifico, living in this house, within 40 yards of the great street, within a few minutes walk of a guardhouse, where soldiers were stationed, was attacked by a mob. Fearing injury, when the mob began to assemble, he sent an intimation to the British Minister, who immediately informed the authorities.

Application was made to the Greek Government for protection. No protection was afforded. The mob, in which were soldiers and gens-d'armes, who, even if officers were not with them, ought, from a sense of duty, to have interfered and to have prevented plunder – that mob, headed by the sons of the minister of war, not children of eight or ten, but older – that mob, for nearly two hours, employed themselves in gutting the house of an unoffending man, carrying away or destroying every single thing the house contained, and left it a perfect wreck.

Is that not a case in which a man is entitled to redress from somebody? I venture to think it is. I think that there is no civilised country where a man subjected to such a grievous wrong, not to speak of insults and injuries to members of his family, would not justly expect redress from some quarter or another... the Greek government were told to 'search a particular house; and that some part of M. Pacifico's jewels would be found there'. They declined to prosecute the minister's sons, or to search the house. But, it is said, M. Pacifico should have applied to a court of law for redress. What was he to do? Was he to prosecute a mob of 500 persons? Was he to prosecute them criminally, or in order to make them pay the value of his loss? Where was he to find his witnesses?... he and his family were hiding or flying, during the pillage, to avoid the personal outrages with which they were threatened. He states, that his own life was saved by the help of an English friend. It was impossible, if he could have identified the leaders, to have prosecuted them with success...

He wanted redress, not revenge. A criminal prosecution was out of the question, to say nothing of the... certainty, of failure in a country where the tribunals are at the mercy of the advisers of the crown, the judges being liable to be removed, and being often actually removed upon grounds of private interest and personal feeling... M. Pacifico truly said 'if a man I prosecute is rich, he is sure to be acquitted; if he is poor, he has nothing out of which to afford me compensation if he is condemned...

[This] was a case in which we were justified in calling on the Greek Government for compensation for the losses, whatever they might be, which M. Pacifico had suffered. I think the claim was founded in justice. The amount we did not pretend to fix... the Greek Government denied altogether the principle of the claim... the demand was not for any particular amount of money. The demand was that the claim should be settled... it came at last to this, either that his demand was to be abandoned altogether, or that, in pursuance of the notice we had given the Greek Government a year or two before, we were to proceed to use our own means to enforce the claim. 'Oh, but' it is said 'what an ungenerous proceeding to employ so large a force against so small a Power!' Does the smallness of a country justify the magnitude of its evil acts?... We are to be generous to those who have been ungenerous to you; and we cannot give you redress because we have such ample and easy means of producing it.

Well, then, was there anything so uncourteous in sending, to back our demands, a force which should make it manifest to all the world that resistance is out of the question? Why, it seems to me, that it was more consistent with the honour and dignity of the Government on whom we made those demands, that there should be placed before their eyes a force, which it would be vain to resist, and before which it would be no indignity to yield.

The revolutions of 1848 were still very much in the MPs' minds and Palmerston took the opportunity of comparing the British attitude during those tumultuous times with those of other nations on the Continent:

We have shown that liberty is compatible with order; that individual freedom is reconcilable with obedience to the law. We have shown the example of a nation in which every class of society accepts with cheerfulness the lot which Providence has assigned to it, while at the same time every individual of each class is constantly striving to raise himself in the social scale – not by injustice and wrong, not by violence and illegality, but by persevering good conduct, and by the steady and energetic exertion of the moral and intellectual facilities with which his Creator has endowed him...

I contend that we have not in our foreign policy done anything to forfeit the confidence of the country... [we] think ourselves bound to offer protection to our fellow subjects abroad ... and whether, as the Roman, in days of old, held himself free from indignity, when he could say *Civis Romanus Sum*; so also a British subject, in whatever land he might be, shall feel confident that the watchful eye and the strong arm of England, will protect him against injustice and wrong.

Palmerston sat down at twenty past two in the morning and his supporters hammered their approval. For a man of over 60, it had been a tour de force which even his opponents acknowledged as brilliant. As Sir Robert Peel, the former prime minister, described it: 'that most able and temperate speech, which made us proud of the man who delivered it'. Gladstone, who would be prime minister four times before the end of the century, described the speech as 'a marvel for physical strength, for memory and for lucid and precise exposition of his policy as a whole'. He recalled that 'through the livelong summer night the British House of Commons, crowded as it was, hung upon his words'.

It was a generous tribute and it came from a politician who spoke for more than three hours against the government the following night. Gladstone found Pacifico's claim outrageous: 'a greater iniquity had rarely been transacted under the face of the sun... the subject of M. Pacifico's claim... would really afford no bad material for some ingenious writer of romance... Sir, the whole statement bears on the very face of it outrageous fraud and falsehood.' Like everybody else, however, his criticism of Pacifico's claim was based on the belief that the claim was for possessions, rather than stock:

> [Pacifico] who thus surpassed nearly all subjects and equalled almost any prince, according to his own account, in many articles of luxury, who had £5,000 worth of clothes, jewels and furniture in his house, had not outside of it, except plate pledged to the Bank of Athens for £30, which he had not been able to redeem, one single farthing! So, Sir, having this house crammed full of fine furniture, fine clothes and fine jewels, Monsieur Pacifico was in all other respects a pauper.

Gladstone made a fine and wide-ranging speech against the government's policies but he took care to make one specific point on which he felt very strongly throughout his life:

> I say fearlessly whatever may be the difference of opinion in this House as to the admission of Jews to political privilege, that no person could dare to stand up among us and allege his religion as a ground for mistrust or for the denial of justice, without drawing down upon himself, from all quarters of the House alike, universal scorn and indignation.

That was Gladstone's position and, indeed, that had been the law of the country for nearly 200 years. During the debate, Pacifico's Jewishness was mentioned by most speakers, and in every case sympathetically.

Among the many well delivered speeches aimed at the government's policy, after Palmerston's oration, was the contribution of Richard Cobden. The man who, more than any other, achieved the repeal of the destructive Corn Laws, was also intent on keeping Britain out of foreign entanglements. He believed that free trade, without interference, would lead to world peace. Cobden accepted the Greeks were at fault, but 'admit they were wrong, and what I want to know is whether the wrong was not one that might have been readily settled by other means than by sending 15 ships of war into the Bay of Salamis'. It was a fair question but the answer was almost undoubtedly 'No'.

Cobden knew spin-doctoring when he saw it. He had been responsible for a good deal of it during his own political lifetime. When it came to the policy of Palmerston, the machinations behind the scenes seemed obvious. As Cobden said: 'I am tempted to ask whether there has not been some little plot, conspiracy and cabal to get up an artificial excitement in the country on the subject. Yes, I have seen placards and circulars; I am not speaking without knowledge'.

In the course of a long speech, Cobden had the grace to admit that 'Mr Pacifico had his house outrageously attacked; that no one can deny.' Those were the only words he uttered, however, that were in Pacifico's favour. He then laid into the claim with vigour:

> For a bedstead £150, he charges for the sheets £30, he charges for the pillow case £10, for two coverlids £25. This inventory is so deeply disgraceful to all concerned in it, that, first, you tried to evade the question, by saying the case was not one for nisi prius details, and then you turned round, and said that Pacifico bought all this furniture to Athens, to sell it to the King of Greece.

Cobden was typical of those who did not know the value of luxury goods in Athens at the time and, because he would not have paid such prices, he assumed that nobody else would either. He did make the valid point that Palmerston didn't use the same tactics with a powerful country as those he had employed with Greece:

> The moment the Court of Russia hear of this demonstration, I find that they send a remonstrance against the government of this country – a remonstrance couched in language I never expected to hear from a semi-barbarous country like Russia to this: read, I ask you, the extraordinary language used by Count Nesselrode to Lord Palmerston, and then read the answer of the latter, and see how different is the tone adopted by him to a country which is powerful compared to what he makes use of to one that is weak.

What Cobden chose to ignore was that diplomacy, like politics, has much to do with the art of the possible. He also set no store by the potential impact around the world of the grand gesture: the threat to dictatorships, that Britain might go to extraordinary lengths to make them treat her citizens fairly. They couldn't be sure that, just because they were a long way from the Channel, and just because the victims were poor or unimportant, they would get away with it.

Cobden also refused to recognize that Palmerston had been absolutely clear from the start of negotiations with the French that he was not going to accept arbitration. Cobden muddied the water: 'He higgles [a variant of haggles] with M. Drouyn de Lhuys over the different words to be used – over "good offices", "mediation" and "arbitration". He won't take "arbitration". It must be "good offices" ... I think it is evident Baron Gros had the most earnest desire to settle the matter'.

That wasn't Palmerston's view at all, but it supported Cobden's view that Pacifico's claim was 'a barefaced attempt at swindling'. Furthermore, he said, the settlement was a defeat in itself: 'Our whole claim on the Greek government was £33,000. The whole amount we have actually received is £6,400.' Cobden was sure that '...if the people of England understood the merits of the question...they would be so disgusted that they would raise a subscription to pay back the Greek Government the money it has given you'.

Cobden's position on the correct attitude for the government was: 'That no foreign state has a right by force to interfere with the domestic concerns of another state, even to confer a benefit on it, with its own consent.' Instead, it would be better to rely on 'the universal outbreak of public opinion and public indignation in Western Europe'. Cobden favoured a policy of appeasement and pacifism and, if it had been applied, there is no doubt that the Greek government would have got away scot-free.

Although the debate ran on for four days, interest remained at a high level. It was generally agreed that the standard of debate in the House was very high and a number of telling points were made very cogently. Finlay's profit from the land came in for a lot of criticism, although why he should be philanthropic in the first place was not explained. The principle seemed to be that you shouldn't be a professed philhellenist on the one hand and a property speculator on the other. It was, however, easier to abhor double standards if you weren't the one trying to make both ends meet. One MP, Mr Wood, had been struck by the unfair reaction to Pacifico's claim: 'What was the answer when he reclaimed redress for these outrages? That he was a Jew and that he had exaggerated his claims for compensation.' Another MP tried to put the riot into perspective: 'the mob, excited as Sir E. Lyons says, by a number of brigands who desired an opportunity of plunder'. All the right points were made by the speakers but subsequent records have ignored many of them, just as so many MPs and newspapers did at the time.

On the last night of the debate there came one of those speeches which make a career. Alexander Cockburn was a QC by the time he was 39 and the Liberal MP for Southampton. He had been elected to the House only three years before and although well known in the law courts, had done little in Parliament thus far. He was a short man but he had great dignity and a melodious voice. A very charming Scottish bachelor, he was always scrupulously fair and his approach was fluent and persuasive rather than learned.

Cockburn had prosecuted the serial poisoner, Dr William Palmer, for murder and seen him hanged. He had defended the maniac who killed Sir Robert Peel's secretary in mistake for the great man. In that case Cockburn established that madness was a defence against a charge of murder and ensured that his client, McNaghton, escaped execution. From his pleading came the present defence in such cases, the McNaghton Rules. The case the public probably savoured most though, arose from Running Rein winning the Derby in 1844. This was the only occasion when the classic race for 3-year-olds was actually won by a 4-year-old, and Cockburn prosecuted the crooks who had carried out the audacious deception.

Cockburn took his parliamentary opportunity and cogently destroyed the opposition. To those who wanted Finlay to go to court, he asked: 'Was the Right Honourable Gentleman ignorant of the first principle of law, that you cannot sue the sovereign?' (in fact, you could in England, but nowhere else). In Cockburn, Pacifico found a champion. A noble lord 'spoke of Don Pacifico as a Jew broker, an usurer, a hybrid Jew. But he was told that this was not done with a view to prejudice the case; he should like to know, then, for what other purpose it was done.' Since when, he asked, was a man tried on his character rather than the facts?

Would Members of Parliament try to sue the rioters? Cockburn could quote chapter and verse without difficulty:

> Nottingham Castle was destroyed by a mob. Did the Duke of Newcastle, to whom it belonged, bring his action against them? ... Londonderry House was attacked by a mob. Was any action brought against them? It was the silliest dream that ever entered into the imagination of men to conceive ... England, with wiser legislation ... provides ... that ... in the case of such injuries the local community, the hundred, should be responsible for the property demolished.

Cockburn also gave examples of what had happened to judges who gave judgements against the government or the king in Greece.

He gave the names of specific judges who had, as a consequence, been removed from office. He accepted that there had been occasions when improvements had been attempted, but pointed out that when Armansperg had tried to introduce fairer processes, he too had been dismissed.

Where others had generalised about the state of the law in Greece, Cockburn quoted cases. He agreed that the constitution forbade torture but 'the constitution was violated in every respect'. There were any number of cases of the torturing of women. The Greek authorities had a habit of tying cats to women's naked bodies so that they would lacerate their victims. Where others had said only that Kolettis had gone easy on brigands, Cockburn spoke of the fifteen brigand chiefs who had been given an amnesty. If he had been challenged, no doubt he would have read out the names.

It was not surprising that Cockburn was soon afterwards offered the position of Solicitor General and then Attorney General.

The Prime Minister watched the battle rage and saw his troops attacking the weaknesses in the arguments of the tories. When he rose to address the House himself, there was still one point about which he felt strongly that had not been covered; he hated the fact that the words of any foreign witness appeared to be preferred by the media and the opposition to the statement of one of his own countrymen: 'Sir E. Lyons is a man distinguished in two professions, of the highest honour and great ability; but we are told that he is ready to adopt every idle story and pass it on without examination...that no credit can be given to his representations.' Russell deprecated this, but it is another illustration that politicians are not trusted.

Towards the end of the debate there came the contribution of Sir Robert Peel. No one could know that this would be the last speech the great man would give in the House. The next day Peel fell off his horse, which rolled on him and caused a rib to puncture his lung. The former Prime Minister died four days later. His last message would be remembered but not honoured, for Peel wanted the country to stay away from disputes involving 'the wildness of democracy and the iron rule of despotism'. He still suggested the House should support the present government in its efforts to take the middle road.

In summing up for the opposition, it was Disraeli's responsibility to endeavour to finally swing the debate against the government. Earlier in May in the House, he had derided 'the somewhat ludicrous suspicious claims of Mr Pacifico'. Even so, for a man capable of coruscating sarcasm, devastating wit and damning condemnation, Disraeli was remarkably restrained when he addressed the assembly. First, he suspected that he was on to a loser. Palmerston had put up a masterly defence of his position and, as Disraeli admitted privately: 'He is a name which the country resolves to associate with energy, wisdom and eloquence.'[3] Second, could Disraeli be basically against the action in Greece? He was no lover of anti-Semitism, given how much he suffered from it himself. Converted or not, Disraeli was always publicly regarded as a Jew. In addition, if he was going to try to bring the government down, he would surely choose an issue that would have the public behind him, and the blockade of Greece didn't come into that category.

The House divided after four long sessions and the still-crowded Commons held its breath as the tellers returned to give the Speaker the verdict of the Members. The voting was 310 for the government and 264 against, a majority of forty-six.

Palmerston's own reaction to his triumph was summed up in his letter to Normanby on 29 June.

> My dear Normanby, – our debate in the House of Commons finished at near 4 o'clock this morning, and we had about the majority which we had reckoned upon...our triumph has been complete in the debate as well as in the division; and, all things considered, I scarcely ever remember a debate which, as a display of intellect, oratory and high and dignified feeling, was more honourable to the House of Commons. John Russell's speech last night was admirable and first-rate; and as to Cockburn's, I do not know that I ever, in the course of my life, heard a better speech from anybody, without any exception.

Lady Clarendon, whose husband would become Foreign Secretary and who was an opponent of Palmerston, wrote: 'He has triumphed over the great mass of educated public opinion, over the great potentate, *The Times*, over the two branches of the legislature, over the Queen and Prince, and most of the cabinet he sits in, besides all foreign nations.' Greville went for a ride with Brunnow, the Russian ambassador, and was told that the Russian Emperor Nicolas I 'cannot comprehend our political condition and is at a loss to know why the Queen does not dismiss Palmerston'.[4] Of course the Queen's hands were tied if Russell stood his ground, and he had done so. Furthermore, her views on her Foreign Secretary were not for public consumption. The Palace would issue no statement on matters of that nature, but the queen told her Uncle Leopold: 'The House of Commons is becoming very unmanageable and troublesome.'[5]

Palmerston could have breathed a small sigh of relief. He had won the debate and the Greeks had paid the compensation without a whole string of awkward facts coming out. It was highly unlikely now that it would ever come out that Pacifico's father was, in fact, a former British diplomat in Rabat. The Emperor of Morocco's refusal to accept David Pacifico's appointment by the Portuguese as minister to that country could be safely forgotten. Nobody wanted to embarrass the Moroccans or the Portuguese. There could be no suggestion that the Foreign Office was simply looking after the families of its former employees. Nothing had come out about Pacifico's work for Pedro and the British government's involvement in the overthrow of Miguel. That meant the Portuguese had been let off the hook.

Palmerston, in his speech, however, had pointed to the British contribution to the recent creation of an acceptable constitution in Portugal and used the event to tackle the accusations which were always made that he acted on a personal, rather than government, agenda:

> Portugal is now in the enjoyment of a Constitution, and practically it is working as well as under all circumstances... could perhaps have been expected. 'Oh, but' said the right hon. Baronet, 'you have Costa Cabral as Minister and your object was to get rid of him.' Now the fault I find with those who are so fond of attacking me... is that they try to bring down every question to a personal bearing. If they want to oppose the policy of England, they say 'Let us get rid of the man who happens to be the organ of that policy.' As long as England is England, as long as the English people are animated by the feelings, and spirit, and opinions which they possess, you may knock down twenty foreign ministers one after another, but depend upon it that no one will keep his place who does not act upon the same principles.

That was what made Palmerston so popular. He really did represent the views of the majority of the population. The case had been made for protecting British citizens abroad under all circumstances. Nobody had picked up the point that the law officers of the Crown had studied Pacifico's claim and said it was worth pursuing, which put it into a much more credible category than a simple principle. All in all, the Foreign Office's cards remained firmly close to their chests and the files could be closed without such awkward facts being out in the open.

The French had agreed to stop quarrelling over the incident. De la Hitte had announced this in the French Assembly on 21 June, before the debate in the Commons, and he had received applause for the decision. Basically, the French had made a lot of fuss, received a lot of European attention and the new government felt important. Palmerston could live with that.

It had been a hard grind at the Foreign Office. The midnight oil had burned for weeks on end. Palmerston generously turned this to the Chancellor of the Exchequer's advantage. When asked in Parliament a few weeks later why British passports cost £3 but French passports only 25p, Palmerston pointed out that the Foreign Office staff couldn't cope with the inevitable rush which would follow a reduction in the fee. They were all too exhausted from their recent labours.

The Times took the defeat of its position in the Commons in its stride. The morning after the debate finished, it shifted its guns from Pacifico to fire a broadside at the triumphant Palmerston: 'We ascribe to the Foreign Secretary an ambition to remodel the Constitution of all Europe, and to recast its territorial divisions in subservience to that end. We also ascribe to him a restless spirit of interference, of insolent dictation to foreign Governments and unwarrantable advances to their political opponents.' But it got worse: 'To this we must add what is patent and undeniable, a mode of getting up cases, and tampering with official correspondence, that would not be thought honest in the private transactions of one gentleman with another.' To accuse the Victorian viscount of not behaving like a gentleman was not armistice-seeking language but Palmerston, on that happy day, couldn't have cared less what *The Times* thought.

Almost as soon as the debate was concluded, Lhuys was packing his bags to return to London. He had come out of the tortuous negotiations with his reputation intact, which was more than could be said for most of the other participants.

On 28 July Otho signed the Convention of London, agreed between the French and the British. The money Wyse had insisted on, as a deposit for guaranteeing the compensation, was returned to the Greek government. O'Brien in Athens was still singing from Otho's hymn book and gushed: 'The sympathy shown for Greece by the majority of the British public during the late question has completely won the hearts of the people of this country.' With

Palmerston the most popular politician in Britain, the sympathy of the British public was perhaps a little less positive than O'Brien portrayed.

NOTES

1   Francoise de Bernardy, *Victoria & Albert* (Harcourt Brace, 1953).
2   Sir F. Thesiger, House of Commons, 25 June 1850.
3   Evelyn Ashley, *Lord Palmerston* (Richard Bentley, 1879).
4   Edward Pearce (ed.), *The Diaries of Charles Greville* (Pimlico, 2005).
5   Albert Hyamson, *Jewish Historical Society of England* (1953).

16 The aftermath

David Pacifico missed all the excitement of the debates in the House of Lords and the House of Commons, although he should have made it to London in time. By the end of the blockade he had been on the battleship *Caledonia* with his family for eleven weeks. He now wisely considered that going back to Athens with his compensation, after humiliating the Greek government, could well make him a doubly-attractive target for any passing Greek brigand. So he set sail for England as quickly as he could after the Greeks gave in.

It had been a long three years since the mob first gathered. The family had been in suspended animation since that time, hanging on, hoping against hope that sufficient outside pressure could be brought to bear on their behalf to repair the damage. Pacifico must have asked himself many times whether it was fair on the women to make them go through such privations just because he was, himself, determined not to give in. Orthodox Jewish husbands are invariably very family-minded.

Many in the local Jewish community would certainly have wished him to stop making waves. They would have feared the consequences of waking the sleeping tiger of anti-Semitism by giving the Greek government such a hard time. Pacifico would obviously have been blamed for the blockade as well. Undoubtedly, the family would not have won a popularity contest in any community in Athens during those three difficult years.

The odds had always been heavily against Pacifico, but then so had they been when he had agreed to take on the commissary's job with Terceira. It hadn't been that much fun being besieged in Porto, either. Still, he would have thought, with the help of God, everything had worked out all right in the end. Kolettis was dead and Tzavellos out of office: the king had been forced to capitulate and the whole rotten regime hadn't been able to get away with robbing him. Admittedly, nobody had been punished and, for the looters, crime had paid. Nevertheless, the Greek government had learned the hard way that it couldn't always get away with ignoring daylight robbery.

After so many ups and downs in his past life, Pacifico must have wondered where the next thunderbolt would be coming from, and he was soon to encounter it. When the ship reached Malta, Pacifico was a very sick old man, suffering from cholera. He was taken off the ship, and the dread disease kept him in bed for three months. Presumably he was lucky to survive, remembering that he was nearing 70. Pacifico finally arrived in the British capital, safe and sound, on 8 August 1850.

Pacifico discovered he was a celebrity; his name was bandied about in the newspapers and everybody knew of the lengths to which the government had gone in order to get him justice. As nobody knew what he looked like, he could still walk the streets without being recognized, and he apparently gave no interviews and kept a low profile.

David and Clara settled down quietly in the City of London and rejoined the Bevis Marks Synagogue in February 1852. The beautiful eighteenth-century building in the heart of the metropolis was elegant proof of the difference in attitude of British governments towards religious toleration, compared to those of Portugal and Greece. Where both the Greek and Portuguese authorities still refused to allow the building of a synagogue in their capitals, Bevis Marks in London had replaced a former synagogue almost exactly 150 years before. Queen Anne had donated a beam to its construction and the Jews had lived in peace in Britain for 200 years. The Pacificos paid the level of dues which was appropriate for a couple in comfortable circumstances (about £240 in today's money) but they were certainly not among the richest. They set up home in St Mary Axe, which was a quarter much favoured by the better off members of the community, and looked forward to peace and quiet.

Even though the affair was over, Pacifico soon discovered that the government continued to be concerned about his welfare. They had blockaded Greece because they maintained he was an honest man with a real grievance. It would not be helpful to their standing if any subsequent event threw doubt upon the truth of this. Pacifico still had plenty of enemies and, now that Greece had suffered such a loss of face, they might well redouble their efforts to drag him down. The government would advise him if he was likely to finish up in court and they would then make sure that he was represented by a first-class legal team. It would be good public relations for the government, in any case, to illustrate the difference between British justice and what was available in Athens. When and if Pacifico had to fight a case in England, no matter how minor the matter, the government's senior law officers would organise his defence.

Others did try to get their hands on parts of Pacifico's compensation. There were two court cases brought by Greek merchants for damages they suffered due to the blockade: *Tambisco vs Pacifico* in 1852 and *Vanzetti vs Pacifico* in 1855. These were brought in spite of the fact that the Greek government had promised not to encourage any Greek claims for compensation when they signed the agreement which ended the blockade.

The family's interests were defended by the Attorney General or the Solicitor General. That involved a lot of expense but, even five years after the final settlement in Athens, the government was, apparently, still not prepared to be undermined by an adverse court decision, unless, of course, their best law officers were unable to prevent such a result. They must have ensured that Pacifico was able to field the first team and they got the result they wanted when the plaintiffs lost.

The emotions aroused about the affair dwindled rapidly. As early as 5 July 1850, the House of Lords had shrugged off the Commons' decision with good humour. They were discussing the forthcoming Great Exhibition and the Earl of Ellenborough proclaimed himself concerned about foreign visitors. In an obvious reference to the Pacifico case he asked what would happen if they formed a mob and rioted and pillaged a house. Would the government pay compensation? The Marquis of Lansdowne was happy to reassure him: 'I have no doubt that if the son of the secretary of war shall excite and lead the mob to the spoliation, which the noble lord so mirthfully anticipates, we shall give compensation.' There was reported to be a laugh.

The last elements of the affair had to be wound up. Part of the settlement with Greece involved the setting up of a commission to adjudicate on Pacifico's claim for the loss of the Portuguese papers in the riot. Pacifico didn't go to Lisbon as an observer when the commission gathered in February 1851. He wrote that the 'impaired state of his health' made this impossible, and a man in his late 60s, just recovered from cholera, could certainly be legitimately excused such a journey. Instead he asked his nephew, Abraham Hassan, to go in his place. Hassan was only 20 years old but he was well liked in the family and would eventually marry Esther. The commission met a few months before Saldanha, the commander of Pedro's second division in Porto in 1833 and a colleague of Pacifico at that time, overthrew the government of Costa Cabral.

France appointed Leon Beclard, Secretary at the French Embassy in Lisbon, who was to act as a commissioner and take the chair. It was a further attempt to assuage French sensibilities, by putting them in charge of another piece of the negotiations. For Britain there came Patrick Campbell Johnston, the British commissioner in Greece, and the Greeks chose George Torlades O'Neill, the Greek consul-general in Lisbon. It was a strong committee. The commission examined the list of claims, which was dated 21 December 1844 and which Pacifico had sent to it in September 1850. After due consideration the commission reported back to its respective governments.[1]

All of a sudden, lost papers started to turn up. The Portuguese had denied having them, but now gave evidence that they had copies of all the papers Pacifico had lost. They were in the archives of the Cortes in Lisbon and they had the details of Pacifico's initial claim in 1839. They said there had been no further move on his part since that time. The actual dating of the document they were examining was five years later.

When Palmerston wrote to ask Pacifico if he had any evidence to back up his claim to the commission, Pacifico at first said 'No'. Then he sent the Foreign Secretary the 1834 document which had been drawn up by the judge in Faro, complete with the supporting proof of his witnesses that he was telling the truth. He still said he had lost 'ministerial orders, certificates, receipts and other vouchers for official duties and liabilities incurred on behalf and at the instance of the government of Portugal and of the valuation of losses sustained in their service'.[2] He went on to say that he had been 'reduced to the necessity of supplicating as a favour, a settlement which I might otherwise have sought as a matter of right'. Paul Midosi, the Portuguese councillor, also wrote to say that he had presented Pacifico's claim in 1837. The point was that if Pacifico could find one key paper, was it so certain that he had lost the others? Cheated by the Portuguese and looted by the Greeks, had he taken the view that it didn't matter who paid him his due, so long as one conniving country did?

The Portuguese said that although Pacifico was in Portugal between 1834 and 1839, he had taken no other steps to recover what he claimed he was owed. It sounded so convincing, if nobody pointed out the labyrinthine attempts by Loulé to find some way for the two parties to settle their differences out of court, and with the Portuguese unable to find the money they owed to Pacifico.

What the commission did find was that Pacifico had certainly petitioned the Portuguese Chamber of Deputies as far back as 1834, 'but the Chamber had taken no action since Pacifico had failed to appear in person to present his claims, nor taken any other known steps, in support of his claims, some of which went back as early as 1828'.³ Of course, he wouldn't have done so, if Loulé was negotiating with him privately to take the Moroccan appointment as a settlement in kind, or when he was appointed to be consul in Greece. 'Most of those that had not lapsed would, if pressed, have been dealt with by the Portuguese government.' Midosi said they hadn't and if Pacifico had a valid claim for a large sum of money, why else would he fail to press his case? He'd been pressing ever since he'd been sacked in 1842.

The commission eventually awarded Pacifico £150 damages against the Greek government, effectively for administrative inconvenience. The anti-Pacifico press scoffed that this was a derisory award and a fitting comment on the fraudulence of the claim. This was either a mistaken conclusion or a deliberate distortion of the commission's views. The commission, in its report, said that it could make no other recommendation because 'the case was still unresolved'.⁴ Nobody was saying that the claim wouldn't be found to be justified; just that it was still unresolved. The commission also stated that Pacifico would be entirely justified in pursuing his claim against the Portuguese government for his outstanding expenses as consul-general in Greece. The Greeks paid Pacifico his compensation for the robbery on 17 January 1851 and paid £150 in June of that year.

It seems that the Portuguese claim never was resolved and that, at the end of the day, Pacifico had paid his own costs to carry out the duties of Portuguese consul-general in Athens for three years. As far as the papers were concerned, it has to be remembered that Pacifico had been trying to get parts of his claim settled for the best part of twenty years. The arguments advanced by the Portuguese against paying up would have needed rebuttal by Pacifico. The Portuguese could have denied making promises in writing; denied overestimating the value of the consulship in Athens; refused to accept the existence of authorisation; and conveniently mislaid important documents. They could have interpreted the material in any number of ways which would have attempted to undermine Pacifico's case. As the Rothschilds had told each other, the Portuguese authorities were not reputable people.

Any plaintiff in a court of law depends very much on accurate paperwork. Pacifico had chapter and verse in his own records. As a former commissary, he had been held responsible for every cartload of supplies, every bullock and horse. Pacifico had always needed to be prepared to justify his account of their eventual use, but then a merchant is accustomed to keeping careful records. It would have been second nature to him to have the paperwork in order. Now Pacifico's own records had been destroyed and he had to rely on the administrative efficiency of the Portuguese, who were acting in their own defence. There could be no doubt that his chances of success could be seen to be substantially weakened.

Of course, that wasn't the way it looked to many of the newspapers in 1850. The comments of *The Times* that March were typically sarcastic:

> Abroad, you would scarce have met a needier man in Athens – within his chambers you would find the furniture of palaces and the ornaments of the great – but above all, in a few scattered leaves of fumbled paper, there lay the grand arcanum of the PORTUGUESE CLAIMS. You imagine they are as worthless as the dead leaves of the magician's casket, but they are bearing interest at a higher rate than you can count. You know that Portugal recognises no such demands, which date from the days of Dom Miguel. Portugal will not be troubled with them, for Greece is to pay them. Therein lies the grandeur of Don Pacifico's invention. Other men have sometimes transferred their liabilities; he transfers his active claims...when one considers the imaginary qualities he is dealing with, one is much astonished at his modesty as at his address. That box might just as well have contained the national debt of a German principality, the repudiated bonds of Mississippi, or the crown of Hungary. Whatever it contained, was not there: so Greece must pay for all, and a bill is drawn in full on the Treasury of Athens.[5]

Palmerston recognized the behaviour of the Portuguese government for what it was. As he wrote to Wyse in March 1850: 'It is to be remembered that what he lost was everything of every kind that was in the house of a person represented as having been in easy circumstances at the time...It must be borne in mind that the Portuguese Government is not much more ready than the Greek Government to acknowledge or to satisfy even the best founded pecuniary demands.'

As far as the British were concerned, the difference between Greece and Portugal was that Portugal was a long-time ally. The British government was not going to treat Lisbon in the same way as Athens. The accusations of financial irregularities, which were readily directed against the Greeks, would have been seen as belonging to a far more delicate area of diplomacy when it came to the Portuguese, who took a great deal in the way of British exports, and the British had many major commercial interests in that country. Palmerston could recognize that Pacifico's claims against the Portuguese were probably justified, but he couldn't bring pressure to bear on the Portuguese government on Pacifico's behalf, in the way he had with the Greeks.

Back in Greece the government publicity machine went into overdrive to minimise the adverse effects of the capitulation. The official line was that brave little Greece had been bullied into admitting to faults which were, in reality, quite unfounded: 'The measures adopted by Lord Palmerston offended the national pride so much as to render King Otho extremely popular on account of the obstinate resistance he offered to the English demands.'[6] It wasn't the story Palmerston had put out of a people rejecting the excesses of their monarch. The Prime Minister, Antonios Kriezis, was actually enabled to remain in power for four-and-a-half years until 1854. As there had been seven Greek prime ministers in the six years before he gained office, this was no mean achievement. Kriezis died in 1865.

On 29 April 1850, immediately after the settlement, Sir Patrick Wyse went back to his post as the British minister in Greece. He loved the country, warts and all, and never left it until he died in 1862, at which point the Greeks gave him a state funeral. Laetitia Wyse outlived her husband by ten years, but died little mourned. As her son, William, wrote: 'Her husband's bane, her children's curse / the filcher of her children's purse / Beneath, what fiend eternal lies? / No fiend, but only Lady Wyse.' Today, the term 'dysfunctional family' would spring to mind.

The probable initiator of the 1847 riot, Kitsos Tsavellos, died in 1855. George Finlay produced his multi-volumed *History of Greece* and died in 1875, highly respected, at the age of 76. Where his history deals with Finlay's own claim for compensation, it couldn't be described as entirely even-handed.

Not surprisingly, the Greek Jews were affected by the national humiliation brought on by Parker's blockade: 'the strength of public feeling against him [Pacifico] does not suggest a secure position for the Jewish community in Athens at the time'.[7]

In 1852 the council of Athens withdrew its permission for the building of a synagogue, and the duchess withdrew the gift of the land because she didn't want the ground used for any other purpose. When she died in 1854, she once again gave the community a site on which to erect the building. The Jewish community, however, were too frightened to take up the offer and allowed the gift to lapse after another thirty years. They were only awarded their official charter as a religious body in 1889, but that was three years before the Jews were officially recognized in Portugal and allowed to build the Shaare Tikvah Synagogue – as long as it didn't face the street! In 1895 the synagogue in Athens was a one-story building in an alley in Ermou Street. There were only forty to fifty Jewish families.

Even if the Greek government had been humiliated, they still felt there was no reason to adopt a low profile internationally. They still adhered to the Great Idea of joining up all the Greek communities in the Mediterranean and Balkans into one much larger country. The Greeks looked to Russia for help. The czar was still furious that he had been prevented from getting his hands on the 1848 rebels to whom the Turks had given political asylum. He wanted to make trouble for the Ottoman Empire and the excuse was his claim that he had the responsibility for protecting Christian communities within the Turkish fold.

One of those communities was the Montenegrin Christians who lived in a particularly inhospitable part of the Balkan world. Getting the land to produce sufficient crops for more than a subsistence economy was almost impossible. Far too many of the people were in real need and the only activity which could be reasonably guaranteed to produce a decent living was the ever-popular brigandage. So a lot of the Montenegrins went over the borders to pillage the surrounding countryside of their neighbours. When Turkey proved uninterested in stopping this, the Montenegrin independence movement grew stronger. The Greeks invaded Montenegro, ostensibly to help the Montenegrin resistance movement.

To raise the necessary fighting force, Otho opened the prisons and recruited any desperado prepared to fight for the cause. A vicious collection of 6,000 predators poured into Montenegro in 1853 to steal anything in sight, with the addition of the usual looting and rape which accompanies such expeditions. 'King, court, ministers and people rushed blindly forward to attack the Ottoman power and trample on the treaties which insured them the protection of Great Britain and France.'[8]

The Russians, for their part, invaded Moldavia and Vallachia, other Balkan provinces. War with Turkey was imminent, and Britain and France had to decide whom to support. The Russians believed that any uprising of the Christians in the Ottoman Empire would quickly result in a general insurrection against the Turks, but this didn't happen. As the Christians in Montenegro were being pillaged by the Greeks just as severely as in any Ottoman segment of the country, the relative stability of governance by Turkey was preferred to the depredations of the invaders. When the Turks lost patience and announced that all Greeks would have to leave Turkish territory within fifteen days, the rush of Greek expats, to get Ionian papers and insist they were English, was immediate. The Ionians themselves were still demonstrating for union with Greece and were surprised when the British suddenly agreed at this point, declaring that they now had no objections, and abandoning the irritating responsibility.

As was to be expected, Otho proclaimed to the world that Greece was strictly neutral in the Russo–Ottoman conflict, even as the Greek papers announced that he and Amélie would shortly leave Athens to join Greek forces on the frontier. Otho denied any suggestions that his forces were rampaging across Montenegrin territory. He might have got away with it if Wyse hadn't made the true position perfectly clear to Palmerston.

The behaviour of the Greek army in Montenegro was atrocious and the image of Greece as the classical birthplace of democracy and European culture took a terrible hammering. Whenever the Greek army met a Turkish force, it crumbled almost instantly, because brigands are not trained soldiers, but piracy now started to proliferate on the seas and this brought France and England down on the Ottoman side. They threatened Otho with the one demand which would break his resistance; they said he must either withdraw his forces or they would demand payment of the interest on the original Greek loan.

For their part, the Russians were now bent on revenge and Greece had to be firmly neutralised. French and British troops landed in the Piraeus in May 1854 and stayed until 1857. Otho was told that unless he stayed neutral, the troops would occupy Athens – and he'd have to pay for them. As a consequence the Greeks did not take part in what became known as the Crimean War.

King Otho was eventually overthrown by yet another Greek revolution in 1862. It was a classic coup d'etat scenario. Otho and Amélie left Athens to drum up support on a countrywide tour, and when they got back to the capital, they found the revolutionaries in control and their frigate's crew preparing to join the rebels. The British navy came to the rescue again. Just as Otho had arrived on a British warship thirty years before, so the royal family left Greece on

HMS *Scylla*, ostensibly to avoid plunging the country into civil war. It would have been a very short war, as Otho had little support left. He retired with his dignity intact to Venice, with the Greek royal regalia. He died of measles there in 1867, at the age of only 52, and was buried in Munich. Amélie survived until 1875. The old royal palace, over the gardens of which there had been so much contention, now houses the Greek Parliament, whose constitutional government is what Palmerston had always wanted.

Pacifico, having survived cholera in 1850, contracted another infection in the early spring of 1854. It arose from the same low standards of urban hygiene, and this time was erysipelas, which can easily be treated today with antibiotics. In Pacifico's day, however, there would be no antibiotics for another ninety years. It was the same disease which had killed Frederick the Great, and after five days, with the streptococci doing their worst and his face grossly red and swollen, Don Pacifico died on the second day of the Jewish festival of Passover, Wednesday, 12 April 1854, at the age of 70. It was almost exactly seven years since the riot. He was buried in the Bevis Marks cemetery at Mile End on the Friday, in the traditional manner.

Like most other journals, even those who had found him such good copy for selling newspapers in 1850, the *Jewish Chronicle* didn't honour him with an obituary when he died. It simply printed a single paragraph stating that he had been involved in the affair four years earlier and left it at that. The *Chronicle* was just another part of the media that had accepted the views of Pacifico's critics at face value and, with a sigh of relief, the Jewish community wrote finis to the whole affair. Pacifico, right or wrong, had been an embarrassment to them. The respectable and low profile they always adopted in public affairs had been damaged in those tumultuous days in 1850, and the sooner the whole thing was forgotten, the happier they would be.

The final irony was that after all the fuss about the money, Pacifico actually died intestate. He had settled two houses in London on his granddaughter, Clara, for her benefit during her lifetime, but otherwise his intentions were unclear. An attempt to clarify who was entitled to the residue of his money was made in court in 1903, years after Clara's death, but was not resolved.[9] The case was brought at the request of Abraham Hassan's son, David, who was Clara's nephew and living at the time in Buenos Aires; the family continued to be widely spread. It is ironic in the extreme that a great deal of the compensation paid by the Greeks is still locked up in the Court of Chancery. It seems highly unlikely that its proper distribution will ever be agreed now.

Aaron Pacifico had died in 1850 and David's wife, Clara, passed away in 1868. Solomon, David's brother, disappears from sight, but their sister, Hannah, died in Lisbon in 1869.

David Pacifico's son-in-law, Jacob, came back to London with him, but Jacob's wife, Clara, probably didn't. She died in Smyrna in Turkey in the same year as her father. She would have been only in her early 30s. There seems no reason why she should have been just visiting Smyrna at the time. Turkey was safe for the Jews, so Smyrna was a logical refuge, and her being there probably indicates that the marriage was no longer a happy one. When Clara died, her daughter, also Clara, was brought up in London by Jacob, who lost his wife and his father-in-law in the same unhappy year. Jacob became a photographer, which seemed to be a clever choice of profession because photography was a very new industry at the time, hardly twenty years old, and everybody wanted to have their picture taken. Jacob even hedged his bets by selling tobacco as well, but he appears not to have been a very good businessman, because he went bankrupt in 1865.

In 1855 Jacob had married again and his new wife was Golding de Fonseca Pimental. They had at least ten children, but in those days many children didn't survive childhood. Dinah succumbed to bronchial pneumonia before her first birthday and David was 10 when he died of cerebral spinal meningitis. In the 1880s Jacob and Golding emigrated to America, where Jacob died in 1898 and Golding in 1907.

Esther Pacifico married Abraham Hassan in 1855 when she was 19, but then the Hassans and the Pacificos had been marrying each other for generations. Esther and Abraham had five sons and a daughter.[10] There was little reason for them to be in the public eye, but in 1865, Golding, Esther's sister-in-law, lost touch with her and Abraham kept putting Golding off when she tried to make a date for them to meet.

Eventually, Golding went to the Hassan house when she knew Abraham would be out. Sitting in the kitchen was a dishevelled Esther, nearly bald, who looked at her with mad, unrecognizing eyes. When Abraham was confronted with this sad state of affairs, he refused to explain the circumstances and Golding went to court. She tried to get a judgement that a qualified medical examiner should see Esther in order to decide if she was insane or not. This plea was rejected on the grounds of insufficient evidence. It seems likely that this was a case of post-natal depression because Esther subsequently gave birth to three more sons and a daughter. Only one son married. There is far more to this than meets the eye because Jacob told the court that his daughter was living with Esther against his will.

That daughter must have been Clara, who would have been 18 at the time and was obviously close to her Aunt Esther. Unfortunately the trail goes cold at that point. David Pacifico's other daughter – the one who married Captain Lante and got thrown out of the house – also disappears. It seems very unlikely that she ever saw her father again. A Pacifico relation called Mrs Charney lived in Athens later in the century – possibly a Lante daughter or granddaughter.

Emmanuel, the respectable medical man and director of the Atlas, died in 1851, not long after David arrived from Greece. Emmanual left £1,000 in bank stock and £100 in Consols (gilt-edged stock) to buy land for almshouses for the Sephardic poor. The houses were built in Hackney but by 1880 the capital was exhausted. By 1895 there were only seven inmates and in 1897 the Charities Commission gave permission for the building to be sold. The sale realised £1,200 and, as there was deflation over the period, there was only a small profit for the Sephardic community.

When Peel died in 1851, the only British politician who could rival Palmerston in the public's affection left the scene. Palmerston became the public's favourite politician, even if Victoria and Albert didn't join in the cheering. They remained determined to get rid of the Foreign Secretary, and Palmerston could still always count on a proportion of his own Cabinet colleagues to try to undermine him as well. In 1851 he finally made one indiscreet comment too many, welcoming the coup d'etat which brought Louis Napoleon to the head of French affairs: 'He had expressed approval of Louis Napoleon's coup on December 2nd and had repeated his expressions after the Queen and Russell had censured him, in a despatch that he submitted to neither.' Palmerston was totally out of line and this time it was too much. Russell capitulated to the cumulative cries of rage and dismissed him in time for Christmas. Just two months later the Prime Minister had a very unwelcome New Year's gift in return, when Palmerston led the radicals in a revolt against a government bill on military spending and brought them down. Russell had always known this was a distinct possibility and must have bitterly regretted that he had allowed himself to be talked into getting rid of his old friend.

After another election, Palmerston was comfortably returned to Parliament and was appointed Home Secretary in Lord Aberdeen's administration. He became Prime Minister in 1855 in the depths of the Crimean War, which he had had a major role in starting, even if he was at the Home Office rather than the Foreign Office at its outbreak. His chosen weapon was public relations, working hard on the newspapers to support his viewpoint. With one short break, Palmerston remained in power until he died in the autumn of 1865, after another resounding general election victory in that summer, still in harness at the ripe old age of 81. He had been a member of every government for fifty-eight-years, from 1807 to 1865, except for those of Peel and Derby. Palmerston sat in sixteen Parliaments and was elected to sit in the seventeenth. He was given the tribute of a public funeral and was buried in Westminster Abbey. He well deserved to take his place among the great British political leaders of the nineteenth century.

As Russell said of Palmerston: 'his heart beat ever for the honour of England'. Gladstone was invariably critical of Palmerston in his lifetime but he recalled an occasion late in his life when a Frenchman said to the old man: 'If I were not a Frenchman, I would wish to be an Englishman', to which Palmerston replied: 'If I were not an Englishman, I should wish to be an Englishman.' Queen Victoria attempted a more balanced judgement:

> He had many valuable qualities, though many bad ones, and we had, God knows, terrible trouble with him about Foreign Affairs. Still, as Prime Minister he managed affairs at home well, and behaved to me well. But I never *liked* him or could ever the least respect him, nor could I forget his conduct on certain occasions to my Angel. He was very vindictive and *personal* feelings influenced his political acts very much. Still he is a loss.[13]

The Queen had been delighted when the Pacifico furore finally ended. She called it 'a most disagreeable business'. Emily Palmerston survived Harry for only four years, dying in 1869.

Palmerston had approved George Gilbert Scott's design for the new Foreign Office in 1856 and within its massive walls today there is still a memorial to, arguably, the greatest British Foreign Minister – the Palmerston canteen! When Peel died, Lord Aberdeen took over the leadership of the Peelites, and in 1852 Victoria asked him to form a government. He said at the time: 'The new government should not be a revival of the old Whig Cabinet with the additional of some Peelites, but should be a Liberal Conservative government in the sense of that of Sir Robert Peel.'

With Russell given the Foreign Office and Palmerston safely at the Home Office, all might have been well. Unfortunately Russia and Turkey went into battle in 1853 and Palmerston achieved his objective when the British were dragged into what became known as the Crimean War. In 1855 things were going so badly that Arthur Roebuck, who had opened the House of Commons debate in defence of Palmerston, proposed a committee of enquiry into the conduct of the war. This was agreed by 157 votes and Aberdeen resigned the next day, leaving the way open for Palmerston. Aberdeen died in 1860 at the age of 76.

When Russell lost the leadership of the liberals to Palmerston, he agreed to serve under him, as Foreign Secretary. The previous year, he had introduced Lionel Rothschild to the House of Commons as the first Jewish MP, when the problem of taking the oath as a Christian was finally resolved. When Palmerston died, Russell briefly took over again, but the government fell, over a measure to further increase the franchise. Russell went to the Lords in 1861 and took Cabinet office again, but he was far less successful as a subordinate than he had been as Prime Minister. He finally resigned in 1866 and died at the ripe old age of 86 in 1878.

Edward Stanley succeeded his father to become the Thirteenth Earl of Derby in June 1851 and died in 1869, in time to leave Disraeli as Prime Minister for his one full term. Derby was Prime Minister on three occasions, leading minority administrations when the liberals were temporarily defeated. He was never in office long but his obituary could have pointed out that during those three minority terms he still managed to pass bills to enable Jews to sit in the House of Commons, to remove the administration of India from the East India Company to the Crown, and to further extend the franchise in 1867.

As far as blockades are concerned, the Hague Convention in 1907 laid down the law that a blockade is permissible only if the blockaded nation has refused to accept arbitration in arguments about contract debts.

Human beings don't change a great deal over the centuries. The Don Pacifico affair seems almost modern in its personalities and diplomatic behaviour. The leaders of great powers continue to act in much the same way. It might be gunship rather than gunboat diplomacy today, but they are still trying to safeguard their interests – legitimate and otherwise – through the unusual channels.

Miguel lived on in exile in Germany from 1851 until he died in 1866. He was blessed with a son and six daughters by his second wife, Princess Adelheid of Löwenstein-Wertheim-Rosenberg but he returned to Portugal only to be buried in the church of S Vicente de Fiora in Lisbon. Marshall Beresford ended his career as the Master General of the Ordinance in Wellington's government from 1828 to 1830. Then he retired and devoted a number of years to arguing with the historians of the Napoleonic Wars whether he'd done a good job or not. He died aged 86 in 1854.

In Portugal the Marquis of Loulé, as prime minister, had one of the longest nineteenth-century Portuguese administrations, from 1860 until 1865. He died in 1875. Queen Maria died in childbirth in 1853 when only in her 30s. The Duke of Terceira continued to serve the Crown and was asked to form a new Cabinet when the government fell in 1859. He died in May 1860 to universal regret. Saldanha was made a duke and died in 1876 whilst serving as ambassador in London. Sá da Bandeira died in the same year but Costa Cabral, now Count Thomar, went on to become ambassador to the Vatican until 1885 before dying in 1889. As *The Times* reported in 1875: 'The Portuguese rulers of the old school – Saldanha, Sá da Bandeira, Loulé and the rest – are either superannuated or have been swept off by death.' Jeremiah Meagher finally retired after fifty-seven years' service with the British Embassy in Lisbon and died in 1871.

Sir Edward Lyons was transferred to the Swiss Embassy but recalled to the navy for the Crimean War. He distinguished himself against the Russians as second in command to Admiral Dundas, and was made Baron Lyons of Christchurch in 1856. He died in 1858. His mentor, Sir Richard Church, outlived him and died in 1873. There is a commemorative window in a Greek church with a dedication written by Gladstone, the then British Prime Minister: 'This window is dedicated by the British government to the memory of General Sir Richard Church who, after distinguished service in the British army, on the shore of the Mediterranean, devoted himself to the cause of Greece as a soldier and a citizen, and won, by the example of a long noble life, the affection of the people for himself and for England.' It seems likely that the Greek love of England was still a slight exaggeration.

The Sea Wolf, Admiral Lord Cochrane, rejoined the British navy and was given back his Order of the Bath in 1847. He continued to serve his country so well that when he died in 1860 he, too, was buried in Westminster Abbey. Rear Admiral Parker came home after completing his stint as commander-in-chief in the Mediterranean and was made a full admiral in 1852. He died in 1866. 'Mad Charley' Napier was put in charge of the Channel Fleet in 1847 but he was as insubordinate to the Admiralty as ever. Eventually they lost patience and he was dismissed in 1849. He spent much of the remainder of his life writing somewhat biased memoirs in which he was always the hero and invariably hard done by. He died as Sir Charles in 1860.

Sir Alexander Cockburn remained in Parliament until 1856, serving as Attorney General from 1851 to 1856. He then returned to the Bar and finished up Lord Chief Justice. He passed away, laden with honours, in 1880.

John Thaddeus Delane continued as editor of *The Times* until 1877, serving thirty-six years in the post. He is remembered as one of the greatest Victorian press chiefs. His relationship with Palmerston improved as time went by, and during Palmerston's ministries, Delane very much took the government line. For their part, the government reduced the stamp tax on newspapers in 1855 to $1/2$p, making it possible for the popular press to be massively expanded over the coming years. Peter Borthwick of the *Morning Post*, Palmerston's staunch ally, died in 1852.

Edouard Druyn de Lhuys went on to have a distinguished career as the French Minister of Foreign Affairs. He occupied the post three times: in 1851; from 1852 to 1855; and from 1862 until 1866. He died in 1881 at the age of 76.

Baron Jean-Baptiste Gros went on to be the French minister in China in 1857 and concluded a historic agreement with the Japanese in 1859. He returned to Europe to take up the post of ambassador to London in 1862 and died in 1870 aged 77. Edouard Thouvanel served in the French Foreign Office until he died in 1866 at the age of only 48.

For some years after Pacifico's death, any man who claimed questionable compensation in a foreign country, and asked for the help of the British government, was known as a 'Don Pacifico'. Eventually memories faded and a version of the facts became enshrined in the history books, believed to be accurate through constant repetition. He continues to get a bad press. Even in modern times Albert Hyamson, who did most work on the subject for the Jewish Historical Society of England, referred to him as 'a somewhat picaresque individual', which is a convoluted way of saying he was a rogue. Francoise de Bernardy, in *Victoria and Albert* in 1953, referred to the 'dubious claims', and on 15 July 2004, *The Scotsman* commented on 'The disgraceful Don Pacifico affair'. Even the *Jewish Encyclopaedia* referred to 'this rather preposterous claim'. Elizabeth Longford, the distinguished author, wrote that 'never was a gentleman more misnamed'.[14]

The truth now appears very different. Pacifico spent his entire life being, at best, tolerated. He was allowed to live in Gibraltar on tolerance, he was tolerated in Portugal and for some time in Greece. After joining with the rest of the Gibraltar Jewish community in the fight against Napoleon, he was finally allowed to own a house. After spending years helping the Portuguese Liberal Party against a tyrant, his reward was to be conned out of his rightful compensation for his consequent losses, and to go unpaid for the years he spent in the service of Pedro.

He could have ducked out at the first sign of civil war in Portugal, as his brother, Aaron, did, but he stayed to fight in what appeared at the time to be a losing cause. The decision to act as commissary in the War of the Two Brothers was foolhardy, to put it at its best. He stood an excellent chance of finishing up either dead, or in prison in Africa.

In Greece there was an initially successful plot, by some of the greatest in the land, to steal every penny he had and he fought against that injustice too. He could have given up hope of getting compensation for his wrongs from both Portugal and Greece at any time over three long years. Pacifico spurned any solution of this kind. He was a very, very obstinate man. Yet through all his problems he cherished his family and his religion and he was loyal to Britain and to Portugal.

David Pacifico was a fighter. Only the British treated him fairly; in return for helping them when they needed it, the British government reciprocated handsomely when he was in trouble and otherwise friendless. Palmerston was a pretty good judge.

NOTES

1 Foreign Office File 881.
2 Pacifico to Palmerston, 27 July 1850.
3 Albert Hyamson, *Jewish Historical Society of England* (1953).
4 Ibid.
5 *The Times*, 1 March 1850.
6 George Finlay, *History of Greece*, vol. VII (Clarendon Press, 1877).
7 Nicholas Stavroulakis, *The Jews of Greece* (Talas Press, 1990).
8 Finlay, *History of Greece*, vol. VII.
9 *The Times*, 30 May 1902.
10 Abraham and Esther Hassan had a son called David in 1857. If he had been their first son, his name would have been Moses,

after Abraham's father. It looks, therefore, as if they had a son in 1856 who didn't survive for very long.

11 *The Times*, 9 January 1865.
12 James Chambers, *Palmerston* (John Murray, 2004).
13 Francoise de Bernardy, *Victoria & Albert* (Harcourt Brace, 1953).
14 Elizabeth Longford, *Queen Victoria: Born to Succeed*.

Appendix

The key document in unravelling the story of Don Pacifico is the detailed claim he sent, on Palmerston's instructions, to the Foreign Office about his claim against the Portuguese government. Typical items read:

> 2nd Class. For my voyage from Lisbon to Genoa, and from Genoa to Greece, by order of Her Majesty's Government, in order to carry on the Portuguese Consulate-General in Greece, in the same way as Her Most Faithful Majesty's Government have paid the expenses of M. Vidal, of M. Joachimo Barassor Ferrera, and others; and I have in my possession an order from the very excellent nobleman, the Marquis of Loulé, Minister at that period, to undertake that voyage at the expense of Her Most Faithful Majesty's Government, amounting to 1550 Spanish taliaris, with interest for five years at 12%, according to the rate of interest of the Royal Bank of this country (Athens), which added to the sum of 1 conto of reis for my return to Lisbon, which makes a total of 3,160,000.

> Four documents

> 2nd Class. Expenses of the chancery of the Consulate-General in 1842, according to the accounts sent in to the minister of Foreign Affairs, amounting for the four quarters to 94,915.

The major items were for the loss of 4 commanderies held at Alentejo for 3 years. Confiscated by Don Miguel 'Because I had done good to all the Liberal emigrants'. Adding interest at 5 per cent this came to a claim for 48 million reis. Then, 'by a judicial decision dated 13 February 1834 in Faro' for the pillage of his house in Mertola and of his corn warehouse in 1833 when the Liberal troops entered the town, he claimed 1,700,000 reis. For the rent for the two furnished houses in Gibraltar, 'one occupied by Archbishop Ataite and suite', the other by Liberal emigrants – the agreed rent was 120,000 reis a month – he claimed 18,144,000 reis.

For muskets 'given to Colonel Almeidas for the defence of Olhio, as proved by Baron de Faro's receipt', he claimed 1,200,000 reis. For his two years' service in the Algarve as paymaster and commissary of the Operations Division, he claimed 2,800,000 reis. It all added up to 94,645,315 reis, or £21,295.07.

What had to be unravelled was what he was talking about!

The documents are in FO 881 443, The National Archives, Kew, London.

Bibliography

Abecasis, José Maria, *Genealogia Hebraica, Portugal e Gibraltar* (Lisbon: 1991).

Ashley, Evelyn, *The Life and Correspondence of Viscount Palmerston* (Richard Bentley, 1879).

Benady, Tito, *Aaron Cardozo: Life and Letters* (Gibraltar Books, 2004).

Benady, Tito, *The Royal Navy at Gibraltar* (Gibraltar Books, 2000).

Billy, George J. *Palmerston's Foreign Policy, 1848* (Peter Lang, 1993.

Birmingham, David, *A Concise History of Portugal* (Cambridge: Cambridge University Press, 1993).

Bradford, Ernle, *Gibraltar* (Rupert Hart Davis, 1971).

Brown, David, *Palmerston and the politics of Foreign Policy* (Manchester: Manchester University Press, 2002).

Chamberlain, M. E. *Lord Aberdeen* (London, 1983).

Chambers, James, *Palmerston* (John Murray, 2004).

Clogg, Richard, *A Concise History of Greece* (Cambridge: Cambridge University Press, 1992).

Dakin, Douglas, *The Greek Struggle for Independence* (B. T. Batsford, 1973).

Dakin, Douglas, *The Unification of Greece* (Ernest Benn, 1972).

Dalven, Rae, *The Jews of Ionnina* (Cadmus Press, 1990).

de Bernardy, Francoise, *Victoria and Albert* (Harcourt Brace, 1953).

Ellicott, J. T. & D. M., *An Ornament to the Almeida* (Portsmouth, 1950).

Esdaile, Charles, *The Peninsula War* (Penguin Books, 2002).

Ferguson, Niall, *The World's Banker* (Weidenfeld & Nicolson, 1998).

Finlay, George, *History of Greece* (Clarendon Press, 1877).

Gooch, G. P., *The Later Correspondence of Lord John Russell*, vol. 2, 1840–1878 (1975).

Hills, George, *Rock of Contention* (Robert Hale, 1974).

Jackson, Sir William, G. F., *The Rock of the Gibraltarians* (Gibraltar Books, 2001).

Jenkins, Roy, *Gladstone* (Macmillan, 1995).

Koss, H., *The Rise and Fall of the Political Press in Britain* (1981).

Laski, Neville, *The Laws and Charities of the Spanish and Portuguese Jews Congregation of London* (1952).

Lindo, E. H., *The Jews of Portugal & Spain* (Longman, Brown, Green & Longmans, 1848).

Livermore, H. V., *A New History of Portugal* (Cambridge: Cambridge University Press, 1966).

Livermore, H. V., *Portugal* (Edinburgh: Edinburgh University Press, 1973).

Livermore, H. V., *A New History of Portugal* (Cambridge: Cambridge University Press, 1977).

Marques, A. H. De Oliveira, *History of Portugal* (Columbia University Press, 1972).

McGuffie, T. H., *The Siege of Gibraltar* (B. T. Batsford, 1965).

Meyers, Allan R., *Jews among Muslims* (New York University Press, 1996).

Newell, Charles, *Portugal* (Prentice Hall, 1973).

Pearce, Edward (ed.), *The Diaries of Charles Greville* (Pimlico, 2005).

Penell, C. R., *Morocco since 1830* (Hurst & Co., 2000).

Phillimore, August, *The Life of Admiral of the Fleet, Sir William Parker* (Harrison, 1880).

Pocock, Tom, *Stopping Napoleon* (John Murray, 2004).

Postal, Bernard & Abramson, Samuel, *The Travellers' Guide to Jewish Landmarks of Europe* (Fleet Press, 1971).

Russell, Jack, *Gibraltar Besieged* (Heinemann, 1965).

Samuel, Edgar, *At the End of the Earth* (Jewish Historical Society of England, 2004).

Schaumann, A. L. F., *On the Road with Wellington* (Greenhill Books, 1999).

Shaw, Stanford, *The Jews of the Ottomon Empire and the Turkish Republic* (New York: New York University Press, 1991).

Sheppard, Francis, *London: A History* (Oxford University Press, 1998).

Strachey, Lytton, *Queen Victoria* (1921).

Stavroulakis, Nicholas, *The Jews of Greece* (Talas Press, 1990).

Thomas, Donald, *Cochrane* (Cassell, 1978).

Waterfield, Roni, *History of Athens* (Macmillan, 2004).

Webster, C., *The Art and Practice of Diplomacy* (1961).

Wells, John, *The House of Lords* (Hodder & Stoughton, 1997).

Index

Jews in Glasgow 1879–1939
Immigration and Integration
Ben Braber
Foreword by **Tom Devine**

'Ben Braber's study is both accessible to a wide readership and a substantial contribution not only to Jewish history but to the broader field of immigration to Scotland and the United Kingdom. At a time when the subject of immigration to Britain remains a highly controversial and politically charged issue, this important analysis of an example from the past demonstrates the continued relevance of historical understanding.'
Professor Tom Devine, University of Edinburgh

This book is a case study of Jews from eastern and central Europe who settled in Glasgow between 1879 and 1939. In individual chapters it looks at aspects of their immigration and integration into Scottish society, namely: the reaction of the native population and the Jewish responses; the education of immigrant children; the participation of Jews in the Glasgow economy; their involvement in the political and the arts world; and changes in Jewish organisations, religious habits and lifestyle. A special chapter is devoted to post-1945 developments bringing the history of the Jews in Glasgow up to the present date. The final chapter compares the Jewish experience in Glasgow to that of Jews in English cities and to the experience of other immigrants in Glasgow such as the Irish, Italians, Germans and Asians.

2007 256 pages
978 0 85303 709 5 cloth £49.50/$65.00
978 0 85303 710 1 paper £19.95/$27.50

Chinese and Jews
Encounters Between Cultures
Irene Eber

The essays in this important book span an entire millennium, from the arrival of Jews to Chinese shores during the Tang Dynasty in the 9th Century to modern times, illuminating the fascinating encounters between the two cultures.

The first part of the book deals with the arrival of Jews in China and their organisation and life in the remote and isolated community of Kaifeng, the settlement of Jews after the Opium War in the mid-nineteenth century and finally the story of the Jewish refugees who flocked to China to find a haven from Nazi persecution in the twentieth century.

The second part reflects on the intellectual exchanges between Jews and their Chinese hosts, how the Jewish communities maintained their identity and how their respective cultures met and merged in surprising and powerful ways through scholarship, literary exchange, the translation of Chinese and Yiddish works and through religious reciprocation.

Unique in its breadth and depth of analysis, Irene Eber's account of the intellectual and inter-cultural history of these two civilisations, at first sight so diverse, is of great value to scholars and general readers alike.

2008   172 pages
978 0 85303 673 9   cloth   £45.00/$85.00
978 0 85303 674 6   paper   £19.95/$35.00

Arms and Disarmament in Diplomacy
Keith Hamilton and Edward Johnson (eds)

War has historically been the *ultima ratio* of diplomacy. Negotiations have often been undertaken in the near-certain knowledge that the alternative to achieving agreement might well be a resort to force. But armaments, their acquisition, employment and manufacture, have, frequently in conjunction with initiatives aimed at avoiding and regulating conflict, also become the subject matter of diplomacy. Since the mid-nineteenth century governments have increasingly sought through multilateral dialogue to secure general acceptance of rules governing warfare. Meanwhile, technological advances in weapons production, a growing public awareness of the cost and destructive capacity of modern armaments, and a desire to contain and mitigate the international rivalries to which they have contributed, resulted in arms control, limitation and disarmament being placed firmly on the diplomatic agenda.

This book presents a selection of nine case studies by historians with a specialist interest in this field in which issues relating to armaments have figured large in diplomacy, from the Hague Peace Conference of 1899 through until the early years of the United Nations.

2007   288 pages
978 0 85303 756 9   cloth   £50.00/$85.00
978 0 85303 757 6   paper   £19.95/$30.00

Israel on Israel

Michel Korinman and John Laughland (eds)

Contributors include: Shlomo Ben-Ami, David Horovitz,
Efraim Inbar, Raphael Israeli, Shimon Peres, Ariel
Sharon and others

Nowhere is the debate about Israel and its future stronger than in
Israel itself. Politicians, academics and journalists from Israel and the
wider world join forces in this volume to discuss the various existential
questions which face their state. What, if anything, has changed in
Palestinian politics since the death of Yasser Arafat? What are the
differences between European and American approaches to the Israeli
question? Why does the Palestinian cause continue to excite so much
support in the West? Is the idea of a two-state solution still viable?
What is the reality of Zionism and why is it so often demonised? What
is the role of historians in understanding the history of the state of
Israel and influencing the policies of today? What is the role of Arab
citizens in Israel? How was the construction of the security barrier
decided, and how was the precise route traced? What has been the
effect has the immigration of Russian and Ethiopian Jews to Israel?
What is the role of religion in Israeli politics?

**Contributors include: Shlomo Ben-Ami, David Horovitz, Efraim
Inbar, Raphael Israeli, Shimon Peres, Ariel Sharon and others**

2008 368 pages
978 085303 657 9 cloth £49.50/$85.00
978 085303 658 6 paper £18.50/$27.50

Jews and Europe
in the Twenty-First Century
Thinking Jewish
Nick Lambert
Foreword by **David Cesarani**

'*A compellingly written and meticulously researched review of Jewish life in western Europe today.*'
Professor Stefan Berger, Chair in Modern German and Comparative European History, University of Manchester

'*Nick Lambert's subtle and persistent questioning peals back the protective layers of European Jewish life to reveal the true picture of a vibrant, passionate and fragmented religious entity, traumatised by its history and fearful for its future ...*'
Rabbi Dr Charles H. Middleburgh, Irish School of Ecumenics, Trinity College, Dublin, and Leo Baeck College, London

'*Eloquently styled and groundbreaking in its implications, Nick Lambert intricately exposes the thoughts, fears and hopes of decision-makers across Europe, revealing that brand new challenges will soon require brand new leaders ...*'
Gidon van Emden, Policy Officer, CEJI, Brussels

The book explores the interplay between minority and mainstream populations, and religious and civic identities in the West, and is based around more than two hundred hours of interviews with prominent Jewish novelists, playwrights, Chief Rabbis, philosophers, sociologists, historians, psychiatrists, economists and parliamentarians in the Netherlands, Britain and Italy.

Parkes-Wiener Series on Jewish Studies

2008   352 pages
978 0 85303 760 6   cloth   £47.50/$75.00
978 0 85303 761 3   paper   £19.50/$35.00